Architectural Design Procedures

Second Edition

Arthur Thompson

ELSEVIER

Architectural
Press

AMSTERDAM • BOSTON • HEIDELBERG • LONDON • NEW YORK • OXFORD
PARIS • SAN DIEGO • SAN FRANCISCO • SINGAPORE • SYDNEY • TOKYO
Architectural Press is an imprint of Elsevier

Architectural Press
An imprint of Elsevier
Linacre House, Jordan Hill, Oxford OX2 8DP
200 Wheeler Road, Burlington, MA 01803

First published in Great Britain in 1999 by Arnold
Reprinted 2002, 2004

British Library Cataloguing in Publication Data
A catalogue record for this book is available from the British Library

Library of Congress Cataloguing in Publication Data
A catalogue record for this book is available from the Library of
Congress

ISBN 0 340 71941 9

For information on all Architectural Press publications visit our
website at: architecturalpress.com

Typeset in 10/11.5 Optima by J&L Composition Ltd, Filey, North Yorkshire
Printed and bound in Great Britain by MPG Books Ltd, Bodmin, Cornwall

Dedication

To my wife, Jean Thompson

Contents

4 Architectural practitioners and the law 56

10   Contract procedures   190

11   Standard documentation   209

List of figures

Preface

The first edition of *Architectural Design Procedures* was published in 1990. At the time of writing it, I was aware of the words of a very wise man – someone not hampered by undue modesty – who described himself as wiser than anyone who had ruled over Jerusalem before him, and a builder of great projects. He had stated that there was no end to the writing of books, and that too much study will wear you out. I recall wondering whether I should heed the philosopher's wise words and refrain from adding yet another book to the pile. In the end, vanity gained the upper hand. After nearly 15 years spent as a lecturer in a building college, preceded by over 30 years working in the construction industry, disability led me into early retirement. I had taught design procedures for many years and during that period accumulated a comprehensive set of lecture notes and handouts. A reluctance to accept that there was no further use for this material, and failure during my teaching days to find a suitable textbook on design procedures to recommend to students, encouraged me to set about converting my teaching material into a book.

The book appeared to be well received by students on the Business and Technical Education Council (BTEC) National Certificate in Building Studies, the Diploma in Construction, and the Diploma in Construction and Land Use courses. Several lecturers told me this was because the text met the syllabus requirements of these courses and was written in a straightforward way free of gobbledegook.

Since 1990 there have been radical changes in the construction industry which has prompted the writing of a new edition of the book. 'Lathamism', the philosophy of niceness in construction, has entered the language of the industry, following the publication of Sir Michael Layton's report 'Constructing the Team' in 1994. Important acts have been passed, such as the Construction Design and Management Regulations (1994), the Housing Grants and Regeneration Act (1996), and the Architects Act (1997). Movement in the European Union toward harmonisation, the acceptance of partnering by many clients and contractors, more variation in procurement systems, and greater use of computers have all had implications for the construction industry and are dealt with in this new edition.

The position of those design team members, who in 1990 were known as architectural technicians and today as architectural technologists, has changed. In 1990, rightly or wrongly, they were commonly thought of as performing an assisting role to the architect, who was invariably the team leader and the only one who could design. Today, although most buildings continue to be architect-designed, it is becoming more common for architectural technologists to act as designers and lead the team. Their function has been described as 'to act as the interface between design and construction and thereby bridge the professional gap'. This role is considered to be a complementary one to that of architects rather than an assisting role. With increasing frequency architectural technologists are setting up in practice on their own account or are becoming partners or directors of established architectural practices. This new edition takes account of these changing circumstances, and also of the fact that the British Institute of Architectural Technology (BIAT), the architectural technologist's professional institute, has begun to move towards a degree-level entry.

This new edition should be useful to students on the many degree courses in architectural technology which are now available, as well as continuing to meet the requirements of BTEC students studying for Design Procedures units. It is hoped it will be a useful tool for student architects during the first part of their degree course, and also afford an introduction to the British architectural profession for overseas students, including members of the European Communities (EC) who expect to practice architecture in Britain.

At the suggestion of lecturers teaching architectural students, and others involved in the design process, the book has been considerably extended. This includes significant additions to the chapter on design constraints, the inclusion of new sections on subjects such as quality assurance and management, and the doubling in size of the chapter on words, phrases and abbreviations used in the subject of architectural design procedures. The book includes information on new acts and regulations introduced since 1990.

Relevant material used in the original edition of the book is retained but updated where necessary. As in the first edition the practice of architecture and building design is discussed in simple terms, explaining the way architects and architectural technologists do their work and how they integrate with staff working on construction sites. The various stages of a typical project are explained, from the time the architect or architectural technologist is appointed to the handing over of the finished building. The organisation and business side of architectural practice is also covered, including legal matters and the acts and regulations which affect construction work. Examples of typical letters, standard forms, and checklists used by architectural practitioners are included.

The book has been arranged in the sequence which the author found to be most suitable when teaching the subject, with a few changes from the arrangement in the original edition, at the suggestion of others. There is a certain amount of deliberate repetition between some of the chapters to reinforce the student's learning of key items.

NB In outlining the roles of members of the building team, and elsewhere in this book, the word 'he' is used in a generic sense. All roles listed can be performed equally well by women and men. In fact there is a gradual but welcome trend for women to take on jobs in the construction industry.

Acknowledgements

The author is very grateful to the British Institue of Architectural Technologists (BIAT) for permission to publish some of their standard forms and include extracts from their *Code of Conduct*, the *1988 Yearbook*, and the 1996 report 'Into the 21st Century'. The copyright of the cited publications is held by BIAT. The inclusion in this book of extracts from these publications, and the reproduction of standard forms, is by kind permission of BIAT. Anyone wishing to similarly reproduce this material must first obtain permission from BIAT. He particularly wishes to acknowledge the help of, and thank, BIAT's Chief Executive, Francesca Berriman, for her assistance and guidance, including reading through and giving constructive comments on parts of the draft typescript. Thanks are also due to another member of BIAT's staff, Simon Gallagher, for supplying information on National/Scottish Vocational Qualifications (NVQ/SVQs) on architectural technology.

The author is also very grateful to the Royal Institute of British Architects for permission to publish some of their contract administration forms, together with extracts from the *Architect's Job Book*, the CI/SfB *Construction Indexing Manual*, the *Guidance for Clients on Fees* booklet, and the *Code of Professional Conduct* booklet. The copyright of all the publications mentioned in this book are held by the Royal Institute of British Architects (RIBA). The inclusion of extracts from the publications and the reproduction of the standard forms in this book is by kind permission of RIBA Publications. Anyone wishing to similarly reproduce this material must first obtain permission from RIBA Publications. Thanks are particularly given to Liza Kershaw of RIBA Publications for her help with regard to the RIBA material used in the book.

Thanks are given to the Building Cost Information Service Limited for permission to include their elemental cost analysis for electronics factories, and the histogram in chapter 5 of the book. Thanks are particularly given to Peter Rumble, Technical Editor of BCIS Limited for updating the summary of BCIS, also included in chapter 5.

Thanks are also given to Andrew Finch, Registrar of the Architects Registration Board, for supplying information about the Board, and to the Epsom and Ewell Borough Council, and their Planning and Engineering Officer, for permission to use their Town and Country Planning and Building Regulations application forms.

The author would also like to thank M. P. Nicholson, Ted Randell, Gavin Tunstall, and Sarah Radif for reading through the first edition of the book and giving helpful comments in respect of improving and extending the contents of the new edition of the book.

The author is pleased to acknowledge and give special thanks to Sarah Radif for reading through the draft typescript, checking the technical contents for errors and omissions, and always providing constructive comments and guidance.

The author would also like especially to thank Eliane Wigzell of Arnold Publishers for her help and encouragement.

Finally, the author wishes to thank and acknowledge the help given to him by his wife Jean over the period of preparation of this book. She helped in many ways, including the preparation of the standard documentation in chapter 11 and the various diagrams and illustration, in numbering the pages and the printing, and the checking of the final typescript. It is unlikely that the book would have been published without her help.

1

Setting the scene

1.1 The beginning

Every building begins in the mind of one person. It may be someone wanting a home built for their family, or a speculator wishing to build a block of flats to sell for a profit. It may be a trader seeking a shop to dispose of their goods, or an industrialist needing a factory in which to manufacture products. It may be a Christian with ambition to create a building to advance their religious belief, or an enthusiastic golfer anxious to construct a golf clubhouse. The building may be required for pleasure, income, utilitarian uses, or many other purposes, but almost invariably the initial impetus comes from one person recognising a need and deciding to do something about it.

In most cases other people – family, friends, colleagues, associates – will soon become involved, and may even take over the idea of providing a particular building as being their own, and either jointly or by themselves assume responsibility for commissioning the work.

At some stage too, the innovator, unless he possesses the necessary expertise in design and building – or thinks he does – will seek professional advice to help translate ideas into a completed building.

1.2 Enter the architect

Traditionally, the first person the innovator will generally turn to, although he may not always be quite sure what to expect, is the architect. Nowadays the practice of architecture is extremely complicated. Some see it as a combination of understanding different architectural styles, possessing artistic sense, and being able to create buildings which delight the eye. Others view it as possessing skills in construction technology and applying them to the design of buildings. In truth it is both these things, but to be really successful and efficient architects, as well as having artistic and technological skills, also need at least a working knowledge of laws, regulations, customs, costs, business, and much more, such as spaces, circulation patterns, access, and special needs.

Essentially, the architect is employed by the client to act as his agent and see that he is provided with a building which will satisfy his needs. To achieve this, the architect, with the approval of the client, has to make a series of choices. First, he will be concerned that the building will satisfy the functional requirements of the occupants. Second, he has to decide how to make the building attractive to look at. He will be concerned with massing, proportion, unity of the various parts, and choice of the right materials. Third, he will have to choose a suitable structural form, and appropriate finishes and services, taking care that the completed building will not incorporate any defects. There will also be choices to be made which relate to costs. Often the architect's decisions will affect running costs and maintenance costs for the future life of the building. The architect will be concerned with many other practical matters, such as how to minimise the danger and inconvenience of fire damage, noise transmission, and thermal loss.

In all that the architect does a decision will have to be made as to how the requirements of a complicated network of regulations, standards, and legal requirements are best met. Finally the architect must choose the right way to manage the actual building operations.

1.3 The arrival of the architectural technologist

In the past many architect's practices employed staff known as architectural assistants. Sometimes they worked alongside qualified architects and performed identical roles. In many of the smaller firms the principals were the only qualified architects, and virtually all the drawing work, and much of the design work, was undertaken by 'unqualified assistants'. They may have been employed because they were cheaper than their qualified contemporaries, but some firms preferred to use them because of their wide practical experience.

Occasionally, architectural assistants would set themselves up in business, generally operating as a one-man band and using descriptive titles, such as 'architectural consultant' or 'architectural designer', which would avoid conflict with the Architect's Registration Council (see section 2.6 of chapter 2).

At a conference on architectural education held in 1958, the needs of the architectural assistants, who by now were becoming known as architectural technicians, were recognised. The 1958 conference resulted in a report, in 1962, entitled 'The Architect and his Office', which arrived at the conclusion that 'there should be an institute for technicians, sponsored by the RIBA to ensure the maintenance of standards of education and training'.

In 1964 the Royal Institute of British Architects (RIBA) provided a grant to establish a national organisation which was called the Society of Architectural and Associated Technicians' (SAAT). In 1969 the SAAT became an associated society of the RIBA.

On reflection, many years after the event, there is a case for saying that 'technician' was not the best possible choice of word. Dictionaries define a technician as 'one skilled in a practical art', whereas the technologist is equated with 'the practice of applied science or art'. However, in 1965 when SAAT was founded, 'technician' was a popular job title. It was used by the Business and Technician Education Council (BTEC) for people in various disciplines whose role appeared to be to assist degree-level and chartered qualified members of various professions.

The role of the architectural technicians, as perceived by BTEC, was stated as being 'to interpret, collate and present design information for use by the construction sector; collaborate with, and take instruction from the architect on the design requirements for a project'.

The RIBA had rightly identified the need for an organisation to represent the aspirations of architectural personnel who did not possess any formal qualifications. SAAT was soon firmly established and developed into an influential national organisation. There was, however, some uneasiness about the name, which eventually led to SAAT with the support of its membership, the RIBA and the Architect's Registration Council of the United Kingdom (ARCUK) becoming the British Institute of Architectural Technicians (BIAT).

The function of architectural technicians developed, and to some observers their role appeared to be similar to that of people in certain other countries who were designated 'technical architects'.

A member of the BIAT staff, David Wood, writing in the BIAT *1988 Yearbook*, provided further clarification of the role of the architectural technician at that time:

> The architectural technician is principally an architectural technical communicator, forging the link between theory and practice. The technician's role is therefore complementary to that of the architect, his main overriding concern being the sound technical performance of the building.

In 1994 BIAT again changed its name, this time to the British Institute of Architectural Technology (BIAT). This was attributed in BIAT's 1996 report 'Into the 21st Century', because of 'the development of degrees and S/NVQs in architectural technology, first mooted in the early 1980s, and the need to gain recognition in Europe'.

In their overview of the situation, which was included in the 1996 report, BIAT stated 'the Institute and the discipline of architectural technology are now firmly established as a vital component of the construction industry'.

The role of the architectural technologist is further discussed in section 2.7 of chapter 2.

1.4 The building team

As well as possessing the multitude of talents outlined above, the architect should also possess the ability to work as a member of a team. As has already been stated, in a traditional format the architect is likely to be the designer, and lead the design team, but he is only one member and will rely on the help and cooperation of all the team members to translate his ideas into a finished building.

There are others within the building team, besides the architect, who can act as designer and team leader, and this will sometimes happen.

The four main groups involved in the design and construction of a building are the client, the design team, the contracting team, and the statutory authorities. The roles of team members are summarised below and the relationship between members is illustrated in Figure 1.1.

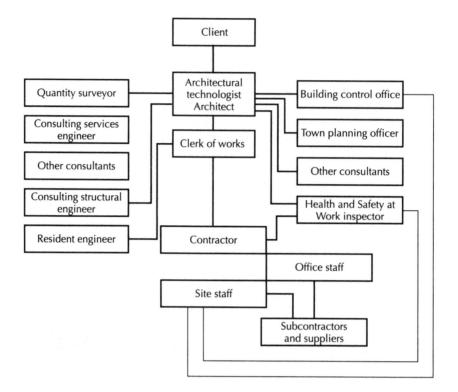

Fig. 1.1 The building team

The client

The client is also known as the building owner, and in the building contract is generally referred to as the employer. The client may be a single individual, a small private company, a large public limited company, a local authority, a state corporation, a voluntary society, or practically any other organisation you can think of.

Essentially, the role of the client is to tell the architect or architectural technologist his requirements, commission the works, and either directly or indirectly 'employ' and pay everyone on the project.

The design team

The structure of the design team is illustrated in Figure 1.2.

Architect

As has been mentioned, the role of the architect is to act as the client's agent in the design and supervision of the building, advising and guiding him as necessary, from inception of the original idea to final completion and occupation of the finished

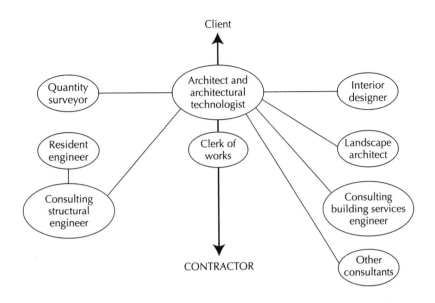

Fig. 1.2 The design team

building. His work will include the preparation of the design and drawings and obtaining statutory approvals.

Architectural technologist
The architectural technologist will work in partnership with the architect, particularly in the field of architectural technology, but he is often involved in all aspects of the work, including contract procedures and administration. Sometimes he will be responsible for the design, and like the architect take on the role of team leader. This matter is dealt with in more detail in chapters 2 and 3.

Other architectural staff
In addition to architects and architectural technologists, practices may use other staff with various designations, such as technician, architectural assistant, and draughtsperson.

Clerk of works
The clerk of works is generally employed directly by the client but acts as the architect's or architectural technologist's representative on-site. The responsibilities of the clerk of works are limited to that of an inspector, without the power to issue instructions on his own authority.

Quantity surveyor
The quantity surveyor is employed by the client as his own and the architect's or architectural technologist's advisor on anything relating to the cost of the job, including preparing the bill of quantities, checking tenders, and carrying out valuations of costs during the progress of the project.

Consulting structural engineer
The consulting structural engineer is also employed by the client, as a member of the design team, to assist in the design, construction, and supervision of the structural elements in the building.

Resident engineer
The resident engineer acts as the structural engineer's representative on the site.

Consultant building services engineer
The consultant building services engineer occupies a similar role to the structural engineer, but in respect of the building engineering services, that is, lighting, heating, drainage, etc.

Landscape architect
On large contracts, particularly where the client is aware of the contribution that well-designed landscaping can make to the appearance of a building, a landscape architect may be employed to take responsibility for this part of the project.

Interior designer
In some prestige buildings, or where the client has special requirements for the internal decor, an interior designer is sometimes employed.

Other consultants
Occasionally the expertise of a specialist consultant will be required, such as an acoustic engineer in the case of a concert hall.

The contracting team
The structure of the contracting team is illustrated in Figure 1.3.

Contractor or builder
The contractor or builder is employed by the client, on the advice of the architect or architectural technologist, to construct the building in accordance with the drawings and other information prepared by the design team.

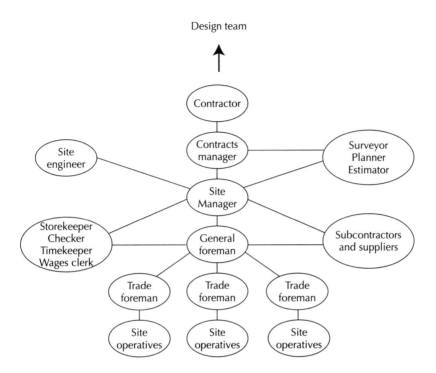

Fig. 1.3 The contracting team

Site manager
The site manager is sometimes called the site agent and is employed by the contractor to control the work on the site.

Contracts manager
The contracts manager is employed by the contractor, generally to run a number of contracts. The contracts manager is the site manager's immediate supervisor and may on a large contract be permanently resident on the site and be given the title of project manager.

Site engineer
The site engineer is responsible for setting out and controlling the accuracy of the building.

General foreman
The general foreman is repsonsible for the day-to-day running of the site. The site manager generally makes contact with the site operatives through him.

Surveyor
The surveyor prepares interim valuations and final accounts and measures work for subcontractors and bonus payments.

Estimator
The estimator prices tenders and is involved with the cost aspects of contracts, especially during the pre-contract period.

Planner
The planner is responsible for planning and scheduling and all aspects of the contractor's programmes.

Other staff
These staff will depend on the size of the project and the contractor, but will include buyers, plant managers, storekeepers, timekeepers and wages clerks.

Trade foremen
These will be in charge of a gang of bricklayers, carpenters, plumbers, etc.

Site operatives
These are the site workforce, including tradespeople, apprentices, and labourers.

Subcontractors
The subcontractors are responsible, under the control of the contractor, for part of the construction work, such as the supply and erection of the structural steelwork.

Suppliers
Suppliers have the responsibility for supplying materials or components used by the contractor in the building, such as the supply of windows.

The statutory authorities
Building control officer
The building control officer has responsibility for ensuring that the building is constructed in accordance with the building regulations, which should mean that when the building is completed it will not be a danger to the health and safety of the occupants. The role may also be undertaken by an approved inspector who is either a private individual or employed by the National House Building Council.

Town planning officer
The town planning officer is responsible for ensuring that the building is appropriate for the area in which it is built and is of acceptable appearance.

Health and Safety at Work inspectors
Previously called factory inspectors, these inspectors have two main roles; first, to ensure that the construction site is a safe place of work, and, second, to make certain that buildings which will be workplaces when completed (e.g. factories) will meet the requirements of all safety, health, and welfare legislation.

Other authorities
On some projects the architect will need to meet with the fire authority to confirm that the design will provide adequate means of escape in the event of fire, and on other contracts there will be a need to consult with authorities such as the gas, water, and electricity companies.

1.5 Summary of the main roles

It can be seen that most people involved in the building process can assume one of four main roles. These are

- to provide the demand and the money (e.g. the client or employer),
- to design the building or help in the process (e.g. the architect and the quantity surveyor),
- to help build (e.g. the contractor),
- to ensure that the building complies with the prevailing legislation and regulations (e.g. with planning and building regulations).

The roles may be combined: for example, the contractor may also be the designer; the employer and contractor may combine; or all three roles may be undertaken by one organisation.

1.6 Main approaches to building

There are two main approaches to building. The first is speculative building in which an entrepreneur buys land and builds upon it, hoping to sell the finished building for profit. The best known example of this is the firm that builds and sells houses to the general public. Speculative building results in a contract of sale. The contract may, in the case of a house, be based on viewing the actual house to be bought, or viewing a show house, or by just looking at the plans and specification. In most case the sale will be finally agreed after construction, but it could take place prior to construction.

The second main approach to building is a contract to build. The essential features of this are that a contract must precede construction, and the building takes place on land owned by the client.

This book is mainly concerned with the second of these two approaches. There are two main variants to this second approach. The first is where one firm is employed to design and build the building. The second is where the client's designer is responsible for the design, and a separate contractor is employed to construct a building to this design. This book is mainly concerned with the second of these two variants.

1.7 Technical terms

In order to gain knowledge of a subject it is necessary to become familiar with the language of the subject. As far as possible the various words and phrases forming the language of the subject of architectural design procedures will be explained as they occur for the first time in this book. However, it is considered useful to provide a summary for easy reference, and this has been supplied in Appendix 1. Readers are advised to refer to this Appendix whenever they come across an unfamiliar word or phrase.

2

Background to architectural practices

2.1 Introduction

This chapter explains how architecture emerged as a separate profession, how architects are educated and derive their authority, and it also looks at the newer and emerging profession of architectural technologists. It goes on to examine the architect's and architectural technologist's relationships and duties to clients and the public, the importance of architects and technologists keeping up to date after qualifying, and other important background matters that affect architectural practices.

2.2 The historic role of the architect

The word *architect* comes from the Greek word *archikton* meaning 'chief craftsman'. During the Middle Ages (about 1000 to 1400 AD) the term 'architect' was seldom used. He was commonly referred to as 'master' in English, *magister* in Latin, and *maestro* in Italian. Whatever the title, the architect in those days was considered to be a chief craftsman or master builder and overseer of works. He would not only plan and design but also engage the craftsmen and labourers needed to build his creations as well as supervise the actual building operations.

It is arguable that by using the term 'chief craftsman' the person who controls the erection of any structure is an architect. Under this definition a properly erected wigwam, a primitive hut, and Stonehenge are all the work of architects. Nowadays, however, most critics would tend to argue that an architect is a person responsible for a building which is not only conveniently planned and properly built but is pleasurable to the eye of the beholder. This is summed up in Sir Henry Wooten's book *The Elements of Architecture* (1624) in which he describes such a building as a 'commodity, firmness and delight', which remains today as the standard by which many judge architecture.

Egyptian architecture

In Egyptian times it was difficult to build structures which met Wooten's criteria. The slave labour used at that time was unskilled, and the buildings were massively formed from huge blocks of stone. The best example is the pyramids which are still standing today. These pyramids were in fact huge royal tombs, and clearly the originators of these gigantic structures possessed great mathematical skills.

Surrounding the pyramids were colleges and temples. The temples were commonly constructed of granite with tapering walls, rather squat pillars, and flat roofs. These Egyptian architects were proving that one of the simplest ways of roofing over a building is to span beams from wall to wall, supported by pillars where required. Outside the more important temples there would be gardens, and at the entrance to the temples a pair of tall tapering shafts, square on plan and known as obelisks.

Babylonian architecture

The Egyptian architects were not responsible for introducing the stepped method of construction which was the basis of the pyramids. The credit for this belongs to the Babylonians, who were responsible for the design and construction of the ziggurats of Mesopotania, built around 4000 BC. They were formed by building a succession of temples, with each temple consisting of a layer set upon the preceding layer, and set back from it, forming stepped, sloping sides.

Greek architecture

When the Greeks came to power the columns and beams used by the Egyptians in their temples were still employed. The Greeks, however, were essentially artists, and their apparently simple, though in reality extremely sophisticated, buildings, such as the Parthenon in Athens (Fig. 2.1) were often used as a background to their sculpture. In Greek buildings all was not as it appeared to be, for they used optical illusion in their buildings. The columns were not vertical, but curved, to give an illusion of straightness. Students of this period of architecture confirm that Greek architects, among other things, had a wonderful sense of proportion and great mathematical skills.

Roman architecture

The practice of architecture continued during the period of the Roman Empire, although the Romans lacked the Greeks' artistic skills. Pointed arches used in the Middle East about 700 AD, which were to be seen in Islamic architecture about

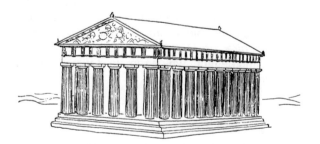

Fig. 2.1 Greek architecture

900 AD, were understood by the Greeks, but it was the Romans who used the arch freely, and this was one of the main contributions of the architects of the Roman period (Fig. 2.2). They also devoted themselves to work which today we would classify as civil engineering, such as roads and fortifications. Roman architecture often reflected the power and might of the Roman Empire.

Norman architecture

With the rise of Christianity came a demand for a new type of building. The Norman style was of heavy construction and very formal. It has been claimed that the man in charge of such a building – who we can call the 'architect' – was sometimes inclined to be a 'Jerry builder', because rubble was often used behind the finely finished surface work.

Gothic architecture

The workmanship improved with the use of the pointed arch during the Gothic period from the twelfth to the sixteenth century. This period included the Early

Fig. 2.2 Roman architecture

English, Decorated, and Perpendicular styles (see Figs. 2.3, 2.4 and 2.5). The stonemasons themselves greatly influenced the detail of the final buildings, and it is not certain where the master's work ended and the mason's work began. In any event, much more was left to the craftsperson than in previous times. Poets and painters of this period are well known to us, but much less is known of the 'architect' or 'master'. Examples are that the architect of Salisbury Cathedral is only known as Master Robert, and the architect of Westminster Abbey is simply known as Master Henry. Many great churches were supposedly designed and built by monks and priests, but whether they had architects or master craftspeople helping them is not known. Some masters were laypeople, and very influential too, occupying important positions such as members of parliament.

The Renaissance period

During the Renaissance period, from about the fifteenth century to the eighteenth century, England produced two of its greatest architects – Inigo Jones and Christopher Wren. Inigo Jones is sometimes referred to as the first architect, but he was also a celebrated theatrical designer and architectural draughtsman. He became surveyor general of the royal buildings. Christopher Wren was an architect, scien-

Fig. 2.3 Early English architecture

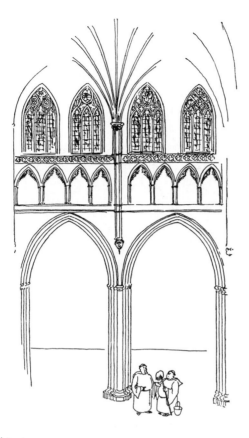

Fig. 2.4 Decorated architecture

tist, and mathematician. He, like many of his contemporaries, was very much involved with the technology and structural theory of buildings, as well as design. During this period, the architect, like the master builder before him, was a man of many skills. He would certainly be a builder and designer, but he might also be an artist, sculptor, scientist, and mathematician.

Engineering
It was around this time that the movement began which was to see the establishment of civil engineering as a profession distinct from architecture. A corps of military engineers had already been formed in France when, in 1716, a body of civilian engineers was established for the building of roads and bridges. A similar development took place in Britain, and by the second half of the eighteenth century engineering was establishing itself as a separate profession, which was taking over many of the architect's traditional roles, particularly in matters relating to science. Early civil engineering concerned itself mainly with the building of canals and

Fig. 2.5 Perpendicular architecture

works associated with transport, but, with the increasing use of machinery and the need for new structures such as mills, they extended their influence.

In some countries architects and engineers were considered to occupy a joint profession. Even in Britain there were those such as Thomas Telford who reckoned themselves to be architect-engineers. In the main, however, architects concerned themselves with traditional materials, such as stone, brickwork, concrete, and timber. It was left to the engineers to involve themselves with the newer materials of wrought iron and structural steel. These materials were first used in mills, and then in the great railway stations, and were largely the work of engineers. It was the engineers too who were most eager to use their scientific skills to make the best use of reinforced concrete and calculated design, as opposed to 'rule of thumb' for timber and masonry structures.

The Victorian era

Architects, for their part, were often engrossed in the artistic side of their profession and frequently continued to hide their buildings behind a veneer of classical detail so that by the Victorian era the architect was more concerned with decoration, while structure was the province of the engineer. An example is the Crystal Palace designed for the Great Exhibition of 1851. It was the work of a gardener, Joseph Paxton, based on his previous experience of greenhouse design, and was adopted by engineers with great success in the design of railway stations previously referred to.

Speculative building

In the nineteenth century, as well as producing buildings for clients, architects sometimes erected building 'on spec'. By the nineteenth century builders had separated from architects, and in the twentieth century builders occasionally employed architects to prepare plans of their speculative housing and industrial schemes. Meanwhile, as buildings became more complicated, with a wider range of components, materials, and services, architects handed over more of their functions to other specialists such as mechanical and electrical engineers and quantity surveyors.

Conclusions

In conclusion, it can be said that the constant role of the architect through the centuries has been to plan or design buildings, including the production of many of the drawings required. Generally, he has been involved to some extent in the construction, either actually building or being engaged in the supervision and inspection of the work. As has been suggested earlier, his detailed role has varied from period to period and his skills have included those of artist, mathematician, and engineer. At the present time we have moved away from the concept of the architect being responsible for everything, towards a situation of shared responsibility. However, even though much of the original role has been taken over by others, the aim remains of producing a building which meets Sir Henry Wooten's criteria of 'commodity, firmness and delight'.

2.3 Design team framework today

It has been previously mentioned that construction work today is more complex, for a number of reasons. As is discussed in chapter 3 there is a wider choice of procurement systems, including traditional, design and construct, develop and construct, and management contracting. There is also a greater variety of materials and techniques, an increase in the scope of work, and it is likely that jobs are more likely to be unique. This leads to the need for a properly structured design team in which everyone contributes their own particular skills. The architect is generally responsible for the innovative design, and more often than not will also have the task of maintaining overall control of the project. The architectural technician will collaborate with the architect on many aspects of the job and is likely in particular to contribute in the field of architectural technology. Sometimes architects and architectural technologists will develop their own specialisations and concentrate on particular aspects. For example, one might provide the perspectives, another the schedules, a third the small-scale location drawings, another could concentrate on more complicated areas of construction, and so on.

Apart from work undertaken by the architectural staff, help will often be required from consultants for specialised areas of work. The Royal Institute of British Architects (RIBA) *Architect's Job Book* includes the following consultancy services: quantity surveying, structural engineering, mechanical engineering, electrical engineering, landscape and garden design, civil engineering, town planning, furniture design, graphic design, industrial design, and interior design. Sometimes these consultancy services are provided within the architect's or architectural technologist's own office by partners, associates, or directly employed staff. Sometimes the service will be by consultants in association with the architects or architectural technologists. Frequently they will be undertaken by consultants in independent professional practices.

Whether or not it is necessary to employ consultants depends on the complexity of the project. For example if the project consists of a single house the architect would consider the design of the structure part of his normal duties. If it were a large office block with a steel or reinforced concrete structure, a structural engineer would generally be engaged and the client would normally pay additional fees for his services. The most commonly employed consultants are probably quantity surveyors, structural engineers, and building services engineers.

Throughout the project the quantity surveyor will be involved with the financial aspects, including the monitoring of costs.

The structural engineer will obviously be responsible for the main building structure. Often there will be a division of duties within the structural work. As well as the division between the designers and detailers or draughtspersons there will often be specialisation between reinforced concrete work, structural steelwork, structural timber work, and structural masonry.

A similar situation will prevail in the building engineering services section. Again there will often be designers and draughtspersons, specialising in electrical, heating and air conditioning, plumbing and drainage, fire protection work, and so on.

The design team will consist of architectural staff, together with staff responsible for the specialised areas of work mentioned above. The architect is the person most likely to be the coordinator of the whole project, instructing the consultants and having regular and frequent meetings with them, but sometimes this role will be performed by the architectural technologist, and less frequently by some other design team member.

On a large job, with many people involved, the system becomes quite complex and it is important that all activities are properly controlled and integrated. It is also vital to define clearly who is responsible for what, to allocate realistic time-scales to each operation, and to make sure that everyone knows what is happening.

2.4 Architects today

Today the architect continues to be widely recognised as the leader of the building team, performing the dual role of building designer, in which he is able to contribute the results of his specialist training in innovative design, and construction organiser, all within the setting of a traditional form of contract. This presupposes that the architect possesses both theoretical and creative skills to produce an acceptable design and working drawings, and practical skills to manage the administration of a functionally satisfactory building.

Sometimes, as was mentioned in the account of the historic role of the architect (see section 2.2), there has been a move away from the traditional form of contract in which the architect occupies a dominant role in the building process. This is discussed in sections 3.3–3.6 of chapter 3. In some other contracts the leader and coordinator of the building team is not the architect but an architectural technologist, quantity surveyor, structural engineer, or building services engineer, with suitable management skills.

The majority of architects are employed either in private practices or by local authorities, government departments, and similar offices. Most of these are salaried, some are partners or directors of practices, and, in a time when the belief that 'biggest is best' has a substantial following, many still operate as 'one-man band' offices. The remaining architects are employed in a variety of situations, including the architect's departments of contractors, facilities departments of large industrial and commercial companies (including property and insurance companies), research organisations, manufacturer's design-and-development departments, consultancies (including interior design consultancies), and in education.

2.5 Education of architects

As has already been mentioned, throughout the years there have been differing opinions as to whether everyone controlling the erection of a structure should be entitled to use the title of 'architect', or whether this term should be reserved for one who bears the responsibility for a building, which, in Sir Henry Wooten's words, combines 'commodity, firmness and delight'. It was only during the twentieth century that there was a successful attempt to restrict the architect's title.

This move began in 1831 with the founding of the Architectural Society, which was intended to establish a school of architecture to educate prospective architects. No formal examinations were set by the Architectural Society, but a condition of membership was that applicants had to complete five years of study.

In 1834 the Institute of British Architects was formed. After only three years it was granted a royal charter and changed its name to the Royal Institute of British Architects (RIBA). Since that time the RIBA has been the recognised head of the architectural profession in the UK. In 1941 Chairs of Architecture were established in Kings College, London. Students successfully completing these courses were awarded a diploma.

In 1847 the Architectural Association (AA) was founded and eventually enjoyed royal patronage. Its chief function was educational, and membership was open to all those engaged in the architectural profession. The AA asked the RIBA to establish an examination in architecture, and the RIBA did so in 1863. By the early 1890s the normal entry to RIBA membership was by means of examination. During 1887 the RIBA instigated an examination system of preliminary, intermediate, and final examinations, which were to last for 80 years and were the forerunner of the present examination system.

In the 1880s the normal method of entry to the architectural profession was by means of training as an articled pupil in an architect's office. During later periods this was supplemented by attendance at evening classes and lectures. The success or otherwise of the training depended to a large extent on the choice of office.

In 1889 the AA set up its own examination system based on full-time education, with studio instruction. Other full-time courses at various colleges and universities followed. These received recognition by the RIBA as giving exemption from the RIBA's own examinations, so that by the early 1930s there were 19 recognised courses. In effect, the RIBA settled the question as to whether it was best to be trained in an architectural school or in an architect's office. Its recognition and encouragement of such full-time schools of architecture had indicated its preference for school training.

Today a minority of aspiring architects continue to work full-time in architect's offices and study part-time for the RIBA's own external examinations. The vast majority, however, study full-time at approved schools of architecture and are granted full exemption from the RIBA's examinations.

A typical course will be a three-year degree course giving RIBA part I exemption, followed by a three-year postgraduate diploma course with the first year being spent in a professional office, with exemption from the RIBA's part II examination. A further year of practical training follows, with an examination giving exemption from the RIBA's part III examination. The student is then able to register as an architect and become a full member of the RIBA.

2.6 Architects' registration acts

Once the formal education system for architects was firmly established the moves to protect the title of 'architect' began. At the time the issue was raised there were differences of opinion as to the motives of those seeking such protection. Nevertheless, Parliament decided it was in the public interest to protect the architect's title and ensure that all who called themselves 'architects' were suitably qualified.

The Architect's (Registration) Act 1931 established the Architect's Registration Council of the United Kingdom (ARCUK), which set up a register of architects. Once set up, the only new admissions to the register were those who had passed the RIBA-recognised examinations. The title 'registered architect' was therefore protected.

The Architect's (Registration) Act 1938 extended the powers of the 1931 Act by restricting the use of the title 'architect' to registered architects. It is still possible for people to call themselves landscape architects, or naval architects. Various titles are used today by people who at least in part undertake the work of architects, although they are not registered, such as architectural designers, architectural consultants, architectural surveyors, and building designers.

In order to escape prosecution under the 1938 Architect's Registration Act, it is no argument to claim that you have the skills of an architect. The question is whether or not your name is on the ARCUK register [now the Architects' Registration Board (ARB) register, see below]. In 1988 a case came before a magistrates court where the ARCUK prosecuted a multidisciplinary small works company for describing themselves as architects on their headed notepaper. The firm was headed by a man who had qualified as an architect, and at one time had been on the register of architects. He had, however, ceased paying his annual fee to the ARCUK and had therefore been struck off the register. He was convicted by the court and fined £500.

In the early 1990s the right of the ARCUK to restrict the use of the description 'architect' to those who had followed an approved course of education and training was put under threat when the Conservative government engaged in an extensive programme of deregulation. Among the targets was the protected status of the title of 'architect', and the government announced its intention to deregulate this title. Their plans were opposed by the RIBA, who launched a vigorous and, what proved to be a successful, campaign. In 1993 the government, handicapped by an overcrowded programme of deregulation, dropped its proposals, while stating that it remained convinced that deregulation of the title was the right way to go eventually.

The next development in the story of architect's registration was the arrival of the Housing Grants, Construction and Regeneration Act 1996. Part III of this important act made provision to amend the law relating to architects. It was decreed that ARCUK be known as the Architects' Registration Board (ARB), and that the ARB appoint a Registrar of Architects. The Registrar has the responsibility of maintaining a Register of Architects in which should be entered the name of every person entitled to be registered under the Act.

The Act sets out the requirements of entitlement to registration which are, broadly, that the right examinations have been passed, the right qualifications have been obtained, and that the applicant has an acceptable standard of competence and practical experience.

The registered person may be required to pay a yearly retention fee to remain on the register, and if he fails to pay the fee, he is liable to have his name removed from the register. He is also liable to have his name removed if the Professional Conduct Committee of the ARB find the architect guilty of unacceptable professional conduct or serious professional incompetence. However, the disciplinary order may result in a lesser penalty, such as a reprimand.

The ARB has the responsibility for issuing a code of practice, laying down the standards of professional conduct and practice for registered persons. The code has to be kept under review, in consultation with those with an interest in architecture.

The Housing Grants, Construction and Regeneration Act 1996 was followed by the Architects Act 1997, which had the declared aim of consolidating the enactments relating to architects. The consolidation covered the key items of the ARB, the Registrar, the register, the Professional Conduct Committee, and disciplinary orders. In addition it provided for the registration of nationals of any state which is a contracting party to the European Economic Area (EEA) Agreement.

The Architects' Registration Board came into being in April 1997. It is made up of eight lay members who are appointed by the Privy Council, and seven elected architects, who are elected by members on the register. The main difference between the former ARCUK and the present Architects' Registration Board is that the Board is more consumer-orientated – its main objective is protection of the consumer. It should also be noted that the Board has a lay majority.

2.7 Architectural technologists today

Architectural technologists are often employed in architects offices, assisting in all aspects of work required on building projects. The work is varied but will generally fall into one of the following four areas:

- technical design;
- investigation and survey;
- management and administration;
- procurement and contracts.

Among the skills required by the professional architectural technologist are:

- to be able to apply, synthesise, and integrate research;
- to perform computer-aided design (CAD);
- to have a knowledge of conservation;
- to have a feeling for contextualisation and a breadth of understanding (e.g. to look at the discipline across Europe and beyond);
- to be able to perform contract administration and management;
- to understand contract economics;
- to have creativity and a knowledge of design;
- to undertake environmental studies;
- to have a knowledge of the science and technology of building;
- to possess legal and legislative knowledge;
- to have a sound professional judgement as well as decision-making and analytical skills;
- to be capable of site investigating and surveying;
- to undertake a study of buildings and their components;
- to have work experience.

Exactly what the architectural technologist does may vary from office to office. In many practices the architect is responsible for the overall design and management of a project, whereas the technologist's task is to ensure the provision of good technical information and day-to-day site liaison. In the matter of design, the architect is more likely to be involved in the innovative design, and the technologist in the technical design, although it could be argued that it is impossible to separate one from the other.

The British Institute of Architectural Technology's (BIAT's) 1996 report, 'Into the 21st Century', summarised the architectural technologist's primary function as follows: 'An architectural technologist applies the science of architecture and specializes in the technological aspects of building design and construction'.

In addition to working in traditional architect's practices, many qualified architectural technologists become directors or partners of architectural practices or are the principals of firms of architectural technologists. Some become heads of departments in a variety of organisations, while others work in education or in the product manufacturing side of construction.

2.8 Education of architectural technologists

When The Society of Architectural and Associated Technicians (SAAT), the forerunner of BIAT, was inaugurated in 1965, under the sponsorship of the RIBA, the academic requirement for membership was the attainment of the Higher National Certificate or Diploma in Building (HNC/HND), plus evidence that the applicant could show, by the keeping of logbooks and interviews, that he had an acceptable level of practical experience. In the case of Business and Technical Education Council (BTEC) certificates and diplomas, the programme followed had to be one appropriate for a career in architecture and, in addition to common skills and core subjects, to include specialised study areas such as architectural detailing and design procedures.

With the development of degrees in architectural technology, first mooted in the early 1980s, the Institute moved towards a degree-level entry. Their 1986 report 'Into the 21st Century' stated that there were eight accredited degree courses in architectural technology, with 10 more courses proposed, and degrees being developed in a further seven academic institutions.

A further development in the field of education for architectural technologists took place in 1997 with the launch of the National/Scottish Vocational Qualificai-tions (NVQ/SVQs) level 4, designed for those working in architectural technology, in both the private and the public sector. The National Council for Vocational Qualificaitons (NCVQ) was set up by the government in 1996 to provide a frame-work of qualifications, reflecting the skills, knowledge, and understanding an individual must possess in relation to a specific area of work. The NVQ in archi-tectural technology is awarded by the Architectural Awarding Body. The lead organisation is BIAT, supported by the Architects and Surveyors Institute (ASI), the Chartered Institute of Building (CIOB), and the RIBA. The NVQ/SVQ level 4 in Architectural Technology is recognised by BIAT as meeting the educational requirements for membership of their Institute.

2.9 Continuing professional development

Professional institutions recognise that the public expect professional people to be well informed and up to date in their area of expertise. This has led the institutions to require their members to continue studying after qualifying to ensure that they keep abreast of the latest developments and maintain and upgrade their skills. This is the general meaning of 'continuing professional development' (CPD).

The RIBA made CPD obligatory for its members in 1993. BIAT states that their members 'have a professional obligation to undertake 35 hours CPD per year'. The way this can be achieved varies to some extent between the various bodies, but can include studying for further qualifications, undertaking research, attending relevant courses, writing technical articles, and undertaking a structured home reading programme.

2.10 The architectural practitioner's relationship with the client

The client's expectation of the architect
Under Section 2 of the Architect's (Registration) Act 1938 an architect is defined as

> one who possesses with due regard to aesthetic as well as practical considerations, adequate skill and knowledge to enable him to originate,

> to design and plan, to arrange for and supervise the execution of such buildings, or other works, calling for skill in design and planning as he might in the course of his business, reasonably be asked to carry out in respect of which he offers his services as a specialist.

This means that the architect must show the care, expertise, and application expected of people practising this profession. It does not mean there will be no mistakes. Building projects are often complicated and unique. Even if an architect works competently, and takes the same reasonable care and application as any other experienced architect, it is possible, as a result of a combination of unfortunate circumstances, for things to go wrong. However, the architect is unlikely to be held responsible if reasonable care, skill, and expertise has been used. This is discussed in some detail in chapter 4.

The architectural practitioner's role as agent

The need for an architect to act as a skilled practitioner of his art is vital because he acts as the agent for his client, or employer, as the client is legally called. He is therefore subject to the law of agency, which is part of the law of contract.

The term 'agency' is used to describe the special relationship that exists when one party, the principal (who in the case we are considering is the employer, or client), employs another party, called the agent (in this case the architect or architectural technologist), to act on their behalf. There are several classes of agency. The usual class for the architect or architectural technologist is 'special', and means they act for the employer (client) in the design and supervision of one particular building.

This means in effect that the architectural practitioner and client enter into a contract. The contract does not have to be in any particular form. It may be written or spoken, but as people's memories are not always reliable it is probably best to put the terms of the appointment in writing.

Terms of appointment

The usual method of formalising the architect–client relationship is the RIBA's Standard Form of Agreement for the Appointment of an Architect. This consists of a Memorandum of Agreement, Conditions of Appointment, and Schedules. Schedule One identifies the information to be supplied by the client; Schedule Two the service to be provided by the architect; Schedule Three the fee arrangement; and Schedule Four deals with any other consultants, specialists, and site staff appointed.

BIAT have a standard form, called Confirmation of Instructions, which the architectural technologist sends to the client confirming the client's instructions to act for him. The form, which provides certain information, such as work stages to be included and the fees to be charged, is reproduced in Fig. 11.40 in the chapter on Standard Documentation (chapter 11). It is usual when sending the Confirmation of Instructions form also to send a copy of BIAT's form 'Conditions of Engagement'. The Confirmation form includes a request to the client to send written confirmation that the conditions are acceptable.

Architectural practitioner's duties

The architect and architectural technologist's duties include entering into contractual obligations with a third party (the contractor) on behalf of the employer. In carrying these out he is expected to use the care and skill which the employer can reasonably expect of his architect or architectural technologist. When agreeing to become the employer's agent, the architectural practitioner will be well advised to satisfy himself that his interests will not be in conflict with the employer's interests.

The employer for his part is legally liable for acts undertaken by his agent – the architect or architectural technologist – if those acts are executed on his behalf. The architectural practitioner has many duties as the employer's agent, but despite his involvement he is not personally liable for claims made against the employer, provided he has acted within the terms of his authority.

Unlike the situation in which an employer engages someone as a salaried employee and can dictate the manner in which the work is performed, in the case of an agent the architectural practitioner can carry out his duties in whatever way he considers most appropriate. Nevertheless there are limitations. He cannot, unbeknown to the employer, hand over his entire duties to someone else. This does not prevent him using the service of other people such as quantity surveyors, structural engineers, building services engineers, and a clerk of works to assist him. Indeed, this is the normal procedure in a project, except small, simple ones.

An architect's power to act as the employer's agent is strictly limited by the terms of the Memorandum of Agreement. In the initial stages he is generally just acting as a designer. However, at some stage, particularly when he is permitted to seek tenders from contractors, he is working as the employer's agent and must take care to exercise his professional skill and to act in the employer's interest.

Although the architectural practitioner is the employer's agent he cannot do as he pleases. During the contract period he cannot instruct the contractor to undertake work which will vary the contract conditions. It is the normal procedure always to make it clear that he is acting as an agent and to disclose the name of his employer.

Possible complications

The fact that the client and architect sign a carefully worded Memorandum of Agreement does not mean that they fully understand the significance of the documents, and complications sometimes arise. A similar situation exists with an architectural technologist who supplies his client with the BIAT current Conditions of Employment and receives written confirmation from the client that the conditions are acceptable. The main complication can occur when the building contract is signed between the employer and the contractor, and the architectural practitioner is named in the contract. This gives him specific rights and duties, during and after construction, in respect of matters such as the giving of instructions and approvals and nomination of people to supply materials and undertake part of the work. Although he will perform all these actions as the employer's agent, the courts have recognised that he derives power from the building contract in an almost independent manner. If disagreements arise between the employer and contractor, this again does not mean he can do what he likes but rather that he must dispense justice between the two parties in accordance with the express terms of the contract. He therefore has the dual and difficult role of being both the employer's agent and an independent arbitrator.

Another possible area of confusion is the matter of fees. When quoting a fee it is important that the architectural practitioner makes the client aware as to exactly what this includes. The fees given in the RIBA Practice Documentation are for a full service covering the work required for all 10 stages of the RIBA Plan of Work. However, there are some items which are not covered, such as locating a suitable site for the client's intended building. Neither do they include the services of other professionals, such as quantity surveyors and structural engineers, even if the architect has qualified people from these disciplines within his own office.

Another matter which surprises some clients is that the bulk of the architect's fees become due before any building work takes place. At Stage G, which is when the bills of quantities are prepared, and before any tenders are obtained, the client could be liable for 75% of the total fees.

Consultants

Under the terms of the RIBA Agreement both the employer and the architect have the right to nominate a consultant, but only if the other party agrees. Regardless as to who initially nominated the consultant, the RIBA Conditions of Appointment makes it clear that the individual consultant, and not the architect, is responsible for the standard of work in the activity assigned to them.

2.11 Codes of conduct

Architects and architectural technologists are expected to show a high standard of professional behaviour. These standards of professional conduct are aimed not only at maintaining the status and uprightness of architects and architectural technologists but also in looking after the interests of the public. To this end they seek to ensure that architects and architectural technologists are not faced with a conflict of interest, by regulating situations where they involve themselves in activities such as land and property dealing and estate agency.

The 11th edition of the RIBA's *Code of Professional Conduct* states three main principles which are obligatory for its members. They are:

1. A member shall faithfully carry out his duties, applying his knowledge and experience with efficiency and loyalty towards his client or employer, and being mindful of the interests of those who may be expected to use or enjoy the products of his work.

2. A member shall, at all times, avoid any action or situation which is inconsistent with his professional obligations or which is likely to raise doubts about his integrity.

3. A member shall in every circumstance conduct himself in a manner which respects the legitimate rights and interests of others.

The RIBA Code of Conduct is a 13-page A5 document which sets out the code in detail, amplifying each principle with rules and explanatory notes.

BIAT also has a *Code of Conduct* booklet for its members. It contains 15 clauses and an introductory note which reads as follows:

> The object of this Code of Conduct is to promote the standard of conduct or self discipline required of members of the Institute in the interests of the public. It aims to ensure:
>
> (a) that all members conduct themselves in a manner consistent with that of a professional person.
>
> (b) that one member does not gain an unfair advantage over another.
>
> (c) that members do not misrepresent themselves.
>
> (d) that the public may rely upon the Institute's members for their integrity and professionalism.

2.12 Quality assurance

Up to now in this chapter consideration has been given to background matters affecting people engaged in architectural practices, such as their education and relationship with each other. Attention will now be directed at issues influencing the management and economic success of practices.

The first of these is the concept of quality assurance (QA), which is now firmly established in the UK and widely accepted as a helpful management tool. Quality assurance can be defined as management systems based on a code of practice but adapted to enable the services and products on offer to meet all customer needs adequately. This aim is achieved by painstaking scrutiny of the organisation, design, production, and installation, and effective control of personnel and resources. All of this needs to be supported by an independent third-party registration, inspection and, certification service.

QA was originally devised for the USA space programme, but today its principles are being increasingly applied to the construction industry. At present it is more widely used by contractors to manage the construction process, but it has been adopted by some architectural practices and members of the design team to improve the control and quality of their services.

2.13 Quality management

The corollary of QA is quality management (QM), or total quality management (TQM). This can be described as the effective administration of quality assurance systems (QAS) and will include correct procedures for matters such as design, planning, control, testing, and training policies.

In 1979 Britain became the first country to introduce a quality management standard. This was British Standard (BS) 5750, and it was promptly adopted, practically unchanged, by the International Standards Organization (ISO). It is now referred to as BS EN ISO 9000, commonly shortened to ISO 9000.

ISO 9000 includes the following items which must be considered when evaluating QAS and QM: management responsibility and organisation; quality manuals and quality planning; design control; document control; process control; inspection and testing; internal quality audits; and training.

2.14 Architects in the European Union

Under a directive which came into operation in 1987 architects in a member country of the European Union (EU) became eligible for registration in any of the other member countries. If architects from countries outside the UK wish to be registered in the UK they have to produce their diplomas, final-year drawings, and dissertation to the Architect's Registration Board (ARB) [formerly the Architect's Registration Council of the United Kingdom (ARCUK)]. They are also required to pay a fee and convince an interview panel of their competence to practise architecture in the UK. The procedure deals with individual architects, and not with architectural practices.

The aim of the directive mentioned above was to bring all EU architectural qualifications in line with each other so that architects are able to work in any part of the EU regardless of which country they obtained their qualification.

In 1993 EU countries became part of a single European market. This had significant implications for architects and others working in the construction industry. As well as formalising the mutual recognition of professional qualifications, they provided for the harmonisation of things such as building contracts and building regulations.

At present only a small number of UK architects practise outside their own country. This may in part be because of the fact that traditional methods of working vary from country to country. In France, for example, the architect generally only prepares the design drawings, and the production drawings are the responsibility of the contractor.

3

Organisation and business side of architectural practices

3.1 Introduction

In order to run a successful architectural practice, an architect or architectural technologist needs to have a range of abilities in addition to design and technical skills. They include an aptitude to organise and manage, and business acumen. This chapter is concerned with that aspect of work and, in particular with the various modes of practice operating under a traditional system, with alternative non-traditional methods, with the function of the various members of the design team, with the need for good communications, and how architects and technologists obtain work and are paid for what they do.

3.2 Types of practice

There are various modes of practice which may be used by architects and technologists, and these are summarised below. The type of architectural practice adopted is important because of the legal and financial ramifications, which will affect employers, employees, and clients.

Self-employed principals
Many architectural practices start with one architect or architectural technologist working alone, possibly from their own home, with the first jobs coming through friends and relatives. If the work expands the principal will employ staff to assist him and probably move into office premises. Alternatively, he may decide to enter into some form of association with other professionals.

Partnerships
Partnerships are probably the commonest form of architectural practice. Architects and technologists enter into partnerships because of the extra strength and flexibility such an arrangement brings. There is some truth in the saying that 'two heads are better than one', and most professionals will sometimes find a second opinion

helpful. It is also useful to have a partner during holiday periods and times of sickness and personal problems. Other advantages of partnerships as compared with single principals are the even distribution of workload between the partners, the effective use of resources (e.g. staff and workspace), and the availability of more funds. The range of partnerships is considerable. It may vary from two life-long friends working together in a single office, to a practice having a dozen branches, twenty partners, a hundred associates, and five hundred employees. However, increasingly, the larger practices tend to be organised as limited liability companies.

A partnership is a relationship between persons carrying on a business in common, with a view to profit. It is possible for a partnership to operate on a very informal basis, but regrettably disputes do arise, so it is generally advisable to draw up a 'deed of partnership' between the parties, using the services of a solicitor. The agreement, drafted by the solicitor, should clearly define the way the partnership will operate, including the proportion of capital to be provided by each partner and how the profits will be divided among the partners. Furthermore, it is vital to state the grounds on which the partnership can be dissolved. These include death, retirement, bankruptcy, and incapacity.

A partnership means that a number of people (i.e. all the partners) are legally liable for the debts of the business. The liability continues to be unlimited, in the same way as it does with a self-employed principal. It is important for individuals who in reality are self-employed principals not to give others the impression that they are in partnership. This could happen in the case of two people who work independently but operate from a jointly owned office.

In most businesses there are restrictions where the number of partners exceeds 20, but professional people, such as architects, can form partnerships with as many partners as they like. Partnerships are often colloquially referred to as a 'firm', but there is no legal significance in this term.

If a partnership, or a sole proprietorship, is carried on under a name other than the surnames of the partners or self-employed principal there are certain restrictions which apply. First, the firm's name must not give the impression, by the use of certain words, that it is connected with the government or local authority. Second, the actual names of the people involved must be given on all business letters and forms.

Sometimes partnerships give senior staff the title of 'associates'. Use of such a title gives senior staff status in the eyes of the 'firm' and other contacts, but no legal liability is attached unless the title 'associate partner' is used. In some instances a retired partner may be retained as a consultant, perhaps continuing to be involved because of a long-standing relationship with a particular client.

Partnerships have to pay income tax on their profits, regardless as to whether they are distributed among the partners or left in the business.

Unlimited liability companies

Companies are mainly controlled by the Companies Acts of 1985 and 1989. They are owned and directed by shareholders and directors who can be generally compared to partners in a partnership. Unlimited liability companies have one main advantage compared with partnerships: directors of companies are freed from liability for the company's debts a year after they have left the company. The other main difference is that the company pays corporation tax at a fixed percentage rate on its net profits. The arrangement governing its financial position is quite complicated, and apart from the one advantage mentioned above there is not necessarily any advantage to be gained. For this reason it is not very common for architectural firms to operate under an unlimited liability company format.

Limited liability company

Fairly recent changes to the code of professional conduct of the Architect's Registration Council of the United Kingdom (ARCUK) [now the Architects' Registration Board (ARB)] now permits architects, and most other professionals, to practise under this form of organisation. The most important and, evident from the heading, obvious difference between a limited liability company and an unlimited company is that in the case of a limited company the personal responsibility of the partners (i.e. shareholders) is limited. The theory behind this situation is that a limited liability company has a separate legal personality from its owners. This means that if the company gets into debt, the personal assets of the owners cannot be claimed to pay off these debts.

This is of great importance when a professional is subject to a claim for negligence. This matter is discussed in chapter 4. As liability for mistakes, and alleged mistakes by architects and other professionals, with the resulting claims for liability, is a real problem for architectural practices, it is likely there will be an increasing trend for architects and technologists to practice as limited liability companies. It can, of course, be argued that a client who feels an architectural firm is practising as a limited liability company so as to protect itself against claims for negligence may lose confidence in the firm and decide to take their custom elsewhere. The above comment represents one viewpoint, which not everyone would agree with.

Public limited company

Even more recently architects have been permitted to operate in the form of a public limited company (plc). A public limited company must use the word limited (Ltd) at the end of its title. A public limited company has the advantage of being able to raise large amounts of money from investors both large and small and to transfer the shares from one investor to another through the stock exchange.

The listing of a company on the stock exchange is also useful because it makes it easier for the company to raise additional capital if it wishes to expand its activities. All the partners in such a firm will be shareholders, although not all will necessarily be on the board of directors.

Integrated practice

An integrated practice is one where the partners come from a number of different professional disciplines. Within the firm there may be one or more architects, architectural technicians, structural engineers, building services engineers, quantity surveyors, town planners, and landscape architects. Such a practice can operate as either a partnership or as one of the types of companies mentioned above. This kind of practice is most useful on large, complicated projects as it means clients can deal with a single firm yet still benefit from the full range of professional skills.

Group practice

In a group practice a number of separate architectural firms combine together so as to offer an improved service to their clients, but they still retain their independence. In a group practice firms do not share profits or responsibilities to clients, although they might share resources, such as staff and telephone lines. The precise arrangement will vary from practice to practice. One possibility is for several partnerships to amalgamate so as to undertake a very large job. One of the group members will have to take responsibility for coordinating the work and accepting liability as far as the client is concerned. Another possibility is that firms in different parts of the country may combine together for their mutual advantage.

Consortia

In the case of consortia, firms from a number of different professional disciplines are grouped together, but each firm retains its separate identity. An example would be when a firm of architects, structural engineers, and building services engineers all cooperate in the design and contract administration of a hospital.

Service companies

Before changes in the code of the ARCUK (now the ARB) permitted architects to practice as a limited company, some architects used a limited liability company to provide non-professional services, such as renting or owning office accommodation, furniture, and cars, and employing non-technical personnel such as secretarial and printing staff. There are sometimes financial advantages in forming service companies of this type.

3.3 Design-and-construct organisations

The architectural practices described above all relate to situations where a traditional arrangement is followed and the architect or architectural technologist is independent of the contracting side of the building team. Consideration will now be given to non-traditional arrangements where the architectural team members are more dependent on the rest of the team and generally adopt a lower profile.

In the nineteenth century, as has been stated in section 2.2. of chapter 2, it had become common practice in the UK for there to be a clear division of responsibility between the design and construction of a building.

In more recent years design-and-construct, or design-and-build, organisations have been set up in which the contractor receives a brief directly from the client and is employed to undertake both the design and the construction work. Design-and-construct organisations employ their own architects, architectural technologists, structural engineers, building services engineers, quantity surveyors, and any other necessary specialists. They are able to involve the contracting staff in the design process in an attempt to achieve the most economic solution in terms of both time and money. In some cases the contractor sublets the design and drawing work to a private architectural firm. In all cases where design-and-construct contracts are used, the architect or architectural technologist will provide all the architectural functions, including briefing, feasibility, design, and production information.

Work can be obtained on the basis of a negotiated price. In order to reassure the client that he is not being asked to pay an excessive price, some design-and-construct organisations recommend the client to employ their own professional quantity surveyor to monitor the costs. Sometimes a 'shared savings' form of contract will be employed, so that surplus profit above an agreed sum will be shared on a 50: 50 basis, or on a 'split' more favourable to the client.

The alternative is for work to be won on a competitive basis. Each design-and-build contractor will prepare a design and price for a building, based on the client's brief. The disadvantage of such an approach is that it may be difficult to ensure that one is comparing 'like with like', and it will probably be more time-consuming, thus losing one of the main advantages claimed for the design-and-build system.

Some of the advantages and disadvantages for the design-and-construct as opposed to the traditional arrangement are given below. The advantages are that:

- the client is able to deal with a single organisation, and often with a single person, thus avoiding divided responsibility and the possibility of confusion;
- communication between the builder and designer is improved, which helps them to be more aware of each other's problems and thus arrive at a better solution;
- it is possible to improve the programme time; one reason for this is that work on-site can commence as soon as the first information is available from the design team; subsequent drawings and other production information can be produced as work proceeds and according to a tight schedule.

The disadvantages are that:

- the quality of the design may suffer, as the organisation may be over concerned with speed and cost of construction, at the expense of the design;
- the client does not have an independent adviser to look after his interests;
- if the work is won in competition the client cannot be sure he is comparing schemes of the same quality, and if the work is negotiated he may be paying above the market rate for the job.

Figure 3.1 illustrates the basic structure of the design-and-construct method.

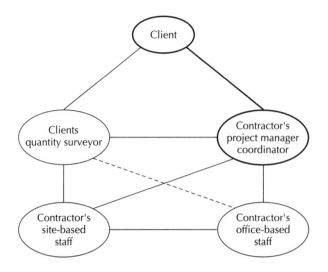

Fig. 3.1 Design-and-construct method

3.4 The develop-and-construct approach

A variation of the design-and-construct method is the design-and-develop approach. In this system the client employs an independent architect or architectural technologist to prepare a sketch design, illustrating the client's requirements in outline, and the contractor develops a detailed scheme and price. The successful contractor will then be responsible for all the detailed production drawings.

The advantages claimed for this approach is that the designer ensures that the client gets what he wants, particularly in regard to the planning and appearance of the building, and the contract is able to ensure that the solution is practicable and economic because he has helped influence the method and details of the construction.

3.5 Management contracting

An alternative way of organising a construction project is by management contracting. This procedure developed from a desire to capitalise on the skills both of the design team members and of the contractor, and to bring them together in a management team whilst retaining the advantage of competitive tendering.

The arrangement adopted is for the client to employ a contractor at the initial stage of the contract, and to pay him an agreed fee to manage the construction work. The management contractor takes responsibility for the site layout and organisation but would not generally undertake any of the permanent construction work. This would be done by subcontractors who would obtain contracts for various parts of the project by competitive tendering and who would be answerable to the management contractor. The architect and other members of the design team are employed by, and answerable to, the client but will need to produce their drawings and other information in accordance with a programme largely dictated by the management contractor. This contractual method is illustrated in Figure 3.2.

3.6 Construction and project management

A variation of the system outlined above is for the client not only to appoint and pay a contractor to manage the project but also to enter into contracts with each individual subcontractor. As with the previous method the client will directly employ the design team. The arrangement tends to place the management contractor, architect, and other design team members and subcontractors, on a similar footing, as they all have direct contracts with the client and work together as equal members of the client's management team. Figure 3.3 illustrates this method.

A further variation is the project management system, where a project manager

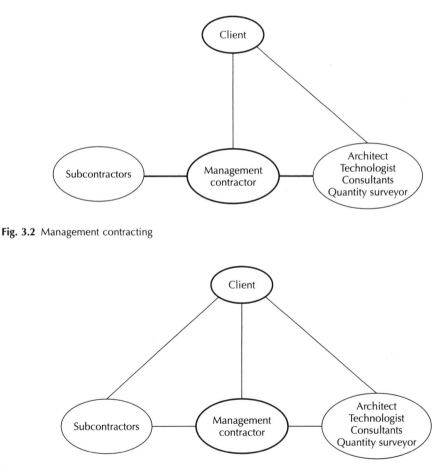

Fig. 3.2 Management contracting

Fig. 3.3 Construction management

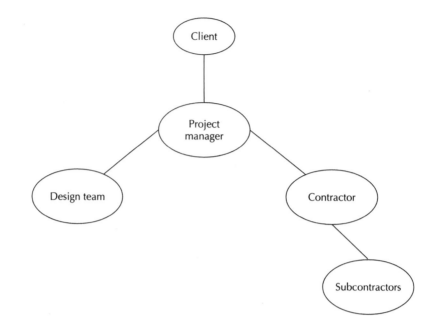

Fig. 3.4 Project management

directs the project for the client. His duties include the selection, organising, and coordinating of both the contracting and the design team members. The main expertise expected of the project manager is the ability to manage a construction project effectively, and the background of the person selected for this role will be influenced by possession of this quality and by the nature of the project. It may be someone with an architectural background but could be a quantity surveyor, contract manager, or some other construction professional. Figure 3.4 illustrates this system.

3.7 The Latham Report

In 1994 a review commissioned jointly by the government and the construction industry, and made under the leadership of Sir Michael Latham, was published. It was entitled *Constructing the Team*, and examined the procurement and contractual arrangements in the UK construction industry. It was a far-reaching review, covering the following areas:

- the role of clients;
- project and contract strategies and briefing;
- the design process (involving consultants and specialist contractors);
- contract choice for clients;
- selection and tendering procedures;
- issues which determine performance;

- teamwork on-site;
- dispute resolution;
- insolvency and security of payment;
- liability post-completion;
- implementation and priorities.

The report included many recommendations to tackle the problems revealed during the consultation process. Among the matters emphasised was the important role that clients should play, the need for more teamwork, an end to the adversarial approach, more equable contracts, improved management, better professional training, increased collaboration, and partnering. Twelve working groups were set up to implement Sir Michael Latham's recommendations.

One result of the Latham Report was to form a partnership between representatives of clients in the public and private sectors and the National Contractors Group. They were given the task of considering improvements which would change the attitudes and atmosphere prevailing in the industry.

3.8 Partnering

Partnering was one of the means identified in the Latham Report to change adversarial attitudes in the construction industry. If successful it brings together individual members of the building team. Ideally it will encompass everyone involved in a project – the client, design team, contractor, subcontractors, and suppliers. It then becomes project partnering. If partnering is to succeed there will need to be an openness and trust between all the parties, a willingness to share the risks and problems, and agreement on the strategies to be followed.

At the heart of it there must be a desire to create working relationships, and this will only be possible if at the outset of the project there is agreement on the basic goals. Typical goals on a construction project are to:

- construct the building to an acceptable standard, within the budget price, and to an agreed time-scale;
- achieve good teamwork and communications;
- provide good and safe working conditions;
- avoid damaging the area adjacent to the construction site and establish good relations with the local residents.

Partnering offers an opportunity to move away from a contract-bound situation, with that situation's adversarial attitudes and a tendency to resort to legal redress in event of difficulties, towards a position of mutual trust and common interests, with differences dealt with by conciliation and mediation.

Project partnership is more likely to be successful if the various firms work together on a succession of projects and build up relationships. However, successful cooperation is possible in 'one-off' situations involving unlikely partners. The Channel Tunnel has been used as an example of a surprising success where an ambitious project was completed by the cooperation of two governments, a consortium of financial institutions, and a mix of construction firms, not all of whom were previously used to working together in unison.

3.9 Professional partnership agreements

In a similar spirit to that shown in partnering there have been moves toward greater cooperation between professional institutions. In 1997 the British Institute of Architectural Technology (BIAT) and the Chartered Institute of Building (CIOB) signed a partnership agreement to encourage such collaboration so as to better serve both their members and the industry in the field of architectural technology.

3.10 Organisational frameworks

Although the practice of architecture is at least in part an art it is also a business. It therefore needs to be organised in an efficient way so that maximum use is made of everyone working for the firm. This organisation takes place at two levels: first, in the matter of the overall organisation, and, second, in the way individual projects are handled. Both of these levels involve the use of what is sometimes referred to as organisational frameworks.

An organisational framework is an arrangement where the total workload of the firm is divided among the staff. Some may be working on their own, but the majority will probably combine together in groups. If the organisational framework is properly devised everyone will know precisely what they have to do, whom they control, and to whom they are answerable.

The simplest framework is a shallow one [Figure 3.5(a)] in which everyone is answerable to a single person. As the number of staff increases this becomes impracticable, so a deep framework may be used [Figure 3.5(b)]. Project leaders are introduced, who receive instruction from the principal of the firm and then in turn direct the work of a group of assistants. The number of tiers could be increased to provide a deeper structure. Also, in the case of an architectural practice, there may be two or more principals (i.e. partners or directors) of equal status, each controlling either a number of assistants or project leaders. A further variation is, in effect, a combination of a shallow framework and a deep framework [Figure 3.5(c)]. The principal controls some people working on their own, as well as a number of project leaders, who in turn control further groups of people.

Reference has already been made to the two levels of organisation. In the matter of general organisation an architectural firm has to decide the degree of specialisation it wishes to pursue. If it is a fairly large firm, employing staff with a wide range of experience, it may decide to make specific groups generally responsible for certain types of projects. One group might specialise in domestic work, another in commercial projects, a third in industrial projects, and so on. Alternatively, there might be a design group responsible for all the projects in the early stages, and staffed with people who are particularly gifted in design and presentation work. They would then pass the project over to other groups when the production-information stage is reached. In both the above arrangements a deci-

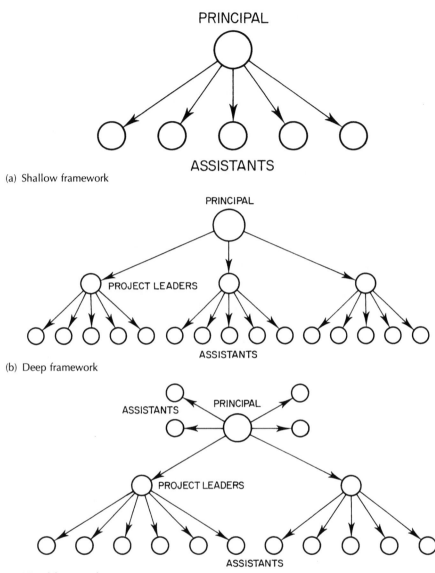

PRINCIPAL

ASSISTANTS

(a) Shallow framework

PRINCIPAL

PROJECT LEADERS

ASSISTANTS

(b) Deep framework

ASSISTANTS   PRINCIPAL

PROJECT LEADERS

ASSISTANTS

(c) Mixed framework

Fig. 3.5 Organisational frameworks

sion has to be made as to whom is responsible for specialist areas of work, such as computer-aided drawing and design (CAD), and non-technical matters, such as administration.

In the organisation of an individual job, as mentioned previously in section 2.3 of chapter 2, there are decisions to be made as to how the various tasks are divided among the individual assistants. Assuming the project is a large one, undertaken by a group of assistants, the overall design would probably be mainly the work of the group leader, although one of the partners is also likely to be involved. Once the production information stage is reached a decision has to be made as to whether a degree of specialisation is introduced or whether most people will undertake most of the different types of tasks. If the first model is followed, one or more assistants may be responsible mainly for the small-scale location drawings, others might work mainly on assembly drawings, others on component drawings; one or more assistants will produce the schedules.

3.11 Some examples of organisational frameworks

Consideration will now be given to the organisation of some typical architectural practices, and the implications for the people involved.

The simplest situation is clearly that of one principal (architect or architectural technologist) working on his own. He needs to make sure only to accept work within his capacity to complete without assistance, and then to plan the work in as efficient a manner as possible.

The second situation is almost as simple, and consists of one principal with one assistant. The principal (architect or technologist) will need to know as much as he can about the assistant's background, interests and ability so that he can allocate tasks to the assistant which the assistant will be able to do in a satisfactory way.

The next simplest case is shown in Figure 3.6(a). This indicates a shallow framework in which a single principal has a sufficiently small staff to be able to control them all individually. It is assumed that the firm undertakes mainly domestic work, with some commercial projects. Where possible the five technical assistants (A1–A5) specialise in one of these areas. There is also a secretary who undertakes the administrative work, and an office junior who does some of the simpler drawing jobs but is employed mainly to run errands, file drawings, and work the plan printer.

Figure 3.6(b) again shows a case where there is a single principal, but this time as the firm is larger he employs three senior assistants whom he calls project leaders (PL1–PL3). They are either architects or architectural technologists, and they each lead a group of people responsible for one or more projects at any one time (persons 1–15). The principal also directly controls a general assistant, a technical information assistant (tech. inform. assist.), and a private secretary who in turn controls two other assistants [an office junior and a word-processor operator (word proc. op.)].

As an architectural practice increases in size it may be best to introduce a further tier in the operational framework. In the example shown in Figure 3.6(c) it is assumed that there is still a single principal. Directly under him there are two associates (assoc 1 and assoc 2), although in a firm of this size they may be made junior partners. Both of these associates will control several project leaders (PL1–PL6), who in turn lead a number of assistants (persons 1–21). The principal (or senior partner) directly controls his own private secretary, and also an office manager, who is in charge of the administrative and support (secretarial) staff (A&S1–A&S4).

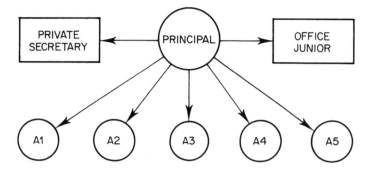

(a) Small firm with sole principal

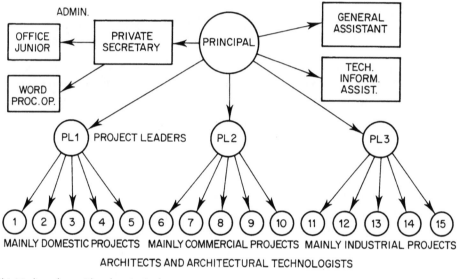

(b) Medium firm with sole principal

Fig. 3.6 Organisational frameworks of firms

Figure 3.6(d) shows the arrangement for a firm in which there are three partners, who have five associates working under them (assoc 1–assoc 5). One of these associates has a special responsibility for the administrative (and secretarial) side of the practice (assoc 1), and the others control one or more projects, under the overall guidance of one of the partners. Each associate has a team to help him. The partners each have a private secretary (priv sec), and one of the partners controls the work of the CAD operators.

A similar arrangement to the last example could be followed in the case of a limited liability company, except that the title of director would be used instead of partner.

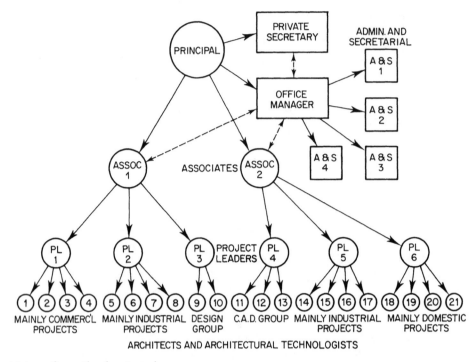

ARCHITECTS AND ARCHITECTURAL TECHNOLOGISTS

(c) Large firm with sole principal

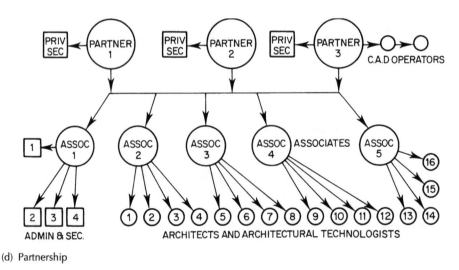

ADMIN & SEC.

ARCHITECTS AND ARCHITECTURAL TECHNOLOGISTS

(d) Partnership

Fig. 3.6 continued

3.12 Organisation of individual projects

As well as achieving good overall organisation of the firm, the principal must also organise each individual project in such a way as to enable the contractor to provide the client with what he wants, and also ensure that his own architectural firm makes a profit.

The organisation of a building project as it concerns the architect or architectural technologist is set out in considerable detail in the Royal Institute of British Architects' (RIBA's) Plan of Work (see section 8.2 of chapter 8), but in general it can be broken down into the following six stages.

Deciding what has to be done

This is the thinking process. Tasks to be done include receiving the client's brief, organising the design team, preparing sketch plans and costing the scheme, preparing a full set of drawings and specifications, obtaining statutory approvals, preparing bills of quantities, selecting the contractor and subcontractors, preparing the contract documents, and administrating the contract.

Programming the work

This will involve setting a time against each individual task and deciding what resources need to be allocated to achieve the required programme.

Organising the work

This will consist of allocating people to each task and deciding exactly 'who does what' and the manner in which they operate.

Coordinating and controlling the work

This means setting up procedures to ensure that everyone is working towards a common aim, with no task left undone or duplicated. It also means ensuring there is a satisfactory chain of command, with everyone aware of who they are answerable to, thus minimising the risk of disagreements between members of the team. Further, it will involve checking that progress is being maintained at the required rate and that the job is keeping within the office budget.

Organising record procedures

Architectural practices will tend to follow standard procedures and will often be guided by the RIBA Plan of Work. The procedures will include the ways instructions and information are issued and the keeping of records for drawings issued and received.

Day-to-day organisation and work philosophy

Whilst most small and medium-sized architectural practices operate satisfactorily without any formal structure or rigid rule, it is sensible to adopt good organisational, philosophical, and behavioural habits in the day-to-day running of a business. Examples are listed below:

- Professional objectives, particularly the need to produce good architecture which is functional and represents value for money, must be a prime objective.
- All activities should be measured against three main criteria – quality, time, and cost.
- The need for profitability and survival must be remembered.
- Every attempt should be made to satisfy client requirements.
- The organisation should meet the needs of the people involved.
- Resources should be utilised efficiently.
- Leaders in the practice must clearly define all objectives, set the expected standards and pace of work, make it as easy as possible for everyone to do what they are supposed to do, and not be over dominant.
- The office atmosphere should be friendly, enthusiastic, and cooperative, with a willingness to admit mistakes where they occur.
- Employment should be as secure as possible.
- Wherever possible the job should provide a challenge.
- Individual employees should receive encouragement and motivation, with every attempt made to assist their personal growth and realisation of their full potential.
- It should be customary to recognise and reward extra effort and above-average performance.
- Delegation of authority should always be provided.

3.13 Local authority and similar offices

Many architects and architectural technologists are employed by local and central government. These departments will have an organisational framework similar to private architectural practices in as much as there will be different levels of responsibility. In a county council's architect's department, for example, there is likely to be a county architect and a deputy county architect at the top of the oganisational framework, and under them there are likely to be two or more assistant county architects, each responsible for a major area of work. In the next-lowest line of command there will be a number of principal assistants, each responsible for a specific area of work. One of these may be responsible for educational buildings and another for social services buildings. Under the principal assistants there will be further levels of senior assistant and assistants. Architectural departments in local authorities may contain specialist staff such as landscape architects, interior designers, and quantity surveyors. Architects may also be employed in planning departments of local authorities to deal with issues such as listed buildings, conservation, and structure planning. Local and central government offices may also employ permanent site staff such as a clerks of works, maintenance inspectors, and supervisors.

3.14 Division of responsibilities within the design team

The number of design team people involved in a project and the division of responsibility will obviously vary from job to job. In a large industrial or commercial project, for example, the roles of the various members of the design team might be as follows:

Partner of architectural practice

The partner will accept the appointment, receive the client's brief, and advise on the choice of quantity surveyor and specialist consultants and is responsible for briefing them. He is involved with the feasibility study and with the outline proposals and scheme design and will possibly be directly responsible for the scheme design.

Job architect or architectural technologist

This person will be responsible for the architectural team and have total involvement with every aspect of the job from start to completion. He will often contribute towards the outline proposals and scheme design and will generally have overall responsibility for the detailed design and production information. Other duties include obtaining approvals under building regulations and town planning, liaison with other members of the design team, attending site meetings, and supervision of the work on-site.

Other architectural staff

These staff will undertake tasks suitable to their abilities. Some tend to contribute more to the preparation of the presentation drawings. Assistants who are qualified architects may be particularly involved with innovative design elements of the job, whilst architectural technologists, although they may contribute towards the design, are often involved with working drawings where a knowledge of construction technology is of particular importance.

Quantity surveying team

A partner in the firm of quantity surveyors, or a senior assistant, will coordinate and direct the work of this section, and in particular will be involved in budget estimates, cost checks, and development of the cost plan. The preparation of the bills of quantities is the chief job of the quantity surveying team. There are a number of separate operations in the preparation of these, and various members of the team will be responsible for different operations. One or more assistants may be involved just with the 'taking off' and others for the 'billing'. The measuring and valuations for interim and final certificates and variations will generally be left to one of the more senior members of staff.

The consulting structural engineering team

A partner or senior assistant of the consulting structural engineers will coordinate and direct the work of this section of the design team, being particularly involved with initial consultation with the architect and advising on a suitable design for the main building structure. Designers will calculate and prepare the design; preparation of the working drawings and schedules will be left to the draughtspersons or detailers.

The consulting building engineering services team

The organisation of this part of the work will follow a similar pattern to that outlined immediately above for the structural engineering team.

3.15 Communications

Good communications (by which is meant successful imparting or exchange of information) between all those involved in the design process is essential. This can be achieved by various techniques, including speaking, writing, and the use of computers, photography, and models. Some requirements of good communications are as follows.

- A pleasant atmosphere is required between all the people involved. This calls for tact, understanding, and consideration on everyone's part. If morale is low and there are bad personal relationships it will be difficult to achieve good communications.
- Good leadership is necessary to inspire confidence and encourage every member to perform to the full extent of their capabilities.
- Everyone should know how the office or offices involved in the design process operate, including the manner in which instructions and information are given. Procedures, such as always confirming verbal information in writing and the use of a standardised way of writing reports, should be strictly adhered to.
- Everyone's role should be clearly established, including status, in the sense of 'who is answerable to whom'.
- As far as possible every person involved in a matter should be given the opportunity to participate.
- People at the top of the hierarchy must pass information on to those under their control. People at the intermediate and lower levels must pass information sideways and downwards.
- Information should be given in a way suited to the background, knowledge, and attitudes of the recipients.

When giving information to others it is useful to ask oneself a few questions. For example:

- Am I certain I have provided all the information required?
- Has all the information I have provided been factually correct, as opposed to being a mixture of facts and opinions?
- Have I given the information in the correct form? (If in doubt give it in writing. This does not necessarily involve a formal memo – it can mean sending a friendly hand-written note.)
- Am I sure the recipient will understand the information? If not, have I taken steps to remedy this?
- Have I made it clear as to the reason for passing on the information? (For example, is the recipient expected to take action?)
- Have I made it clear whether the recipient needs to pass on the information to anyone else or seek the help of someone else? If so, does the recipient have the authority to get the help he needs?

If you have people working under you it is important to be in control of the communication between members of your staff. Ensure that everyone knows the extent of their responsibilities and authority. This will help them decide what to do with information supplied to them, and whom to turn to for help. It is important that people know what they may, or may not, do.

3.16 Telephone communications

Telephone communications can be the cause of strained relationships, and some clients have been antagonised unnecessarily by being left uncared for at the end of a telephone line. A few guidelines are listed below to encouarge better telephone communications:

- Make sure you have enough telephone lines to cater for the calls expected.
- Employ a competent telephone operator or other member of staff to answer calls.
- Answer calls promptly and pleasantly.
- If the person the caller wishes to talk to is not immediately available, he should, if possible, be connected to an acceptable substitute, otherwise he should be given a return call at the earliest opportunity.
- Keep telephone calls as brief as possible, without appearing curt.
- Keep a note of all telephone conversations, particularly when information is exchanged or decisions made.

3.17 Fax communications

Facsimile copying, or faxing as it is commonly called, is a useful method of conveying pages of the written word and drawings. It can be used as an alternative to posting between two addresses which have the necessary fax equipment. They are particularly useful for transmitting architect's sketches which are urgently required by the site staff.

The cost of sending material by fax is more than using the postal services, so it will generally only be used for urgent matters. It should be noted that fax transmissions are not always accepted as legal documents, so it is important that original documents are sent immediately by post.

3.18 Computer communications

A newer, and extremely effective, way of passing on information is by means of computers, including the use of digital telecommunication lines. The equipment used includes a small keyboard which can rest on the lap. This has led to the expression 'desk-top conferencing' and is proving to be an effective way of communication between various members of the building team.

Files, briefs, drawings, and specifications can all be quickly passed between different offices. This means that the various people involved in a project, although separated by distance, can all be looking at the same drawing on their computer screens. Different aspects of the drawing can be discussed, changes can be immediately implemented, and the drawing can be transferred to paper and copies circulated to all the people involved.

This communication facility is becoming a popular means of linking construction sites to offices, and British Telecommunications (BT) now offer a comprehensive and sophisticated service of data, pictures, and videos.

3.19 E-mail communications

An increasingly favoured method of communication is electronic mail, or 'e-mail'. In order to use the system it is necessary to have a mail machine connected to the network. The e-mail message is always typed. Unlike the case with the telephone, the sender and recipient of the message are not synchronised, so the onus is on the sender to check whether any messages have arrived. Like most communication systems, e-mail has advantages and disadvantages. An advantage is that it can be used for group communications. One disadvantage is that it has a low level of security compared with the telephone.

3.20 Written communications

Written communication, delivered by the Royal Mail, or by hand, remains a popular method of communicating information and instructions, despite the various alternatives now available.

Care needs to be taken when communicating by letters and memorandums. There are various principles worth following and some of these are set out below:

- Decide what you want to say, and then say it in a brief, clear, and orderly manner.
- A good rule is to write as you would speak, if you had time to think before you spoke. For example, it is better to write 'Thank you for your letter', than 'I acknowledge receipt of your written communication'.
- Write in a way the reader will understand. This means avoiding the use of technical terms to someone, such as a client, who has no technical knowledge.
- Avoid slang and words which do not have dictionary definitions.
- Devote separate paragraphs to each item you are dealing with.

3.21 Reports

The essential purpose of a report is to present information to someone in a clear, concise way without any 'padding'. Care must be taken to ensure that the reader completely understands what the report is saying. This means tailoring the style and language of the report to suit the recipient.

A typical report will consist of the following parts:

- headings – these should state who the report is to and from, the title of the report, and the date it is sent;
- introduction – this should summarise the purpose of the report;
- the body of the report – this is generally best divided into sections with sub-headings; the subjct matter should be arranged in a logical order, with facts given first, followed by opinions;
- conclusions – these should include recommendations, where appropriate.

3.22 Fees

Percentage fees
Although architects and technologists may not have entered the profession primarily to become rich, like everyone else they need money to live. They will therefore nearly always charge fees for their services. The RIBA publishes a scale of indicative fees, but these are not mandatory. Traditionally, fees are charged as a percentage of the total construction cost. The fee system takes account of the complexity of the building, as well as the cost. Buildings are classified from classes 1 to 5, 1 being the simplest. The full list is as follows.

- class 1
  - industrial: storage sheds,
  - agricultural: barns, sheds, stables,
  - commercial: speculative shops, single-storey carparks;
- class 2
  - industrial: speculative factories and warehouses, assembly and machine workshops, transport garages,
  - agricultural: animal breeding units,
  - commercial: speculative offices, multistorey carparks,

- community: community halls,
- residential: dormitory hostels;

- class 3
  - industrial: purpose-built factories and warehouses, garages and showrooms,
  - commercial: supermarkets, banks, purpose-built offices,
  - community: community centres, branch libraries, ambulance and fire stations, bus stations, police stations, prisons, postal and broadcasting buildings,
  - residential: estate housing, sheltered housing,
  - education: primary, nursery and first schools,
  - recreation: sports centres, squash courts, swimming pools,
  - medical social services: clinics, homes for the elderly;

- class 4
  - commercial: departmental stores, shopping centres, food-processing units, breweries, telecommunication and computer accommodation,
  - community: civic centres, churches and crematoria, concert halls, specialist libraries, museums, art galleries, magistrates, county, and sheriff courts,
  - residential: parsonages and manses, hotels,
  - education: other schools (see class 3, education), including middle and secondary schools and university complexes,
  - medical social services: health centres, accommodation for the disabled, general hospital complexes, surgeries, nursing homes;

- class 5
  - commercial: high-risk research and production buildings, recording studios,
  - community: theatres, opera houses, crown and high courts,
  - residential: houses for individual clients,
  - education: university laboratories,
  - recreation: leisure pools, specialised complexes,
  - medical social services: teaching hospitals and laboratories, dental surgeries.

The scale of fees for 'new works' range from 5% to 11.25%; for 'works to existing buildings' they range from 7.75% to 16.5%. Professional fees, like all other charges, are liable to change from time to time, and in cases where current accurate figures are required a copy of the RIBA publication *Guidance for Clients on Fees* may be referred to. At the time of writing this book, the 1996 edition of the *Guidance* book was in use.

When paid as percentage amounts of the cost of the job, the fees are generally paid at intervals based on the stages of the RIBA Plan of Work, as follows:

A/B	inception/feasibility	generally paid on a time charged basis
C	outline proposals	10%–15% of fee
D	scheme design	15%–20% of fee
E	detail design	20% of fee
FG	production information	20% of fee
HJKL	tendering, planning, site operations	25%–35% of fee

Percentage fees are a traditional method of payment, but nowadays they may not be the most common way of calculating fees, particularly in the early stages of a project. Alternative methods are given below.

Lump-sum charges

Sometimes a client will want to know at the outset the amount he will have to pay his architect or architectural technologist for their professional services. He may request a quotation for a lump sum, or all-inclusive fee. There may also be circumstances where the architect or architectural technologist considers a percentage fee would be an inappropriate method to charge for his services, such as when the scope of the job or the time-scale are unclear.

It is generally more difficult to arrive at an equable lump-sum charge than by using the percentage method. It is therefore important to define the extent of work included in the lump-sum charge and to state whether expenses and disbursements are included.

Time charge

A third method which may be used is to charge the client a fee based on an hourly rate for all technical staff engaged on the project. This will comprise the aggregate of the staff member's salary and overheads, plus a sum to enable the practice to make a profit. The current salary of each employee will be readily available, but if the job is likely to extend over a long period an allowance will need to be made for salary increases. Most practices will also have reliable figures, built up over the years, of overheads. This includes the cost of providing each employee with a space to work, together with the use of facilities such as lavatories, communal rooms, lighting, heating equipment, and general services. As a rule the cost of overheads will be roughly equal to the salary costs. The profit margin is more variable and will be influenced by how anxious the practice is to obtain the job, but it is not unusual for the profit margin to be set at the same level as the salary. This means that the hour rate charged for a member of the architectural staff will be three times the hourly rate.

Other fees

The quantity surveyor's and the consultant's fees are charged additionally to the architect's or architectural technologist's fees, generally at rates recommended by their professional institute.

3.23 Value added tax

People using the service of architects, architectural technologists, and other people supplying goods and services have to pay a tax known as value added tax (VAT). This is an extra percentage which is currently set at 17.5% in addition to the cost of the service – in this case the architectural services, including expenses.

It is not necessary to charge VAT if the turnover is below a certain figure, but most architects and architectural technologists working full time for themselves will normally earn enough in fees to make them responsible for collecting this tax for the government. They will need to be registered and prepare three-monthly accounts in enough detail to show how much tax is payable.

3.24 Disbursements and expenses

In addition to professional fees the client will also be charged for disbursements, which are sums paid by the architect or technologist on behalf of the client, such as prescribed fees payable to the local authority when applying for town planning and building regulations approvals.

Expenses such as hotel and travelling costs, printing, postage, telephone, and other day-to-day expenses may be charged to the client but only if this has been agreed with the client beforehand. Otherwise, the client is entitled to assume that all out-of-pocket expenses are included in the architectural practice's fee.

3.25 Termination of architectural practitioner's services

It is possible that at some stage of the project the client may wish to dispense with the services of his architect or technologist. This may be because of financial reasons or because he has lost confidence in his professional advisor. Whatever the reason, the client has the right to abort the appointment, providing he gives reasonable notice of his intention. Equally, however, the architect or technologist has the right to be paid for all the work he has done up to the time of termination.

Termination is always a possibility so it is sensible to recognise this fact at the outset and to make provision for such an eventuality in the formal agreement, which should be signed before any work commences.

3.26 Involvement of the client

The client is obviously the first person to be involved with the project, and his involvement continues throughout. Initially, he considers the need to build, appoints the design team, and briefs them. Then he approves the initial sketch design, provides whatever information is necessary for the more detailed design, and approves the architect's or technologist's proposals. He provides further information to allow the detailed working drawings to be prepared and approves them where necessary. The contractor's tender then has to be approved by the client, and the client then signs the contract.

During the building operations the client continues to supply information as required by the design team. Throughout the project the client pays all the bills and, on completion, accepts the finished building.

3.27 **Influence of the client organisation**

If the project is to proceed satisfactorily it is important to create a good relationship between the design team and the client. As a rule the design will be required to match the client's organisational needs.

The first requirement is that the architect or technologist must keep the client fully informed of the progress of the project. This is fairly straightforward if the client is one person, such as a woman wanting a house built for her own occupation. Frequently, however, the client will be an organisation, such as a private company, a public corporation, or a voluntary society. In these circumstances it is essential to decide precisely who in the client organisation needs to be informed and has the authority to issue instructions. Ideally, this role will be restricted to one person, although there will invariably be a number of people to assist that person.

Although the best arrangement is for one person to have authority to act for the design team, in practice the design team will take account of the client's organisational requirements and try and satisfy all their demands. This could mean that on a large project several people in both the client's organisation and the design team are actively involved, but the key people should be aware of, and possibly have to approve formally, all decisions taken by their staff. In an industrial project, for example, the factory manager may liaise with the project architect to agree the general factory layout, the plant manager may agree the services with the consulting building services engineer, details of the dock leveller may be agreed between the warehouse manager and an architectural technologist, the client's accountant may agree the method of paying the accounts with the architectural firm's office manager, and so on.

Large commercial organisations may have special departments, such as property or facilities departments, with the express function of briefing the architect or technologist, approving the design, and issuing instructions. Employees in this department of the client organisation may include architects, architectural technologists, building and quantity surveyors, and others with some sort of building background.

Other private companies may appoint a person with technical expertise, even if not expressly related to building, to act for them in day-to-day decision-making. An industrialist requiring a factory to be built may appoint the plant manager or production manager of an existing factory to this role. A voluntary organisation, such as a church or golf club, will probably have a committee to act for it, but it is best if the actual authority to approve the architectural firm's suggestions is vested in one individual, generally the chairperson. Often the person will be someone who has worked in or has some knowledge of, the construction industry.

A central or local government body, or public corporation, will invariably have an architectural department to fulfil the role of client when it engages a private architectural practice to act for it. A county council, for example, will often have an assistant county architect with the direct role of liaising with private architectural firms it appoints.

A fairly common arrangement is for the appointment of the architect or architectural technologist and approval of the basic brief, including budget costs, to be made by a very senior person in the client organisation, such as the managing director, and then for all the detailed decisions to be left to some other person or persons.

3.28 Obtaining work

It is self-evident that even the most brilliant architect or technologist will not succeed unless he is able to obtain work, and successful architectural practitioners are aware of the need to actively promote their architectural practices. At one time this was done in a covert way, but for many years now direct methods have been used. It is openly acknowledged, even by architectural institutions, that professional marketing of architectural services can be worthwhile. Larger firms increasingly turn to public relations and advertising consultants, but even smaller firms need to consider how to sell themselves in the most effective way.

The first requirement is to be aware of exactly what you are able to offer potential clients, what type of jobs you are aiming for, and how to tempt clients to entrust their work to you. Various ways in which work may be obtained are as follows.

Traditional restricted advertising

At one time the only advertising methods allowed to architects by the professional bodies were to fix a nameboard of a specified size outside their office, to write their name and title (again in a maximum size of letter) on the office window, to place their name under the appropriate heading in a classified edition of a telephone directory, or to put their name on a site noticeboard.

Direct advertising

Direct advertising, albeit with limitations, is now permitted. This means, for example, that an architect commencing practice and interested in small domestic work can display an advertisement in a local newspaper offering services for domestic alterations, extensions, and other types of work. It is also possible to publish brochures for handing to people or firms who may need the services of an architect or architectural technologist.

Friends, relatives, and social contacts

These are a useful source of work. The ability to make friends is clearly a useful asset in business and can prove invaluable to professionals starting up in practice. Whilst not many would freely admit to building up a circle of friends and acquaintances solely for business purposes, it is obvious that everyone is a potential source of work and most people needing professional advice tend to think of someone they already know. A cautionary note should be struck about friends representing a useful work source. Although the statement is true, it is equally true that doing business with people known to us can be dangerous, as there is a tendency to act informally, to fail to confirm everything in writing, and generally to fail to be as business-like as we would be if the client was at 'arm's length'.

As a result of previous work

This is one of the most rewarding ways of obtaining work. A potential client may be impressed by a building he passes and seek out the architect involved to ask that architect to act for him too. If the building which arouses the initial interest is not completed, the nameboard which most architects and architectural technologists place on the site of their building project will obviously serve a valuable purpose in linking up the client and architectural practitioner. If the building is completed, the potential client may approach the owner of the building for the name of the architect or technologist involved. Hopefully, the client will have enjoyed a good relationship with his professional advisor and will be happy to recommend him.

From other professionals

Work often comes on the recommendations of other professionals, such as solicitors, accountants, and bank managers. Sometimes architects and technologists will get to know such people as a result of social contacts. Some architectural practitioners, however, on commencing their practice, make a point of visiting near-neighbours of other professions to introduce themselves and make their availability as widely known as possible.

Client's advisory service (CAS)

The RIBA offers a service which seeks to promote the use of its members and introduce potential clients to RIBA architects. The RIBA advertises in some directories and if approached will generally provide information on three or four suitable architects. BIAT also advertises in similar publications to the RIBA.

Competitions

Taking part in competitions is the most difficult way of obtaining work but is worth attempting when the subject of the competition interests the architect. The RIBA provides guidance for its members with regard to competitions and prohibits them from entering competitions which fail to meet the RIBA criteria.

Competitions may be either 'open', when generally anyone on the ARB register can enter, or 'limited', which means that only selected architects are eligible to submit entries. Some competitions are conducted in two stages. In the first stage the competitors are asked to submit fairly simple drawings illustrating the basic ideas of their design. Some competitors are then shortlisted and proceed to the second stage, when they are expected to prepare more detailed drawings.

4

Architectural practitioners and the law

4.1 Introduction

When an architect or architectural technologist agrees to act for a client he is involved in a legal relationship with that client. Among other things this could involve him in being sued for negligence. This and other matters relating to the legal position of the architect and technologist are dealt with in this chapter. Legal information given in this book is limited to what is appropriate for a student architect or architectural technologist.

4.2 Negligence

An architect or architectural technologist, like all other professional people, is expected to show a degree of competence appropriate to a skilled and experienced person. If he fails to do so, he may be faced with legal problems, notably being brought before the courts for negligence.

In this part of the book reference is made to important cases which have come before the courts. These cases must be viewed in a general way, as the rulings may be modified by the specific circumstances of other, apparently similar, cases. The law is a complicated business, and the intention here is merely to provide the reader with an introduction to the law of negligence, and other matters, as they affect the architect and technologist and their staff. If the reader is unfortunate enough to become involved in legal proceedings, the reader will need to seek the advice and assistance of qualified lawyers.

4.3 Professional indemnity insurance

Professional indemnity insurance is very much a fact of professional life. This is because if things go wrong, and the architect is sued for negligence, he may face enormous claims for damages. The purpose of professional indemnity insurance is to provide protection against the financial consequences of such alleged negligence. Negligence is discussed further in section 4.6.

The basic policy offered by the insurance company to the architect or architectural technologist will vary from policy to policy. Typically it will be the payment of all sums which the insured shall be legally liable for as a direct result of his acts of negligence, but will not generally cover *ex gratia* payments to protect goodwill. It can include cover in the event of claims made in the following circumstances:

- legal costs; this can embrace both the architect's costs in defending a case, whether or not the claim is valid, and the plaintiff's costs, where he succeeds in his action;
- physical injuries to a third party or to property;
- costs caused by the action of consultants;
- liability to a third party who has been influenced by the architect's comments or actions.

Some architects may be convinced they will never make a mistake, but they will still generally need professional indemnity insurance. This is because if they fight a case which they win, it can still cost money, and they must also take account of the fact that they are liable for their employees' and partners' mistakes as well as their own. In any case, an architect wishing to undertake work in the 'public sector' must be insured, as public commissions can only be placed with architects carrying a minimum cover of £250,000.

The scope of the claim that can be made against a professional adviser can include the cost of the mistake as well as the cost of remedying the mistake. In other words, it can include the consequential loss – that is, the loss which the employer suffers as a consequence of the mistake.

On a project where the architect has nominated a consultant, the architect is liable to be sued by the client in the event of the consultant's negligence. It is therefore important that the architect ensures that either the consultant has adequate professional indemnity insurance or else covers the eventuality of the consultant's negligence in his own insurance.

Architects also owe a duty of care to third parties. Even if they have no contractual relationship with them, the third party can sue the architect because advice he gave proved to be faulty and resulted in the third party suffering a financial loss. In a court case in 1997, *Machin* vs *Adams & Orr*, an architect wrote a letter to a houseowner, who in turn sent it to a third party who was influenced by remarks the architect had made in his letter. In this particular instance the third party was not successful because the architect was unaware that the third party would be influenced by his statement. It was, however, clear from comments made in this and other cases, that if the architect had known that his advice would influence the actions of a third party and cause him to lose money he would be liable to pay damages to the third party, even though he was not contractually answerable to him.

The period of cover given to the architect is generally for claims within the period of insurance; that is, it relates to when a claim is made for negligence, not when the negligence occurred. The procedure for notifying claims is for the architect to notify the insurer immediately a claim is made against him, or immediately he is aware of an occurrence which may give rise to a claim.

The fact that claims for negligence can be made some time after the negligent act occurred means that an architect could be sued for negligence after retiring. This is likely to be particularly significant for sole practitioners, and they need to consider whether to continue insurance cover after retirement.

The most difficult question the architect has to decide is the amount of indemnity insurance required. The minimum cover of £250,000 has already been mentioned for those who wish to do public sector work. Apart from this consideration, architects are advised to obtain as much cover as they can afford bearing in mind inflation, the growth of their practice, the fact that people are more likely to sue nowadays, and that courts are more inclined to award large amounts of money to employers making claims.

Architects need to be aware that professional indemnity insurance, like most other legal matters, is complex and should be approached with care. In particular, when taking out an insurance policy, architects need to know precisely what cover they are obtaining. This is illustrated by a case which came before the Court of Appeal in 1988. A firm of architects, practising as an unlimited company were appointed to act for a housing association in the refurbishment of about 350 properties. There were 17 separate contracts of engagement between the architect and client for work to the properties.

The architects had an insurance policy to protect them against claims for negligence with a limit of indemnity of £250,000 for any one claim. There was an excess of £2,000 for each and every claim – in other words the architects would have to pay the first £2,000 of every claim themselves. Serious defects occurred in the houses, and the client sued the architects for negligence claiming they had not shown sufficient care and skill. It was claimed that the total cost of repairs was likely to be about £5.7 million.

During the course of the case the issue arose as to what constituted a single claim. If there was a single claim covering all 350 properties, the limit of indemnity would be £250,000 less (17 × £2,000) of excesses; that is, £216,000. If, however, there were 17 claims (i.e. one for each contract of engagement between architect and client) the limit of indemnity would be (17 × £250,000) less (17 × £2,000) of excesses; that is, £4,216,000.

A further complication arose when the insurers made the architects an offer in full and final settlement of their claims under the insurance policy. The client for their part did not want this settlement to take place, as they were afraid that if the architects did not have the financial resources of the insurance company behind them they would be forced into bankruptcy. This would mean that they (the client) would not be able to obtain the damages awarded if, and when, they won the case. They therefore brought proceedings under the Third Parties (Rights Against Insurers) Act 1930 to prevent the insurers being released from their obligations. The ramifications of this and other cases is beyond the scope of this book but helps to illustrate the complexity of professional indemnity insurance and the care architects and technologists need to take in these matters.

Some of the professional institutes insist that their members hold professional indemnity insurance (PII) for any project in which they are involved. Mandatory PII is an essential element of BIAT's code of conduct.

4.4 Legal duties of the architectural practitioner

Contract law

The duties of an architect or technologist are contractual because, generally before beginning work, they will make an agreement to act for the client. This Agreement of Appointment is a contractual arrangement. It will usually be in a written form. In theory there is no reason why a contract should be in writing, but experience suggests that verbal agreements are not advisable, as they can lead to problems, such as misunderstandings or uncertainty of terms.

There are certain principles governing contracts which can be summarised as follows.

- The parties to the contract must intend to make, and reach, a legally binding agreement. It is an important fact of contractual liability law that it is based on consent between the parties to the contract.
- Under the contract each party must give something and receive something in return. The architect and architectural technologist will generally give their expertise in the form of a design, drawings, specifications, advice, and use of the skills listed in section 2.7 of chapter 2. In return they will receive a sum of money for these services.
- The parties must not be acting illegally, and the contract must not have been agreed under a misrepresentation.

Law of tort

The architectural practitioner's duties may also be imposed by the law of tort. It is not easy for the layperson to grasp the legal idea of 'tort'. The word 'tort' means a civil wrong, and the idea of the law of tort is to compensate a person who has been wronged by another. Unlike liability under contract law, which is essentially liability based on consent, law of tort is a liability imposed by the law.

4.5 Under which law can the architectural practitioner be sued?

The architect and architectural technologist, like other professionals, are liable to be sued for negligence either under contractual law or the law of tort. Generally, the plaintiff will claim under the law likely to provide him with the most favourable results and will take account of factors such as time limits for claims and the basis on which damages are likely to be awarded.

The Defective Premises Act of 1971 may also affect architectural practitioners as a means by which they can be brought before the courts. This act relates to dwelling houses and it places on architects and others an additional duty to that imposed on them under contract law and the law of tort. It requires anyone who undertakes work relating to the provision of a dwelling, including conversion work, with the duty of ensuring that the work is done in a professional and workmanlike manner, so that the dwelling when completed is fit for human habitation. An additional factor is that sometimes the architectural practitioner, by acting in a negligent way, may find himself liable under criminal law.

4.6 Definition of negligence with examples of court cases

Section 2 of the Architect's (Registration) Act of 1938 defines an architect as

> one who possesses with due regard to aesthetics as well as practical considerations, adequate skills and knowledge to enable him to originate, to develop and plan, to arrange and supervise the execution of such buildings and other works as he might in the course of his business reasonably be expected to carry out in respect of which he offers his services as specialist.

Glasgow University vs *William Whitfield and John Laing Construction (1988)*

This case concerned a claim by the university against the architect for negligence, as a result of the architect's design for an art gallery built at the university. The university claimed that the architect's design was defective in the following areas:

- dry linings resulting in condensation;
- roof parapets resulting in leaks;
- wood wool decking resulting in condensation;
- roof monitors resulting in condensation.

In giving his ruling, the judge maintained that the architect owed duties towards the university, both in contract and tort, and that the standard of care owed was the standard of the ordinary, competent architect, using reasonable skill and care.

In the case of the dry linings, part of the trouble arose because there was no provision for sealing the vapour barrier behind the dry lining at the edges and on the faces. The judge held that, by the standards of 1976 (the date when the work was undertaken) such a seal was required and accordingly the architects were guilty of negligent design.

In the case of the roof parapets, the trouble arose because the felt roof covering was dressed up the parapet and tucked into a mastic-sealed chase in the top of the parapet. Eventually the freezing and thawing action of the weather loosened the mastic seal and allowed water to penetrate. The judge held that by the standards of the time (1972–76) it was difficult to accept the architect was negligent in his design.

In the case of the wood wool decking, the judge ruled that while it would not be right to design the roof using wood wool today, it could not be criticised by the standards appropriate to the time it was designed. Accordingly, there was no negligence on the part of the architects.

In the case of the roof monitors, condensation dropped off the glass and metal windows of the roof monitors. The design was not a fully-sealed double-glazing system but a cheaper system for use in industrial buildings. The judge held that the architects were negligent.

Most observers reading the full account such as the one referred to above would probably feel that architects and other professionals walk a tightrope in the matter of negligence.

D&F Estates vs The Church Commissioners (1988)

In 1963 the plaintiff, D&F Estates were sold a luxury flat which was owned and built by the Church Commissioners through a joint venture company with Wates Ltd. In 1980 it was discovered that all the plasterwork was defective. Wates were held liable on the grounds that it was in breach of its duty to provide adequate and proper supervision of the plastering work. The plaintiff was awarded damages in respect of the remedial work completed in 1980, with further sums in respect of future remedial work and in respect of the loss of rent while the work was carried out.

However, later, the House of Lords decided that none of this is recoverable as damages because a contractor is not responsible for the torts of an independent subcontractor. Moreover, remedial work necessary because of defects, or even potential dangers, is not recoverable as damages for negligence.

Warwick University vs YRM/Sir Robert McAlpine/Cementation Chemicals (1988)

This case involved a lengthy legal battle, which ended with a High Court ruling in 1988 and concerned the architects YRM, the contractors Sir Robert McAlpine, and the tile manufacturer Cementation Chemicals. It was in respect of tiles which were fixed to the outside of a number of buildings at Warwick University. When it was found that water had got in behind the tiles, remedial work was carried out, which consisted of injecting an epoxy resin adhesive behind the tiles, causing some of the tiles to crack and fall off.

The architects and contractors were both absolved from responsibility generally on the basis that they had followed the best advice available at the time. The judge said that in the 1960s and early 1970s when external tiled cladding was 'much in vogue' it was not generally appreciated that a weakness of the system was that ceramic tiling did not provide an impervious cladding. The judge stated that the university's expert had said there was no way in which the architect would have been aware of the risk. The adhesive manufacturers were, however, found liable for the massive repair bill involved. The judge stated that at the time the remedial work was carried out, Cementation Chemicals were the only UK firm licensed to use the epoxy resin techniques.

Presumably it can be assumed from this case that the architects were not liable because they had taken the same care that any other competent architect could be expected to take, whereas the tile manufacturer had been found liable because they had not taken the care expected from an expert in their field of expertise.

Sutcliffe vs Thackrah (1974)

The plaintiff appointed the defendants to design a house for him and act as his architects and quantity surveyors. Building work began and the defendants, as part of their job, issued interim certificates to the builders, from time to time, authorising payment to them for work they had done. Before the building of the house had been completed, the plaintiff terminated his employment of the builder and requested the builder leave the site. Subsequently, the builder went into liquidation. A second firm of builders was employed to complete the work.

The plaintiff claimed that the defendants had been guilty of negligence because they had certified work not done, or improperly done, by the original builder, which meant in effect that the original builder had been overpaid. The House of Lords ruled that the defendants were liable in negligence for overcertifying.

Walmsley Lewis vs Hardy (1967)

The plaintiff employed the defendant to survey a house for him, and as a result of the survey bought the house. The defendant noticed dormant dry rot but did not mention it to the plaintiff and did not inspect the loft. The defendant later asked the plaintiff if he would like a further report with the carpets removed and an examination of the loft. No mention was made of the dry rot, and the plaintiff decided he was satisfied with the original report. Subsequently, the plaintiff had to sell the house at a loss. The judge's ruling was that the defendant should have warned the plaintiff about the dormant dry rot and was also negligent in not discovering extensive dry rot and damp.

4.7 Period of liability

Once it is decided that there is a possibility that an architect, or other professional person, has been negligent, the question arises as to whether it is possible to sue that person or whether it is too late to take any action.

The general position is that in England, Wales, and Northern Ireland the period of limitation – that is, the period during which legal action can be taken – is six years, but twelve years for contracts made 'under seal'. The period of liability is unlimited where fraud is involved.

The next factor is, from when does the period of six or twelve years commence? Does it commence from the time the faulty work is done, or from the date when the faults caused by the negligence were discovered? For example, if the foundations of a building have been laid at the wrong level in the ground, the mistake may not be noticed when the work is done. The building might be completed and occupied by the client without any indication that some of the work was faulty. Then, many years later settlement could take place, and serious faults develop in the building. If it were more than six years since the foundations were laid, the client would be unable to sue for negligence. It is even possible in the case of a large contract, built over a long period of time, for the limitation period for the foundations to end before the building is completed and handed over.

Many law cases have been concerned with the question as to when the period of liability for negligence dates from. The rulings do not always appear to be consistent, which leads to the conclusion that the situation has changed through the years. Some important cases are mentioned below.

Prior to 1977 it was generally accepted that the architect's liability was for a period of six to twelve years, depending on the type of contract. This seemed to change in 1977 when the *Amis vs London Borough of Merton* case suggested that the architect's liability could last practically forever. Fortunately for architects and other professionals, later rulings qualified this situation.

Bagot vs Stevens Scanlon and Co. (1966)
The architects were sued for negligent supervision of defective drains. The judge ruled that they were not liable because more than six years had elapsed since the drains were constructed. At that time it was held that the Limitations Act 1939 provided for claims in ordinary contract or in tort being extinguished six years after the cause of the action occurred.

Dutton vs Bognor Regis UDC (1972)
The Bognor Regis Urban Development Corporation was sued for negligence because its building inspector had approved inadequate foundations on an infilled site. Lord Denning ruled that the six-year period of limitation should begin from when the foundations were badly constructed and not from when the defects were discovered. This meant that the plaintiff was not successful in his action.

Sparham-Souter vs Town and Country Developments (Essex) Ltd. (1976)
In this case Lord Denning appeared to have changed his mind over the previously mentioned case. This case was also to do with foundation problems. Lord Denning stated:

> I have come to the conclusion that when the building work is badly done and is covered up, the cause of the action does not accrue, and time does not begin to run until such time as the plaintiff discovers that it has done damage, or ought with reasonable diligence to have discovered it. It may seem hard on the builder or council surveyor that he may find himself sued many years after he has left the work, but it would be harder on the householder that he should be without remedy, seeing that the surveyor passed the work and the builder covered it up and thus prevented it being discovered earlier.

Amis vs London Borough of Merton (1977)
Following a House of Lords decision in this case, which again was concerned with foundation problems, it appeared that architects, builders inspectors, and other professionals would be liable for negligence for long periods after leaving the site.

The plaintiffs were owners of maisonettes which they bought 15 years previously.

In 1970 structural movement began to take place, which caused the walls to crack and the floors to slope. It was claimed that the foundations were not taken down as deeply as shown on the plans which Merton Council had approved. The Council were sued in 1972, more than six years from the time when the building was completed.

A unanimous House of Lords decided that the limitation period began to run when the defect first appeared in 1970. 'The cause of the action can only arise when the state of the building is such that there is present imminent danger to the health and safety of persons occupying it', said Lord Wilberforce.

D&F Estate vs The Church Commissioners (1988)

In this case, previously referred to in section 4.6 above, the House of Lords reversed a series of key court cases, including ones mentioned above. The ruling was that under current legislation the limitation for a breach of contract runs out six years from the date when the breach takes place, not when the damage was discovered or should have been discovered.

Glasgow University vs William Whitfield and John Laing Construction (1988)

This case, also previously referred to in section 4.6, threw some light on another interesting aspect of the law relating to negligence. In respect of the alleged design defect in the dry lining resulting in condensation, it was noted that the defect became apparent in the building after completion, and the architect gave advice on how to overcome the problem at that stage. It was ruled that when this happened 'the duty could be reactivated or revised'. The judge quoted from a ruling in a previous case:

> I am now satisfied that the architect's duty of design is a continuing one, and it seems to me that the subsequent discovery of a defect in the design, initially and justifiably thought to have been suitable, reactivated or revised the architect's duty to take such steps as were necessary to correct the results of the initially defective design.

The continuing duty was considered to be a duty both under the law of contract and under the law of tort.

4.8 Persons to whom the architectural practitioner may be liable

One of the rulings in the *D&F Estates* vs *The Church Commissioners (1988)* case, previously referred to, was that the architect and other professionals are only liable to their clients under the terms of their engagement. In the current situation, architects are not generally liable to third parties, such as the future occupiers of the building. However, as discussed in section 4.3 it was indicated by a court case in 1997 that architects do owe a duty of care to third parties, even if they have no contractual relationship with them.

4.9 Extent of liability for negligence

The *D&F Estates* vs *The Church Commissioners (1988)* case further resulted in the judgement that architects are not liable in tort for the cost of remedial work, as this is considered to be what is termed 'economic loss'. If the plasterwork was defective and fell off the walls as a result of faulty supervision, the architect would not be liable to pay damages for the necessary remedial work. He would, however, be liable if, because of his negligent design or supervision, physical damage resulted to the plaintiff or his property.

4.10 Collateral warranties

Owing to the fact that recent court decisions have tended to reduce the extent of the architect's liabilities for negligence, some clients are now trying to replace the third party's liabilities by asking architects to sign collateral warranties. A collateral warranty is a contract which runs alongside, and supplements, another contract. Provisions of such warranties include the architect guaranteeing that the building he designs is fit for the purpose for which it is built, as well as assigning a warranty for future purchasers or tenants of the building. It gives third parties the right to sue architectural practitioners for negligence. This reinforces the case for the architectural practitioner always to ensure he has adequate professional indemnity insurance. It is necessary to check the amount of cover regularly and to increase it where necessary.

Developers and large financial institutions are in a strong position to dictate such terms to architects. If an architect wishes to obtain a lucrative design contract he may have no option but to sign a collateral warranty on the client's terms first. However, he puts himself in the dangerous position of increasing the area for which, if anything goes wrong, he can be sued for negligence. There is the added danger that the architect's professional indemnity insurance (discussed in section 4.3) may not cover all the requirements of the collateral warranty.

The fact that since the late 1980s collateral warranties have become an increasing part of everyday life for professional design consultancies has led the British Institute of Architectural Technology (BIAT) to introduce a collateral warranty vetting system for the benefit of their members. One of the concerns is that as well as standard forms of warranty which have been drawn up by interested parties, and agreed as being equitable, there are also non-standard documents which may be unreasonable to architectural technologists and others.

4.11 Architectural practitioners limiting their liability for negligence

Clients are not the only group of people anxious to protect their interests. In the past some architects have insisted that as a condition of their engagement they limit their liability for negligence. However, the Unfair Contract Terms Act of 1977 sets out to restrict exemptions of liabilities clauses. This means, for example, that an architect is no longer able to say: 'I will act as your architect provided that if anything goes wrong my liability will be limited to £1,000'. In particular, this act provides a total ban on contractual terms aimed at excluding or restricting liability for death or personal injury.

4.12 Liability of architectural partners

Partners in an architectural partnership are considered to be agents for each other in respect of the business of the partnership. They are therefore responsible for each other's business debts and torts, including such matters as the making of contracts, hiring and firing of staff, payments of money by the partnership, and for the damages awarded against the partnership for the negligence of the partners in the course of their business activities.

4.13 Liability of architectural directors

It is now becoming increasingly common for architectural firms to operate as limited liability companies rather than as partnerships. One effect of this is to change the liability for negligence of the architects or architectural technologists involved.

A partner in an architectural firm who is successfully sued is personally liable for the full sum awarded against the firm, even if the negligence is due to the actions of the partner. This could mean having to hand over his personal assets, including his home, to pay the debts of the partnership.

Architectural directors of a firm practising as a limited liability company are less vulnerable. In law a limited liability company has a separate legal personality, quite distinct from its employees, including the directors. Up to now the law appears to have adopted the position that the employees cannot be sued for the company's negligence. This does not necessarily rule out the possibility of a future claim against an architectural director being successful. An aggrieved client might attempt to sue, jointly, a limited liability company of architects and technologists and one or more of its directors, for tactical reasons.

However, if such a situation were to arise, architectural practitioners might then try to persuade their clients to introduce a clause in the contract absolving the architectural directors, or other employees, from personal liability for negligence proved against the company. The ultimate answer, apart from all architectural staff taking the utmost care in their work, lies in architects and technologists taking out sufficient indemnity insurance cover, although many firms are already finding this insurance an enormous burden on their financial resources.

4.14 Liability of employees of architectural practitioners

An architect or architectural technologist employed in a salaried position in an architectural practice is liable for his own torts (i.e. any civil wrongs he is responsible for). If the wrong act by the employee occurs during the course of his employment it is held to be the joint responsibility of the employer and the employee.

The employee has a duty to take reasonable care in the way he does his work, as well as an obligation not to pass on confidential matters about his employer's business to third parties. The duty not to pass on such information to others still applies after an employee has left to take employment with a different company.

4.15 Site safety

European law
Most of Britain's recent health and safety legislation originated in Europe. The member states have to agree proposals from the European Commission and are then obligated to make them part of their national law.

Major legislation
The fundamentals of British health and safety law, including the health and safety of people working and visiting construction sites, are contained in the Health and Safety at Work Act of 1974. This lays down the employer's responsibilities to his employees and others, and the employees' responsibilities to each other and to themselves.

The passing of the 1974 Health and Safety at Work Act was particularly important because it introduced an obligation not only to provide a safe place of work, but also a safe system of work.

The next significant event in safety legislation was the introduction of the Management of Health and Safety at Work Regulations 1992 (the Management Regulations). These placed a duty on all employers and self-employed people to make an assessment of the risk to construction workers and others resulting from the construction work. The next major landmark was the Construction (Design and Management) Regulations 1994 which actively involved clients and designers in the task of achieving safe and healthy conditions on building sites. This important piece of legislation is considered below, in section 4.16.

In 1996 there was a further important addition to construction safety legislation when the Construction (Health Safety and Welfare) Regulations 1996 became law. These replaced regulations introduced over 30 years earlier. They cover matters such as excavations, prevention of falls, and working platforms. Although the primary responsibility in these and earlier regulations rests with the contractor, the designer must make sure that all the construction work – temporary and permanent, including materials – will not endanger the health and safety of anyone on the building site.

Architectural practitioners' responsibility for site safety
Traditionally, once a contractor takes over a building site he is responsible for the safety of the people working on, or visiting, the site. However, a case arose in 1987 when a firm of architects were charged with failing to provide a safe system of work on a site they were involved with. A member of the architect's staff, while making

an unaccompanied visit to the site, fell to her death from the fourth floor, through a hole left by the removal of a staircase.

Previous to the case against the architect, the building contractor responsible for the site had admitted breaching the Health and Safety at Work Act 1974, by failing to protect the hole and so prevent people falling through it. The Health and Safety Executive had stated there should have been scaffolding placed around the hole, or boards placed across it.

While accepting liability the building contractor stated that the architects had told him to leave the holes because they had not finished their survey and to fill in the holes would make the job more difficult. The magistrate concluded that site safety was not the architect's responsibility. 'It's up to builders to know the rules and to guard against accidents to their employees and other visitors', he said.

4.16 Construction (Design and Management) Regulations 1994

The Construction (Design and Management) Regulations 1994 (CDM Regulations) place a shared statutory responsibility on designers, contractors, and clients to ensure the safety of everyone on a building site during the whole period of a construction project. This is a major departure from previous legislation when the contractor took virtually sole responsibility for site safety.

An important requirement of the regulations is the appointment of a 'planning supervisor', with the role of overseeing the planning and design of the building to make certain that safe methods of working are followed. Two new documents were introduced – health and safety plans, and safety files.

Certain minor works, namely those lasting 30 days or less and employing a maximum of four persons, those for domestic clients, works in shops and offices which do not interrupt the normal activities in the premises, and minor works to heating or water systems, are exempt from the regulations.

Role of the client
The client has specific duties to carry out, although if they wish they can appoint someone else to act for them, provided they send a written declaration of their intention to the Health and Safety Executive (HSE).

The duties of the client or his agent are to appoint a planning supervisor and a principal contractor, making sure that both of these people have the ability and resources to perform these roles, and to ensure that a suitable health and safety plan, and a safety file, are produced and made available as required.

Role of the designer
Designers can be either organisations or individuals, and may, among others, be architects, architectural technologists, consulting engineers, or principal contractors.

Designers are concerned both with ensuring that their designs can be constructed safely by the construction workers and that the completed building will be a safe place for people to occupy and maintain. The specific duties of the designer are to make the clients aware of their obligations, to give due regard to health and safety in the design, and to cooperate with the planning supervisor and others who are involved in the project.

Role of the planning supervisor

The planning supervisor should be appointed at the beginning of the design and planning stage. He has the responsibility of coordinating the health and safety aspects of the project. When the project is a sizeable one, the planning supervisor will generally be an organisation, such as an architectural practice, with design and construction experience and relevant knowledge of health and safety.

The duties of the planning supervisor are to notify the HSE of the project, to promote cooperation between the designers, to ensure that designers satisfactorily undertake their duties, to make certain that a pre-tender health and safety plan is prepared, and to assemble a health and safety file.

Health and safety plan

The health and safety plan is divided into two stages. In the pre-tender stage the plan is coordinated and managed by the planning supervisor, and at the construction stage this job is undertaken by the principal contractor.

The pre-tender safety plan is essentially a collection of information about the health and safety risks of the construction project. The client will supply information about matters such as the location of services, and the designers will cover issues such as unavoidable risks in the construction process.

The main purposes of the pre-tender plan are to highlight the health, welfare, and safety considerations, to make all requirements clear at the tender stage, and to assess the competence of prospective principal contractors with regard to health, welfare, and safety issues.

The construction stage plan should set out the arrangements for securing the health and safety of all construction workers and site visitors for the total period that work is being done on the site. It needs to deal with the method of managing the construction work to achieve a safe and healthy environment, the monitoring system adopted to ensure that the plan is being followed, and the health and safety risks resulting from the construction work.

The health and safety file

The health and safety file is prepared under the leadership of the planning supervisor, for the benefit and use of whoever will occupy the completed building. It should forewarn those who will be responsible for the future maintenance, repair, and construction work to the building of the key health and safety factors they need to take into account. Typically, the file will include 'as-built' drawings, the design criteria, details of construction methods and materials, maintenance details, and manuals for plant, equipment, and services.

The preparation of the health and safety file should be a continuous process during all stages of the project. The client, designers, and contractors all need to be involved in, and contribute towards, the preparation of the document.

The basic structure, and relationships operating under the CDM Regulations are illustrated in Figure 4.1.

Court cases

Since the introduction of the CDM Regulations on 31 March 1995 there have been a number of court cases brought because of non-compliance with the CDM Regulations, and three of these are summarised below.

Office demolition

The defendants, a firm of building contractors, had to demolish a large brick chimney as part of an office refurbishment contract. The demolition contractor failed to take account of the risks involved in undertaking this operation, particularly in providing a safe system of work. As a result of this negligence one of the site workers was fatally injured.

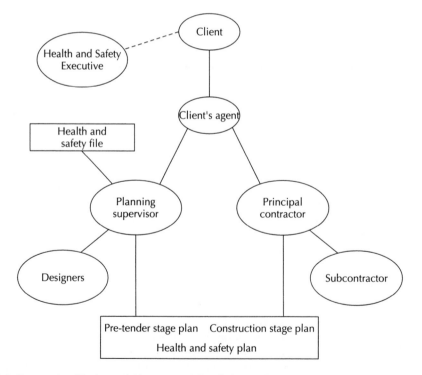

Fig. 4.1 Construction (Design and Management) Regulations 1994

The defendant, who was the principal contractor for the project, was convicted on the grounds that he had failed to provide appropriate safety training, or a health and safety plan. He was fined a total of £4,000.

Radio dish dismantling
The defendants, a firm of engineers, were responsible for dismantling some large radar dishes on an open site. The weight of the dishes was wrongly calculated, with the result that the crane supporting the dishes collapsed. There were no injuries to people on the site.

The defendants, who were both the principal contractor and the planning supervisor, were found guilty as the principal contractor and fined £2,000.

School refurbishment
During some demolition work at a school which was being refurbished a wall collapsed resulting in damage to a vehicle. The consulting engineers for the project denied any responsibility as they had not been appointed to supervise the work and their comments on the contractor's method statement had been ignored.

The HSE decided not to prosecute the engineers.

Indemnity insurance
The introduction of the CDM Regulations may in some cases affect architects', architectural technologists' and other professionals' indemnity insurance. It is not certain, for example, that all insurers will meet the criminal defence costs of prosecutions brought under the CDM Regulations.

Benefits of the CDM Regulations
The main aim of the CDM Regulations is to improve the health, welfare, and safety of all who work on, or visit, construction sites. Other benefits may also accrue, such as improved coordination and cooperation between design and construction, greater awareness at the tender stage of the risks involved, resulting in realistic tenders, and simpler and cheaper maintenance.

4.17 Copyright

The law relating to copyright is governed by the Copyright, Designs and Patents Act 1988. Section 4 of this Act makes it clear that works of architecture are included with artistic works as being given protection against infringement of copyright. Works of architecture include models of the buildings as well as the actual buildings. The copyright period lasts for 50 years after the death of the copyright holder, for example the architect who designed the building.

The nature of copyright was defined as follows in the Gregory Committee on Copyright Law:

> Copyright is the right given to or derived from works, and not a right in novelty of ideas. It is based on the right of an author, artist or composer to prevent another person copying an original work, whether it is a book, picture or tune, which the originator has created. There is nothing in the notion of copyright to prevent a second person from producing an identical result (and himself enjoying a copyright in that work) provided it is arrived at by an independent process.

In the case of buildings, the ownership of the copyright is vested with the architect, architectural technologist, or other practitioner who designed or drew the building. There are two important exceptions to this general rule. If a design or drawing is done by an employee during periods when he is working for the employer, the copyright will be vested in the employer and not the employee. Similarly, if the design or drawing is produced by a partner, the copyright rests with the partnership and not solely with the individual partner who was responsible for the design.

The second exception was highlighted by a court case in 1995 when Cala Homes (South) Ltd sued Alfred McAlpine Homes East Ltd claiming they had infringed the copyright of their 1988 'New Standard' house design. The drawings of the house had been produced, for Cala, by a firm of architectural draughtsmen. Prior to this case it might have been thought that the firm of architectural draughtsmen were the sole copyright owners. However, the judgement included the ruling that because one of Cala's employees had provided detailed instructions to the firm of architectural draughtsmen, they were joint copyright owners. This status enabled Cala to win the case.

4.18 Other legal matters affecting architectural practitioners

There are also various other legal matters affecting architects and architectural technologists which are dealt with elsewhere in this book. They are as follows:

- chapter 2
  - restriction on the use of the description 'architect',
  - architect's and architectural technologist's role as agent;
- chapter 3
  - legal ramifications of partnerships and other types of practices,
  - termination of architect's or architectural technologist's services,
  - architect's or architectural technologist's terms of appointment;
- chapter 6
  - obligations to employees in respect of health, welfare, and safety,
  - legal requirements relating to conditions of employment,
  - position regarding dismissal of employees and redundancy;

- chapter 7
  - constraints placed on a design by legal requirements,
  - building regulations and town planning acts,
  - trespass and nuisance,
  - boundaries and party walls,
  - easements and ancient lights;

- chapter 8
  - contracts, including determination,
  - building regulations and town planning acts,
  - Housing Grants, Construction and Regeneration Act 1996;

- chapter 9
  - contractual responsibilities during the pre-contract period;

- chapter 10
  - contractual responsibilities during the contract period,
  - issuing of certificates,
  - death of architect or employer
  - bankruptcy
  - arbitration and adjudication.

5

Technical information

5.1 Introduction

This chapter explains the need architects and architectural technologists have of access to a wide range of information affecting the design and construction of buildings. It explains some of the ways this information can be obtained and the standard method of classifying information for building work. The list of sources of information provided in section 5.2 below is not intended to be comprehensive.

5.2 General design and construction information

In order to be effective, architects and architectural technologists need the back-up of accurate up-to-date information on design standards, materials, construction techniques, and legislation for buildings.

The sources of information to which architects and technologists need to refer include the following:

- manufacturer's and contractor's data on products and materials
- British Standard Specifications (BSS),
- British Standard Codes of Practice (CP),
- European standards and Eurocodes,
- building regulations,
- other acts and regulations,
- government leaflets and publications,
- law reports,
- contracts, standard forms, and documentation,
- checklists,
- professional magazines and publications and technical articles,
- textbooks and technical books,
- design criteria,
- job records and feedbacks.

5.3 Basic library

Traditionally, most architectural practices have had a basic library, housing the various kinds of written information listed above in section 5.2. In recent years, with the advent and increasing use of computers, particularly the arrival of the Internet, the traditional library is likely to be used less, but for the time being most architects and architectural technologists will depend upon, and regularly consult, their practice's library.

The method of storing design and construction information may take various forms. The traditional method is by manual storage, generally by means of shelves accommodating books, box files, lever arch files, or some other type of file. The majority of technical information prepared for such systems is produced to A4 size, though not everyone is willing to conform to this standard size.

Large offices may employ one or more assistants to set up and maintain their reference library. An alternative method is to engage an independent commercial organisation to undertake this work. Smaller offices may use a junior assistant, or a non-technical member of the office staff, to file information, but in this case a senior assistant will generally be responsible for selecting the material and overseeing the work.

Computer information systems are dealt with later, in sections 5.6 and 5.7.

5.4 British Standards

An organisation called the British Standards Institution (BSI) is responsible for publishing British Standards (BS). It also publishes the English-language version of the European Standards [Euronorm (EN)] and is involved in the preparation of the International Standards of the International Standards Organization (ISO).

British Standards describe workmanship, details of materials and components use, testing methods, and information on dimensions. They are not legally enforceable but are accepted as 'deemed to satisfy' the requirements of the building regulations. Also, products carrying the BS 'Kitemark' provide an assurance that they were manufactured and tested to comply with specific standards.

The British Standard Specifications (BSS) lay down minimum standards for materials and components (e.g. walling blocks and doors) used in the construction and other industries.

Codes of Practice (CP) describe codes of good practice covering workmanship in specific areas (e.g. building drainage, and brick and block masonry).

5.5 European Standards: Euronorm

European Standards are standards agreed by all members of the European Committee for Standardisation (CEN), which is the organisation working with the national standards associations (such as the BSI in Britain, AFNOR in France, and DIN in Germany) in all the countries of the European Union. When European standards were first produced they were given a different number from their BSI, AFNOR, and DIN equivalent, even when they adopted a national standard virtually unchanged. For example, as was mentioned in section 2.13, Britain introduced a quality management standard, and called it BS 5750. It was adopted by the ISO and the CEN (which is responsible for producing EN standards) and called BS EN ISO 9000, now commonly shortened to ISO 9000.

Eurocodes (EC) are codes of practice, published by the CEN. When first produced they may be pre-standards (preENVs) and then at a later date changed to an EN.

It is hoped eventually that all national codes will be withdrawn and replaced by a European standard (EN) which will be used in all the countries of the European Union. There is a further expectation that within 20 years most of the rest of the world will be working to these codes.

5.6 Computer information systems

As an alternative to a manual information system using A4 pages, computer information services are now widely used. Many firms provide information on computer disks which can be fed into a computer system to provide a wide range of information, such as the building regulations, contract law, Building Research Establishment (BRE) publications, texts of British and European standards, and product details. The information can be regularly updated. It is displayed on a television-type screen, but paper copies can be obtained as required, by means of a printer.

5.7 Internet

The fastest growing and most popular computer information system is the Internet. It is the largest computer network in the world and is best described as a worldwide network of networks. The Internet has been compared to a public library system where most day-to-day needs can be met if it is a well-stocked local library, but where if a particular book or piece of information is not available locally it should be able to be obtained from a neighbouring public library. The Internet truly converts computers into information appliances. Once connected to the Internet, you have instant access to a vast network of computers and a wealth of information. It can be used to undertake library searches, to gain access to data bases, obtain reports, to read professional journals, as well as to provide many other information functions. Some of the information obtained has to be paid for, but much of it is free.

The Internet is more than an information system, and other aspects are mentioned in section 6.10.

5.8 General cost information

The cost aspect of work is the particular concern of the quantity surveyor, who will generally be employed as the client's financial advisor on all but the smallest projects. However, many architects and architectural technologists will maintain their own cost information.

The information may consist of a detailed build-up of building costs, based on labour and material rates plus preliminaries, overheads, and profit, but will more likely take the form of approximate estimated information. Details of approximate estimating are given in section 9.4. There are many sources of information for approximate estimating, three of which are outlined below.

5.9 Cost analysis of previous jobs

The methods used and the system of recording the information will vary from office to office. One method is to keep a loose-leaf record book with one or more pages for each different type of building. As each job is completed, basic details such as total floor areas, total cost, and price per square metre of floor area are recorded. A note is also made of any special circumstances which made the job more, or less, expensive than average. To use this information as a guide for a new project, it is necessary to update the costs (generally by means of a percentage increase) to allow for the change which has taken place in building costs during the period between the two jobs.

This can be a useful method, particularly if the person using the information is familiar both with the earlier projects and with the current project. However, care has to be taken in applying the correct percentage increase and to take full account of local and national cost trends and any special circumstances for a particular project.

Frequently the available information is recorded on a computer disk.

5.10 Price books and journals

There are a number of excellent price books, still available, providing useful information for preparing approximate estimates, although they are tending to be replaced by computer systems. They include books running into thousands of pages, and clearly contain much valuable information. However good these books are they should be used with discretion, and some quantity surveyors would claim it is foolhardy to use them for anything other than 'back up' information. A number of technical journals for architects, technologists, and builders also provide similar information to that shown in price books.

5.11 Computer estimating systems

Many firms now provide software packages (i.e. disks) with information for feeding into computers. Most of these are comprehensive estimating packages providing thousands of prices of materials, components, and labour costs, to enable detailed prices to be built up for contractor's tenders. However, some of them provide the sort of information the architect or architectural technologist needs when calculating the approximate cost of a building project. The various systems are generally updated at regular intervals.

5.12 The Royal Institution of Chartered Surveyors' Building Cost Information Service

The best known and most comprehensive cost information service is probably the Royal Institution of Chartered Surveyors' (RICS) Building Cost Information Service. This offers cost information for every stage of a building project, from feasibility studies in the initial stage, to cost control during operations on-site. The service is based on the principle of reciprocity; subscribers to the service undertake to provide data from their own sources, and in return receive information made available by all. As a result the service has a 'bank' of information ready for use covering in excess of 12,000 projects.

Included in the service are building price schedules, containing pounds sterling per square metre prices, for over 500 building types. The coverage is exhaustive. For example, the section on factories covers 18 categories, including different sizes and various methods of construction. The information is updated quarterly. There are also concise cost analyses containing data from a large number of projects, to give a range of prices for early cost estimating. The cost is broken down into the main elements of substructure, superstructure, internal finishes, fittings, services, external works, and preliminaries.

Furthermore, there is a library of detailed cost analyses of actual projects, which can be used for budgeting and estimating, to produce probable costs of future projects. As the title suggests, these analyses are more detailed and break the cost down into each individual element. For example, the cost breakdown of the super-structure includes items such as upper floors, roof, stairs, external walls, windows, and external doors, and the services cost breakdown includes items such as sanitary appliances, water installations, ventilating systems, electrical installations, and gas installations.

Figure 5.1 gives the RICS Building Cost Information Service's detailed elemental analysis for electronics factories, and Figure 5.2 shows a histogram for the costs of factories generally.

5.13 Samples

Architects and architectural technologists often maintain a collection of samples of various building products such as bricks, tiles, ironmongery, flooring materials, glazed tiles, and electrical accessories, both for use by their own staff and for showing to clients.

It is important that these samples are labelled with information on the name and address of the supplier, the date they were obtained, and the cost. It is also important that they are arranged in an orderly manner. Generally, they will be on shelving. Large firms may have a special samples room, or use part of their

Detailed Elemental Analysis
BCIS *Online* analysis number: 15606

New Build
BCIS code: A - 1 - 2,865

Job title:	Electronics Factory, Northern Ireland
Location:	Northern Ireland
Client:	
Dates:	Receipt: 13-Apr-1995 Base: 13-Apr-1995 Acceptance: 10-May-1995 Possession: 11-May-1995

Project details:	Single storey factory building, 95×28×4.4m, with attached boiler and compressor house, 9.4×18m, ready for occupation. External works include macadam and insitu concrete paving, chain link fencing, landscaping, services, drainage, security hut and chemical store.
Site conditions:	Level green field site with moderate ground conditions. Excavation above water table. Unrestricted working space and access.
Market conditions:	Project tender price index was 75 on a base of 1985 BCIS Index Base Indices used to adjust costs to base price level: TPI for 2Q95 129; location factor 0.76

Tender documents:	Bill of Quantities		Contract:	GC/Wks/1 edition 2
Procurement:	Selected competition		Cost fluctuations:	Fixed
Number of tenders:	Issued: 6 Received: 6		Contract period:	Stipulated: 4 Offered: Agreed: 4

Contract breakdown

	Contract £	Analysis £	Competitive tender list	Tender £	% above lowest
Measured work	1,078,990	1,078,990	1	1,810,990	-
Provisional sums	51,000	51,000	2	1,858,401	2.6
PC sums	509,200	509,200	3	1,874,212	3.5
Preliminaries	131,800	131,800	4	1,899,439	4.9
Contingencies	40,000	40,000	5	1,914,045	5.7
Contract sum	1,810,990	1,810,990	6	1,953,259	7.9

Accommodation and design features: Factory with offices, canteen, stores and attached utilities block. Concrete strip and pad foundations, ground slab. Steel portal frame. Rendered block dwarf walls, steel cladding to walls and roof. Double glazed aluminium windows; electric steel roller shutter doors. Block partitions, WC cubicles. Flush doors. Plaster and paint only to walls; special screed, vinyl, carpet and tiles to floors; suspended ceilings. Fittings. Kitchen fitments. Sanitaryware. Oil HW heating. Extract fans, electric light and power. Sprinklers. Burglar and fire alarms, CCTV. Ext works.

Storeys as a % of gross floor area		Average Storey Heights		Functional unit		Rate
		Below ground floor	-			
		At ground floor	-			
		Above ground floor	-			

Areas					£m2 incl Preliminaries		
		Element	Percentage	Total cost of element £	£ per m2	Tender prices	1995 constant prices
Basement floors	- m2						
Ground floor	2,865 m2						
Upper floor	- m2						
Gross floor area	2,865 m2						
		Substructure	6 %	109,079	38.07	41.13	54.54
Usable area	2,608 m2	Superstructure	19 %	351,991	122.86	132.74	176.01
Circulation area	88 m2	Internal finishes	6 %	99,733	34.81	37.61	49.87
Ancillary area	169 m2	Fittings	1 %	16,215	5.66	6.11	8.11
Internal Divisions	- m2	Services	25 %	446,572	155.87	168.40	223.30
Gross floor area	2,865 m2						
		Building sub-total	57 %	1,023,590	357.27	386.00	511.83
Area not enclosed	- m2	External works	34 %	615,600	214.87	232.15	307.82
External wall area	1,597 m2	Preliminaries	7 %	131,800	46.00	-	-
Wall to floor ratio	0.56	Contingencies	2 %	40,000	13.96	13.96	18.51
Internal cube	- m3						
		Total		1,810,990	632.11	632.11	838.17

Submitted by: DOE for Northern Ireland

Fig. 5.1 Royal Institution of Chartered Surveyors' Building Cost Information Service: detailed elemental analysis for electronics factories, sheets 1, 2, and 3

Element		Preliminaries shown separately				Preliminaries spread	
		Total cost	Cost per m2	Element unit quantity	Element unit rate	Total cost	Cost per m2
1	Substructure	109,079	38.07	2,865 m2	38.07	117,850	41.13
2A	Frame	122,000	42.58	2,865 m2	42.58	131,809	46.01
2B	Upper floors	-					
2C	Roof	92,920	32.43	3,041 m2	30.56	100,391	35.04
2D	Stairs	-					
2E	External walls	45,967	16.04	1,334 m2	34.46	49,663	17.33
2F	Windows and external doors	35,883	12.52	263 m2	136.44	38,768	13.53
2G	Internal walls and partitions	37,291	13.02	1,798 m2	20.74	40,289	14.06
2H	Internal doors	17,930	6.26	51 No	351.57	19,372	6.76
2	Superstructure	351,991	122.86			380,292	132.74
3A	Wall finishes	25,360	8.85			27,399	9.56
3B	Floor finishes	53,020	18.51			57,283	19.99
3C	Ceiling finishes	21,353	7.45			23,070	8.05
3	Internal finishes	99,733	34.81			107,752	37.61
4	Fittings	16,215	5.66			17,519	6.11
5A	Sanitary appliances	included in	5F				
5B	Services equipment	-					
5C	Disposal installations	included in	5F				
5D	Water installations	included in	5F				
5E	Heat source	included in	5F				
5F	Space heating and air treatment	174,000	60.73			187,991	65.62
5G	Ventilating systems	included in	5F				
5H	Electrical installations	150,000	52.36			162,061	56.57
5I	Gas installations	-					
5J	Lift and conveyor installations	-					
5K	Protective installations	52,200	18.22			56,397	19.68
5L	Communications installations	-					
5M	Special installations	-					
5N	Builder's work in connection	70,372	24.56			76,030	26.54
5O	Builder's profit and attendance	-					
5	Services	446,572	155.87			482,479	168.40
	Building sub-total	1,023,590	357.27			1,105,892	386.00
6A	Site works	442,112	154.31			477,660	166.72
6B	Drainage	118,630	41.41			128,169	44.74
6C	External services	included in	5F				
6D	Minor building works	54,858	19.15			59,269	20.69
6	External works	615,600	214.87			665,098	232.15
7	Preliminaries	131,800	46.00			-	
	Total (less Contingencies)	1,770,990	618.15			1,770,990	618.15
8	Contingencies	40,000	13.96			40,000	13.96
	Contract sum	1,810,990	632.11			1,810,990	632.11

Fig. 5.1 Continued

Element	Specification
1 Substructure	Excavation in unstable ground. 1995m2 Type 3 crushed rock. Concrete C35/20 in foundation trenches, C40/20 reinforced concrete slab, power float finish, 200mm thick. Reinforced concrete stanchion bases. 215mm precast concrete block walling.
2A Frame	PC sum £122000 for single span steel portal frame.
2C Roof	BSC Colorcoat steel cladding, insulated core and powder coated inner skin. Translucent rooflights. KingspanHighline steel gutters. PVC rainwater pipes.
2E External walls	Precast concrete block dwarf walls, rendered, with BSC Colorcoat insulated composite metal cladding.
2F Windows and external doors	Kawneer 102 series double glazed aluminium windows and external screens; Leaderflush doors. 2No electrically operated steel roller shutters.
2G Internal walls and partitions	10.5N/mm2 precast fairfaced concrete blocks, mainly 215mm. Toilet cubicles.
2H Internal doors	51No 44mm solid core doors in softwood frames.
3A Wall finishes	2 coats Carlite plaster and vinyl emulsion to blockwork.
3B Floor finishes	Sealed concrete floor with 2mm Larcote SL or Laybon Sealdeck; 421m2 vinyl flooring; 86m2 ceramic tiles; 261m2 Interface Genesis carpet.
3C Ceiling finishes	1122m2 Armstrong Minaboard Dune suspended ceilings.
4 Fittings	Minor shelving, vanity kitchen units, bench seats, reception desk.
5A Sanitary appliances	14No WCs, 15No wash basins, included in 5F.
5C Disposal installations	Included in 5F.
5D Water installations	Included in 5F.
5E Heat source	Included in 5F.
5F Space heating and air treatment	PC sum £174000 for 2 boilers, calorifiers, compressors, dryer, air receiver, 2 toilet extract fans, 2 general extract fans, 7 smoke ventilators.
5G Ventilating systems	Included in 5F.
5H Electrical installations	PC sum £150000 for electric light, power, switchgear and CCTV.
5K Protective installations	PC sum £52200 for sprinklers.
5L Communications installations	Intruder alarm and fire detection.
5N Builder's work in connection	Concrete bases, tank platforms, holes, pipe casings.
6A Site works	Grassing; 4462m2 reinforced concrete roads; 4057m2 asphalt roads; 1801m2 macadam paving; 2022m2 macadam footpaths; chain link fencing, rendered block retaining wall with galvanised balustrading.
6B Drainage	2915m2 PVC drain pipes, 110mm diameter; 92No gullies; 44No manholes. Pumping chamber.
6C External services	Oil supply, sprinkler mains, water, electricity.
6D Minor building works	Security hut, utility building and chemical store with rendered block walls and composite roof panels.
7 Preliminaries	8.04 % of remainder of Contract Sum (excluding Contingencies).
8 Contingencies	2.44 % of remainder of Contract Sum (excluding Preliminaries).

Fig. 5.1 Continued

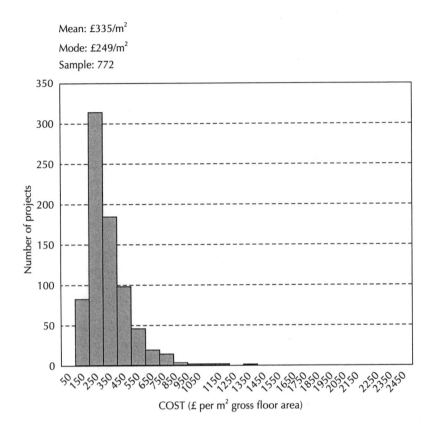

Mean: £335/m²

Mode: £249/m²

Sample: 772

Fig. 5.2 Histogram of costs of factories generally

reference library for this purpose, but in smaller firms the sample shelves will be fixed in some convenient area of the office.

5.14 Record drawings

Even when a building is completed and handed over to the clients, architects and architectural technologists will still need to keep, and have access to, many of the drawings used for the construction of the project. This has always been the case, because queries on the building's construction may arise at some time in the future. There may be extensions or alterations required to the building, or drawings of previously constructed buildings may be useful to the designer for one of his future jobs. Since the passing of the Construction (Design and Management) Regulations 1994 there has been an additional reason for keeping the drawings. The regulations require that the health and safety file includes a set of the record or 'as-built' drawings produced throughout the construction process (section 4.16).

Generally, apart from the set of drawings kept in the safety file only the negatives will be retained. These can be stored in metal tubes and arranged on shelves or racks. They should, of course, be labelled, and if more than one tube is required for a particular project, it is best to strap them together.

This traditional method of filing record drawings has the disadvantage of using up space. If less desirable spaces, such as basement and attic areas, are available, they may become the home for record drawings, otherwise valuable and expensive office space will be lost.

As an alternative to the traditional system, use may be made of a microfilm storage system. The original drawings, reproduced on A3, A2, A1, or A0 sheets are transferred onto 35 mm microfilm copies which can be conveniently filed in a relatively small cabinet. It has been estimated that microfilm copies need only about 5% of the space taken up by traditional drawings.

The microfilm copies need to be indexed accurately, but once this is done they are easily located and retrieved when needed. They have the further advantage of being able to be housed in a lockable, fire-resistant container. Readers are available for viewing the microfilm copies, and printing can be arranged, or a printer can be supplied by a company specialising in microfilming work.

Where computer-aided design (CAD) drawings are produced the information can be retained on the computer disks, but hard (paper) copies are required for the health and safety file (section 4.16).

5.15 Royal Institute of British Architects' products library data

Among the organisations offering information on building products and services is RIBA Services Ltd. They produce A4 information sheets on various products based on information supplied by the manufacturers. The format of these sheets are standardised, so making it easier to compare the different products. The sheets are assembled in a series of binders, which are regularly updated.

5.16 The Construction Industry/Samarbetskommitten for Byggnadsfragor (CI/SfB) system

There are many other systems, in addition to the one outlined above, which could be used for filing technical information about the construction industry, particularly about building materials and products.

At the moment the system most widely used is known as the CI/SfB system. This is of Swedish origin, but was introduced into this country by the Royal Institute of British Architects (RIBA). Eventually, it will be replaced by a new system, Uniclass, which was launched in 1997. However, the widespread use and popularity of the CI/SfB system suggests that it may be a considerable time before this happens.

It is therefore important in the interim period that architectural staff are familiar with it, particularly those involved in the management of such a system. To achieve complete familiarity with CI/SfB it is important to study the CI/SfB Construction

Indexing Manual produced by RIBA Publications Ltd. There is no adequate substitute for this procedure, but, as an introduction, the main features of the system are summarised below.

Everything is classified under five tables. Table 0 covers the physical environment. It includes items such as planning areas but is mainly concerned with different types of buildings or facilities. Each type of building or facility is given a distinctive number, for example:

6   religious facilities generally,
61 religious centre facilities,
62 cathedrals,
63 churches and chapels,
64 mission halls and meeting houses,
65 temples, mosques, and synagogues,
66 convents,
67 funerary facilities and shrines,
68 other religious facilities.

Table 1 deals with particular functions which combine to make up the facilities in Table 0. They include substructure items, such as foundations; primary elements such as window or door openings and suspended ceilings; finishes, such as wall, floor, and ceiling finishes; services, mainly piped and ducted; other services, mainly electrical; fittings, such as sanitary fittings; and external elements. Each item is given a distinctive bracketed number. For example:

(2-) primary structural elements,
(21) external walls,
(22) internal walls,
(23) floors,
(24) stairs,
(27) roofs,
(28) building frames.

Table 2 deals with the construction of forms which combine together to make up the elements in Table 1. Each form is given a distinctive, capital letter. For example:

F blocks, blockwork, bricks, and brickwork,
G large blocks and panels,
H sections such as structural steel sections,
I pipework.

Table 3 deals with the materials which combine to form the products in Table 2. They include formed materials, such as clay to make bricks and metal to make sections; formless materials, such as concrete and mortar; and what are termed 'functional materials', such as paint. Each category can be further subdivided by use of a number added to the lower case letter. For example:

g   clay (dried or fired),
g1 dried clay,

g2 fired clay,
g3 glazed fired clay,
g6 refractory materials (e.g. fireclay).

Table 4 deals with activities which assist or affect construction but which are not incorporated in it. Each item is given a combined capital letter and number set within brackets. For example:

(K) fire and explosions,
(K1) source and types,
(K2) fire protection,
(K3) fire resistance (structures),
(K4) reaction to fire (materials),
(K5) smoke, etc.,
(K6) explosions,
(K7) fire explosion damage and salvage.

Figure 5.3 shows the general concept of the system in diagrammatic form. Figure 5.4 shows how Tables 1, 2, and 3 are used. Lists of the main subject headings for the five tables are given below. The subdivisions of the various tables are equally important, and the reader will need to study the CI/SfB Construction Indexing Manual, published by RIBA Publications Ltd, for this information.

Table 0
0 planning areas,
1 utilities and civil engineering facilities,
2 industrial facilities,
3 administrative, commercial, and protective service facilities,
4 health and welfare facilities,
5 recreational facilities,
6 religious facilities,
7 educational, scientific, and information facilities,
8 residential facilities,
9 common facilities and other facilities;

Table 1
(1-) ground and substructure,
(2-) structures, primary elements, and carcass,
(3-) secondary elements and completion of structure,
(4-) finishes to structure,
(5-) services, mainly piped and ducted,
(6-) services, mainly electrical,
(7-) fittings,
(8-) loose furniture equipment,
(9-) external elements and other elements;

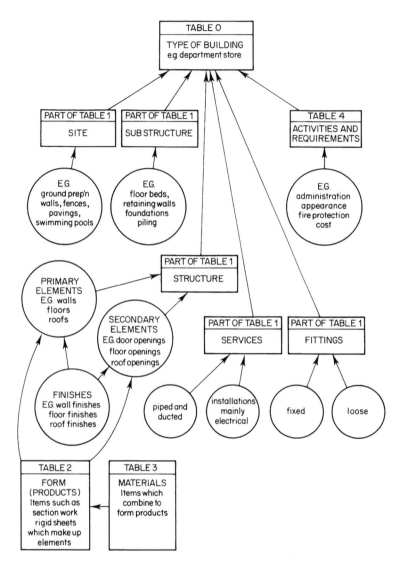

Fig. 5.3 General concept of the CI/SfB (Construction Industry/Samarbetskommitten for Byggnadsfragor) system for technical information

Table 2

A   construction forms,
B   vacant,
C   excavation and loose fillwork,
D   vacant,
E   cast *in situ* work,

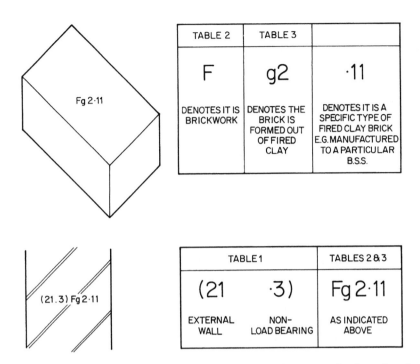

Fig. 5.4 Use of Tables 1, 2, and 3 of the CI/SfB (Construction Industry/Samarbetskommitten for Byggnadsfragor) system

F   blockwork and brickwork,
G   large blocks and panel work,
H   section work,
I   pipe work,
J   wire work,
K   quilt work,
L   flexible sheetwork (proofing),
M   malleable sheetwork,
N   rigid sheet overlap work,
P   thick coatingwork,
R   rigid sheetwork,
S   rigid tilework,
T   flexible sheetwork,
U   vacant,
V   film coating and impregnation work,
W   planting work,
X   work with components,
Y   formless work,
Z   joints;

Table 3

e	natural stone,
f	pre-cast with binder,
g	clay (dried or fired),
h	metal,
i	wood,
j	vegetable and animal materials,
k	vacant,
l	vacant,
m	inorganic fibres,
n	rubbers, plastics, etc.,
o	glass,
p	aggregates and loose fills,
q	lime and cement binders, mortars, and concrete,
r	clay, gypsum, magnesia and plastic binders, and mortars,
s	bituminous materials,
t	fixing and jointing materials,
u	protective and process or property modifying materials,
v	paints,
w	ancillary materials,
x	vacant
y	composite materials,
z	substances;

Table 4

(A)	administration, management, activities, and aids,
(B)	construction plant and tools,
(C)	vacant,
(D)	construction operations,
(E)	composition, etc.,
(F)	shape, size, etc.,
(G)	appearance, etc.,
(H)	context environment,
(J)	mechanics,
(K)	fire and explosion,
(L)	matter,
(M)	heat and cold,
(N)	light and dark,
(P)	sound and quiet,
(Q)	electricity,
(R)	energy and other physical factors,
(S)	vacant,
(T)	application,
(U)	users and resources,
(V)	working factors,
(W)	operation and maintenance factors,

(X)   change, movement, and stability factors,
(Z)   peripheral subjects, form of presentation, time, and place.

5.17 Uniclass system

Uniclass, which is an abbreviation for United Classification for the Construction Industry, is a new classification scheme for the construction industry, which was launched in 1997. It is sponsored by the Construction Industry Project Information Committee, representing the four major sponsor organisations – namely, the Construction Confederation, the Royal Institute of British Architects (RIBA), the Royal Institution of Chartered Surveyors (RICS), the Chartered Institute of Building Services Engineers (CIBSE) – and the Department of the Environment (DoE) [now the Department of the Environment, Transport and the Regions (DoETR)].

Uniclass is a classification system for organising library materials and for structuring product literature, cost information, specifications, and project information.

The intentions of the sponsors is that Uniclass will eventually replace the well established CI/SfB classification system (section 5.16). There are various reasons for initiating this change, including international developments, the advance of computerisation, and the need for a classification system which can include new building types, and concepts involving energy and environmental issues.

The introduction of Uniclass took place shortly before work began on the writing of this book. This means that the author does not have the benefit of any feedback on the degree of acceptance of the new system by the construction industry.

The information in this book about the Uniclass system is taken from the *Uniclass Manual*, with the kind permission of the publishers, RIBA Publications. The copyright belongs to the sponsor organisation listed in the first paragraph of this section, and information given in the manual should not be reproduced without the prior permission of the copyright owners and RIBA Publications.

In order to understand and achieve familiarity with the Uniclass system it is necessary to study the *Uniclass Manual*. As an introduction, the main features of the system are summarised below.

Uniclass comprises 15 tables, each of which represents a different general aspect of construction information, for example Table C covers information on all aspects of management relating to the construction industry, in the sense of the industry as a whole and with regard to the operation of individual companies and practices.

Each table can be used on its own; for example Table D32, which in the Uniclass index is given as the classification for 'office facilities', or Table E853, which is the classification for 'temporary buildings'. Alternatively, terms from different tables can be used to form more complex subjects; for example Table D32: E853 is the classification for temporary office facilities. Signs such as +, <, and > may be used to combine two different items into a single classification; for example D27+D32 includes industrial facilities (D27) and office facilities (D32), D32<D41 gives details of an office facility (D32) which is part of a hospital (D41).

It can be seen that each classification consists of a capital letter followed by zero or more digits, except for tables J and K. Unlike the CI/SfB system there are no combinations of lower case and capital letters. These were avoided in Uniclass because of a belief that some users of information systems find such arrangements confusing, and complex notations also cause problems with computerisation.

Some elements occur in more than one table; for example windows appear in Table G as an element, with the notation G321, and in Table L as a product, with the notation L413.

The numbers used in the notations start off with the table letter, for example D, which represents the general subject of 'Facilities'. Further digits are added to define the item more precisely; for example D8 denotes residential facilities and D81 denotes domestic residential facilities, and housing, and D8151 denotes owner-occupied housing.

The 15 tables in the Uniclass system, with an outline of their contents and examples of notation, are given below. Note there is no Table I or Table O, to avoid confusion with the numerals one and zero.

Table A: form of information
This covers types of reference materials to be found in libraries, such as dictionaries, catalogues, price books, and reports. Examples of notation are: A3, national and international standards; A31, British Standards; A32, European Standards.

Table B: subject disciplines
This covers the body of knowledge centred around professions such as architecture, engineering, and contracting. Examples of notation are: B1, architecture; B11, architecture, by name of the architect; B13, history of architecture; B14, architectural design.

Table C: management
This covers all aspects of management. Examples of notation are: C3, type of business or organisation; C322, partnerships.

Table D: facilities
This classifies construction work according to the user activity. Examples of notation are: D6, religious facilities; D61, cathedrals; D622, cathedral treasures.

Table E: construction entities
A construction entity is an independent piece of construction, with the classification governed by its physical form rather than the user activity. Examples are buildings, bridges, and tunnels. Examples of notation are: E5, bridges; E57, movable bridges; E571, drawbridges.

Table F: spaces

A space is a volume such as a room or corridor within a building or a balcony external to a building. The purpose of the classification is to classify information about the design, costs, regulations, etc. Examples of notation are: F3: circulation spaces; F327, corridors.

Table G: elements for buildings

This classifies major physical parts of buildings such as floors, walls, and services. It can be used for organising both design and cost information. Examples of notation are: G2, fabric (complete elements); G22, floors; G222, upper floors.

Table H: elements for civil engineering works

This generally has the same main headings as for Table E, except that it is for civil engineering works rather than building works. Its primary use is expected to be for cost analysis.

Table J: work sections for buildings

This table is based on the Common Arrangement of Work Sections (CAWS) for building works and is used for classifying trade literature and design or technical information relating to construction products. Examples are curtain walling, warm air heating, and lifts. The use of this table is in organising information in specifications and bills of quantities, classifying literature on particular construction operations. Examples of notation are: JA, preliminaries, JA4, contractor's general cost items; JA41, site accommodation.

Table K: work sections for civil engineering works

This table is based on the Civil Engineering Standard Method of Measurement, and has similar uses to Table J. Examples of notation are: KE, earthworks; KP, piles.

Table L: construction products

This table is used for classifying trade literature and design or technical information relating to construction products such as lintels, bricks, wash basins, and rainwater pipes and fittings. Examples of notation are: L5: coverings and claddings lining; L52, roof coverings, claddings, and linings; L521, roof tiles; L5221, clay roof tiles.

Table M: construction aids

This table is for classifying trade literature and technical information relating to plant and equipment used for aiding construction operations. Examples are scaffolding, construction vehicles, and testing equipment. Examples of notation are:

M3, scaffolding, shoring, and fencing; M31, complete scaffolding; M311, prefabricated scaffolding.

Table N: properties and characteristics

This table is for the arrangement of information on the properties and characteristics of things such as environmental factors, fire, and acoustics. Examples of notation are: N36, optical; N361, sources of light types; N3611, natural light.

Table P: materials

This table is for classifying different types of materials, such as timber, metal, and plastic. Examples of notation are: P2, cementitous, concrete, and mineral-bound material; P22, concrete (general); P222, dense concrete.

Table Q: Universal Decimal Classification

Universal Decimal Classification (UDC) is a book classification system. It is invaluable for general use but less suited to provide information classification for specialist areas such as construction. Table Q indicates how UDC can be used to classify subjects not covered elsewhere in the Uniclass system. Examples are applied arts and crafts, mathematics, and agriculture. The classification method is to use the UDC number and precede this number by Q. For example, UDC classifies sculpture as 73, so the Uniclass system classifies it as Q73.

6

General office practice

6.1 Introduction

As well as organising the technical side of their work, architects and architectural technologists, like all other professional and business people, need to attend to matters such as arranging accommodation, furnishings, and insurance. They also have obligations to the staff they employ, with respect to conditions of work, National Insurance, income tax, and holidays. This chapter deals with such matters.

6.2 Accommodation

Architects and architectural technologists will generally try to obtain the best possible accommodation which they can afford, so as to provide agreeable working conditions for their staff and an inviting atmosphere for visitors, particularly clients. In practice they will be limited by what is available within their price range in the area where they wish to operate and by whether the available accommodation is for rent, lease, or sale.

A reception or waiting area is a useful feature in a professional office, although clients in particular do not expect to be kept waiting. Facilities will also be required within the office accommodation for meetings with clients and others. This space may be arranged within the partners' or directors' offices, although often a separate meeting room will be available.

Further areas will be required for the architectural and other technical staff and for the secretarial and administrative staff. A computer-aided design and drawing system (CAD) will frequently be arranged in separate rooms or areas. Library and other storage space will generally be provided, as will toilets and at least a small kitchen area for tea and coffee making.

6.3 Furniture

The standard of furniture will vary enormously, from fully carpeted and curtained offices, with attractive furniture and internal landscaping, to the distinctly spartan or positively grotty. It is not always easy to know exactly what to expect in the way of furniture and furnishings, as sometimes minimalism is fashionable, so a spartan office could be a sign of keeping up to date.

Partners and directors will generally, as a minimum requirement, be provided with a desk, drawing facilities, possibly a plan chest, and enough chairs for themselves and their visitors.

Other architectural staff will require drawing facilities, chairs or stools, laying-out space for drawings, catalogues, etc., and provision for storing drawings.

Secretarial and administrative staff will require desks, chairs, storage facilities for files and stationery, and typewriters and computer equipment. Computer equipment is discussed further in section 6.10. Equipment for office staff will generally be located in the office work areas.

6.4 Telephones

An adequate number of telephones is essential, with a phone within easy reach of each worker, as even the most junior staff will occasionally have to take phone calls. People, including clients, can get very frustrated if as a result of too few lines being available they have difficulty in making contact with the architectural staff. Mention has been made under section 3.16 of the importance of a pleasant, competent telephone operator to create a good initial impression on callers.

6.5 Stationery

Architects and architectural technologists setting up in practice will need to obtain a whole range of standard forms. These can be individually designed, but many architects and architectural technologists will choose to use the standard forms designed by the Royal Institute of British Architects (RIBA) and the British Institute of Architectural Technology (BIAT). Examples of such forms are included in chapter 11.

6.6 Health, welfare, and safety of employees

Whatever accommodation is provided, the architect and architectural technologist, as employers of staff, are responsible for complying with the requirements of the Workplace (Health, Safety and Welfare) Regulations 1992, the Management of Health and Safety at Work Regulations 1992 (commonly referred to as the Management Regulations), the Health and Safety at Work Act 1974, and various other health and safety laws. They include provision for the health, welfare, and safety of people employed in offices.

The obligation on employers is to provide what is reasonably practicable and appropriate for the health, safety, and welfare of their employees. Legislation on health, welfare, and safety of employees is an area of frequent change. In particular, it is necessary for anyone having responsibilities in this area to keep in touch with

European legislation and directives that affect employers and employees. These are being regularly revised and implemented.

A description of just some of the things the architect and architectural technologist employer, like all other employers of office staff, must provide, are given below.

Ventilation

An adequate supply of fresh or purified air must be provided; warm, humid air must be removed and diluted; and air movement must be provided, giving a sense of freshness without causing draughts. Ventilation may be provided by means of windows, but where necessary mechanical ventilation systems should be installed.

Temperature

The premises must be heated to a reasonable temperature, generally to at least 16°C.

Lighting

Enough suitable lighting must be provided to enable people to work and move about safely. Lighting must not create any hazards, and where the sudden loss of light would create a risk, automatic emergency lighting, powered by an independent source, should be provided.

Cleanliness

Workplaces, including furniture, fittings, and furnishings, should be kept clean, and it should be possible to keep floor, wall, and ceiling surfaces clean.

Room dimensions and space

There should be enough free space to allow people to move about with ease. People should be able to leave their workplace swiftly in an emergency. A minimum of 11 cubic metres of space should be provided per person. In working out the room volume, all parts of the room over 3 metres high should be counted as being 3 metres high.

Seating

Where work can be done sitting down, an appropriate seat with proper support should be provided for each worker.

Visual display units

Visual display unit (VDU) workstations should be arranged to avoid eye strain, and employees spending the majority of their time working at such stations should be sent for an eye test annually.

Floors and traffic routes
Enough traffic routes, of sufficient width and height, should be provided, allowing people to circulate safely with ease. Floors should be strong enough for the loads and traffic placed upon them, with surfaces which are free from holes and obstructions and which are not uneven or slippery.

Fire precautions
A safe means of entering and leaving the building should be provided and sufficient and suitable fire extinguishing equipment supplied.

Staircases
Open sides of staircases should be fenced with an upper rail at a minimum height at 900 mm and with a lower rail. A handrail should be provided on one side of every staircase. Access between floors should not be by ladders or steep stairs.

Lifts
Where lifts are provided they should be safe, state the maximum load they can carry, and be examined by a competent person every six months.

Maintenance
The building and equipment should be maintained in efficient working order, including mechanical ventilating systems which would result in a health risk if a fault were to develop.

Windows
Openable windows, skylights, and ventilators should be able to be opened, closed, and cleaned easily and safely.

Doors
Doors should be suitably constructed and fitted with all necessary safety devices.

Sanitary conveniences and washing facilities
Sufficient suitable sanitary conveniences and washing facilities should be provided, located in readily accessible places. Generally five WCs for men and 5 WCs for women will be enough for up to 100 of each sex, with basins provided on the same scale as WCs. Hot and cold, or warm, water should be supplied, with soap and clean towels or other means of cleaning or drying.

Drinking water

An adequate supply of wholesome drinking water should be provided.

Clothing

Provision should be made for storing, and as far is reasonably practicable, for drying the workers' clothing.

Rest and eating facilities

Suitable and sufficient rest facilities and space for eating meals should be provided, including a facility to obtain a hot drink. Rest areas should include arrangements to protect non-smokers from discomfort caused by tobacco smoke. Rest areas for pregnant women and nursing mothers should be near to sanitary facilities and include the facility to lie down.

Disabled people

Where people with disabilities are among the workforce, the workplaces must be suitable for them, including toilets and traffic routes.

6.7 Insurance of premises and contents

If architects or architectural technologists own their own office building they will need to insure it against loss and damage due to fire, burglary, and other mishaps, such as lightning, explosions, damage by aircraft, storms, floods, and earthquakes.

In any event they will need to take out insurance cover for the contents of their offices. The main thing is to ensure that the cover obtained is adequate to replace the full value of the loss and damage incurred. Most insurance companies offer index-linked schemes which take account of the effects of inflation.

As well as the normal contents of the premises, architectural practitioners also need to cover the cost of replacing drawings, specifications, and other documents damaged or destroyed, including those documents in the course of preparation.

6.8 Employer's liability insurance

Architects and technologists, like other employers, need to take out insurance against claims made on them either by their employees or by members of the public.

There is a legal responsibility placed on employers to take out insurance to cover claims arising out of injury or death of their employees. The premiums are based on the class of employee and the salary paid.

Insurance can, if desired, also be taken out to cover claims by members of the public against the employer – for example a client who, when visiting an architect's office, slips on the floor and injures himself. Protection against injuries sustained during this kind of incident are more important now that the health and safety laws set out the general duties that employees have towards members of the public.

An employer is also liable for any wrong done by a member of his staff which occurs while the employee is engaged on his employer's business, and most employers will therefore insure themselves against such action by their employees. An employer is not, however, liable for a wrong done by an employee outside that employee's normal course of employment.

6.9 Other insurances

Architectural practitioner employers may also need to take out other insurance policies, such as for company cars, travel insurance, insurance to cover special situations such as the death of partners or directors, public health care insurance, and policies covering pensions for partners or directors and staff.

6.10 Use of computers

Like most other professionals and groups of people, architects and architectural technologists tend to show a mixed reaction to the use of computers, ranging from absolute commitment to total distrust. The indications are that they will, for the foreseeable future, play an ever increasing role in business, information and media fields, and in education. Information technology and the use of computers are already firmly established as elements of most architectural courses, and they already make a significant contribution in many architectural offices.

Computers are becoming more compact, able to work faster, and capable of storing huge amounts of information. A computer can take many forms, but commonly will consist of a central processor, a typewriter style of keyboard, and a VDU similar to a television screen (Figure 6.1).

A particularly useful job undertaken by computers is the supply of information. This was discussed in sections 5.6 and 5.7. They can also undertake their original role of calculators, although they are now able to solve far more complicated mathematical problems than were originally envisaged.

Computers can fulfil the function of an office filing system, using a fraction of the space required by a traditional filing system. They are also available to deal with routine office tasks, such as office accounts, payments of salaries, value added tax (VAT), etc.

Architects and architectural technologists can, with the aid of computers, have at their disposal a mass of technical and design information which they can use to drive an electronic drawing board, displaying a pictorial representation of their designs. Computer-aided design and drawing (CAD) systems are discussed in section 8.11.

However, computers are only as useful and reliable as the quality of the programs written for them and the quality of the staff operating them. Many programs are available commercially for architects and technologists to buy. Some architectural

Fig. 6.1 A typical computer draughting workstation

practices employ their own staff to design and write their programs. Trained staff are also required to operate the computers.

Mention was made under section 6.6 of the need to prevent computer operators from suffering eye strain. Glare-free indirect lighting is required, and surfaces surrounding the computer work area should not be too light. The aim should be for the computer operator to see the VDU display against a dark, rather than a bright, background.

6.11 Employment of staff generally

Architects and architectural technologist employers employing staff will have certain legal responsibilities relating to matters such as contracts of employment, dismissal, redundancy, National Insurance, and income tax. These will be discussed in the following sections.

6.12 Employment protection

At one time employers, including architects, could hire and fire at will, but the influence of trade unions and others, and various laws, have changed the situation.

One of the most important laws governing employment is the Employment Protection (Consolidation) Act of 1978. The principal matters dealt with by the Act are the contract of service, pay, time off work, notice, dismissal (including unfair dismissal), lay-off and short-time working, redundancy, maternity leave, and trade union rights.

Men and women have protection regarding equal pay under the Sex Discrimination Act 1975, and advice and help for those seeking redress against racial discrimination at work is available from the Commission for Racial Equality.

6.13 Conditions of employment

Most genuine full-time employees will have a contract of service. This will be issued within 13 weeks of starting work and should include the names of the parties involved in the contract, the date employment commenced, pay details, hours worked, holiday arrangements, sickness pay, discipline, pension arrangements, and notice.

Benefits to the employees include firm rights as to the payment of their salary. It is sensible to agree all details at the job interview. As well as the amount of the commencing salary, this should also include details of any bonuses or profit-sharing schemes, whether there are regular salary reviews and details of how and when these take place, full information of any 'company perks' such as company cars, expenses, private medical insurance, and payment of professional subscriptions.

Ideally, the employees' hours of work should be stated in their contract of service, but this information is often omitted. This may be because it is thought to be unprofessional to work too rigidly to prescribed hours. Payment for overtime is another 'grey area', perhaps because it is considered professional to contribute extra effort and time during crisis periods. Some firms who do not pay overtime compensate their staff by granting them time off during the slacker periods in return for the unpaid overtime worked in the busy spells. This may be a reasonable arrangement if working overtime does not happen very often. However, if it is a regular occurrence, possibly because of understaffing, it seems only fair to pay overtime at an hourly rate. If unsocial hours are worked, an hourly rate of one and a half times the regular rate is generally considered reasonable.

Employees also have legal obligations to their employers, in as much as they are expected to render faithful service. This can be relevant for architectural staff who may be tempted to run a small private practice of their own from their employer's office, for they are not entitled to make a secret profit from their employer or to compete with him. Also, confidential information is expected to be kept confidential.

A serious breach of contract on either side can result in the ending of the contract without notice. An aggrieved employee can take his case to an industrial tribunal.

6.14 Dismissal of employees

Minimum periods of dismissal are fixed by the 1978 Employment Protection (Consolidation) Act. Employers must give a minimum of one week's notice for each year of service, up to a maximum of 12 weeks. Employees must give a minimum of one week's notice. Periods of notice can be more, or less, by agreement. Employees who consider they have been unfairly dismissed can apply to an industrial tribunal, but they must do this within three months. The possible results of such action may be re-instatement (i.e. given their old job back), re-engagement (given a different but comparable job), or compensation.

6.15 Redundancy

Unfortunately, the construction industry, including architectural practices, are more susceptible than most to changes in the nation's economic climate. Financial cutbacks frequently lead to a reduction of architectural work, and from time to time some architectural practitioners will be faced with the unpleasant task of reducing their number of staff.

The minimum amount of continuous service necessary to qualify for redundancy is two years. In calculating the amount of the redundancy payment, account is taken of the employee's age, his basic rate of pay, and his length of service, up to a maximum of 20 years, commencing from the age of 18 years.

Valid reasons for redundancy are defined as:

- the employer has ceased to carry on business;
- the demand for the employer's business has diminished or ceased;
- the employer has moved office, and the employee is not prepared to move to the new location.

The procedure is that the employer normally pays the redundancy money, but he may be able to obtain 47% from the Redundancy Fund, which is a fund financed by employers and administered by the Department for Education and Employment. If need be the employee can claim directly from the fund. He can also appeal to the industrial tribunal.

6.16 National Insurance

All employers have legal obligations regarding deductions for National Insurance. They both deduct the employees' contributions from their salaries and make their own employer's contributions. The system is administered by the state under the Social Security Act 1975; benefits include unemployment pay, sickness and industrial injury retirement pensions, and mobility allowances.

Payments are generally linked to income rather than risk. Full-time employees pay Class 1 contributions, which entitles them to a fuller range of benefits than self-employed people, who are Class 2 contributors.

6.17 Income tax

Employers have to deduct tax from each employee's wages (unless they are self-employed) at rates specified by the Inland Revenue. The Inland Revenue issues a code number to each individual, which is worked out by a system of allowances which are deducted from the total earnings to give the taxable pay. Architectural employers, like other professionals, unfortunately have to pay tax. They are covered by Schedule D of the tax schedules, as opposed to Schedule E for employees. A full-time working director of a limited liability company is treated as an employee and is therefore covered by Schedule E. Schedule D covers sole principals of an architectural practice as well as partnerships. Any profits made have to be declared, and the Inland Revenue require to know the net profit for the accounting year, supported by a statement of accounts.

6.18 Holidays

It is not always appreciated that, generally, holidays are a matter of agreement between employer and employee; they are not covered by the Employment Protection Act.

However, most employees in Britain get three weeks paid holiday a year, and many receive more than this. Holiday entitlement will normally be fixed by the contract of service, and this is legally binding on both parties.

Generally, there will be a qualifying period before a new employee is allowed holidays with pay.

Design constraints

7.1 Introduction

At the beginning of this book reference was made to the varied skills and breadth of knowledge the architect and architectural technologist need if they are to undertake their roles effectively.

In developing the design the designer must take account of many constraints, including those imposed by the client's specific and preferred requirements, factors related to sites and the environment, cost considerations, the effects of legal rights and responsibilities, planning and building legislation and procedures, together with the constraints arising from the attitudes and actions of those involved in the design, management, and construction of the building. These and other constraints are discussed in this chapter.

7.2 The client

Client groups

Clients can be broadly divided into two main groups: those who build for their own use and those who build for profit. The first group includes the married couple who want a house to live in, a shopkeeper who needs a shop to trade in, a giant industrial company which wishes to have a new industrial complex to manufacture its products, a government department requiring an office block to house its staff, and a church needing a new building in which to worship. The second group includes the contractor who builds houses, shops, and factories to sell and let for profit, and insurance companies who build office blocks as a source of investment for their funds.

Building occupier
Both of these main groups of clients will exercise constraints on the design of the building. There is likely, however, to be more variation in the constraints imposed by the first of these groups – the client who will occupy the building he is financing. He will always conceive the idea, but sometimes the concept may be no more than

him wanting a house, shop, or factory built. This means that the designer has to do more work to produce a building matching the client's needs, but he will have the maximum freedom to introduce his own ideas into the design. Another client may have very fixed ideas as to what he wants, sometimes to such an extent that the designer will begin to wonder why he has been employed. In such a case the designer will have to be firm enough to ensure that the client does not take over the designer's role and exceed his rights and responsibilities under the terms of the contract.

Speculator

The client who builds for speculation will generally have a different attitude from the owner-occupier. His main aim will be to make a profit from the sale of the completed building, so he will generally go to considerable trouble to find out what the public wants and what they will pay for it. He will then, with the aid of the designer, set himself the task of meeting these requirements, while still making a profit from the enterprise.

Client's relationship with designer

Architects and architectural technologists must always remember that their role is to act as agents for their clients and to translate their needs, and not always their precise ideas, into the finished building. This is particularly important with the owner-occupier type of client mentioned previously who appears intent on doing the designer's job for him. It is not unknown for such a client to bring considerable pressure to bear on the way the building is designed and constructed, and then to lay all the blame at the feet of the designer when the completed building does not match up to his expectations.

Client and costs

Another major constraint the client will exercise will be the amount of money he will have to finance the project. It must be remembered that the client, either directly or indirectly, pays for everyone involved in the building process and for all the materials used. The effect of cost limits will be considered later, but for now it is sufficient to state the obvious fact that the amount of money available will influence both the size and the quality of the finished building. One of the first questions the architect must therefore ask the client is how much money he has at his disposal. In some cases the answer might be none, because the client is hoping to fund the entire project with some form of outside financial assistance. In this case the designer will need to proceed with caution until he is certain that the anticipated financial backing has materialised.

Client and the site

The third constraint the client generally brings with him when he first approaches his design will be the site. Again this is dealt with in more detail later, but clearly the site the client wants to use for the proposed building will greatly influence the design.

7.3 The designer

Three conditions

Reference was made in chapter 2 to Sir Henry Wotten's dictum that three conditions were necessary to build well and create a good building – commodity, firmness, and delight. Commodity can be achieved by organising the plan to meet the social needs of the people who will use and occupy the building. Firmness is concerned with ensuring the building will provide a safe and comfortable shelter. The designer comes into his own with the third condition – delight – when he uses his designing skills to integrate the conditions of commodity and firmness and create a building which will be visually pleasing to the viewer.

Designers and designs

Although the designer is concerned with all three conditions, it is, as was hinted above, in the matter of design that his influence on the nature of the building will have the greatest impact. This influence will depend on two factors; first on the designer's views of his role in the total building process, and, second, on his views on architecture.

Designer's role

First, with regard to how the architect considers his own role: does he see himself as the boss, or as a member of a team, putting his skills of designing and administrating at the team's disposal, so as to provide the client with a building which will meet all the client's needs?

There may be a small minority of designers who adopt a prima donna attitude and act as though buildings are intended to be monuments to them, but the common philosophy of designers is to produce buildings which will satisfy the expectations and aspirations of the people who will occupy them. This should override any misconception about the need of a building to reflect the personality and viewpoint of its designer.

Designer's views on architecture

The second factor influencing the finished form of the building is the designer's views on architecture. There are two main bodies of opinion. First, there is the aesthetic approach, in which the designer expresses ideas in a physical form, aiming to produce an aesthetically pleasing building. The designer who follows the aesthetic path will not be unduly influenced by the planning arrangement or the practical demands of the building. He will be prepared to design in the abstract to produce a beautiful building. Second, there is the functional approach, which takes account of the structure and plan of the building, and often expresses them in the finished building. It is in fact a gross simplification to label every designer as either an 'abstract aesthete', or a 'functionalist'. In reality there are numerous variations and combinations, resulting in a wide variety of differing points of view regarding the subject of architecture.

Three great architects

Similarly, the three architects – Le Corbusier, Mies van der Rohe, and Frank Lloyd Wright – who can arguably be credited with having had the greatest effect on twentieth century architecture, can all be grouped together as part of the Modern Movement, yet they are each responsible for a distinctive type of architecture.

Le Corbusier's early interests included town planning and mass-production housing. The introduction of the sun terrace, open plans, and roof gardens have been attributed to him. Later, he became interested in the proportioning system – The Modular – which was based on mathematics and proportions of the human body. His Modular was illustrated in the Pilgrimage Chapel of Ronchampe, France. His remark 'a house is a machine for living in' is often quoted, but he merely meant that a building should work as anything else should work. Le Corbusier's favourite material was raw concrete; he produced sculptural concrete architecture, with horizontal windows and flat roofs. There is much of the functional about Le Corbusier's work, but in one of his books it was stated that he saw things from the viewpoint of a creator of human forms and not of an inventor of merely functional forms.

Mies van der Rohe produced buildings with steel frames sheathed in glass, with the floor and roof horizontals emphasised. He appeared to make clear the constructional form and function of his buildings. He had a particular interest in construction technology and the way it could help solve contemporary problems. Mies van der Rohe was famous for his philosophy that 'less is more' in architecture, on which he based most of his buildings.

Frank Lloyd Wright is remembered for buildings with strong horizontal lines, bold overhanging eaves, with buildings sweeping over the surrounding ground with no apparent support, and the breaking down of barriers between buildings and landscape. He explored ideas throughout his life, from the Prairie House of Chicago to the Guggenheim Museum in New York. Toward the end of his life he was asked 'What is your favourite building?' His answer was in tune with his character and philosophy: 'The next one'.

Architectural composition

Despite their differing views, these 'three architectural greats' had some things in common. They all disliked the practice of dressing up buildings constructed of new materials, such as steel and reinforced concrete, in neoclassical facades. Also, they all, perhaps instinctively, followed the principles of architectural composition. These principles represent another constraint which the designer has to take into account.

In order to introduce the reader to this subject the significance of some of the terms used in architectural composition are summarised below. Readers who wish to gain a fuller knowledge of the subject are strongly advised to obtain one of the excellent books dealing with architectural composition. A book particularly worth studying is '*The Principles of Architectural Composition*' by Howard Robertson (1955).

Unity
The first requirement of good architecture is to produce buildings that present an appearance of being a unified whole rather than a collection of unrelated elements. This unity can be helped by creating a centre of interest in the building. Often this means the introduction of a dominant central element, as illustrated in Figure 7.1.

Duality
Unity will not be achieved if there are dualities in the composition. A simple example of a duality is shown in Figure 7.2. The position of the rainwater pipe

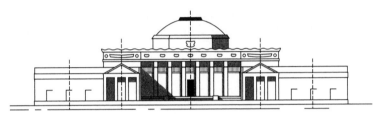

Fig. 7.1 A building unified by a dominant central element

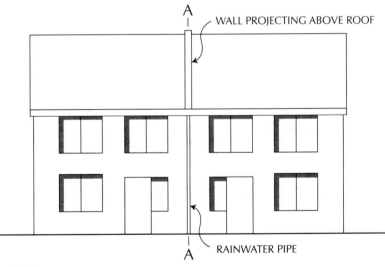

Fig. 7.2 A duality

and the wall projecting above the roof divides the building into two equal elements on the line A–A. The duality can be removed by introducing a new element in the centre of the facade as illustrated in Figure 7.3.

Dominance
If unity in architectural composition is to be preserved it is imperative that the composition be dominated by a key element or group of elements.

Mass
When the word 'mass' or 'massing' is used in architecture it refers to the basic three-dimensional shape of the composition – shapes that can be seen only against a background of light. It is important, if the massing is to be visually pleasing, that the forms used are primary geometrical shapes – the cube, cylinder, prism, cylinder, and pyramid. These definite shapes produce a bold outline which delight the eye and satisfy human emotions. Great architecture of the past, such as the Pyramids, the Parthenon, and the Coliseum, all used these beautiful primary forms. The composition need not necessarily consist of a single element. It can be composed of any number of primary forms, providing there is no hesitation or indecision in the massing, and providing a strong definite shape results.

Proportions
One of the more difficult areas to resolve is the fixing of the building's proportions. This includes both the mass of the building, which involves three dimensions, and two-dimensional elements, such as elevations, right down to a single window. There are certain rules that can be followed, for example making squares exact squares, and circles exact circles. There are also geometrical solutions governing proportions which are discussed in some books on architectural composition, but

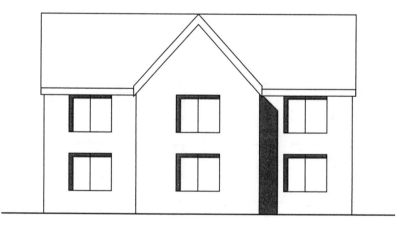

Fig. 7.3 Removal of a duality by introducing a central element

often it is a matter of experience and an ability to decide by looking at a building, or a porch, or a window, whether or not the proportions are right. In mentioning the matter of proportions in relation to architectural composition, the contribution of the Greeks should be mentioned. Their designs were based on a harmonic modular relationship of part to part, and part to whole. The Parthenon in Athens is a great example of this. In his book on architectural composition, Howard Robertson (1955) wrote 'the golden rule of proportion is that there must be no hesitation or weakness'.

Scale

John Belcher, in his book *'The Essentials of Architecture'*, first published in 1907, described scale as 'the proper relation of the several parts to one another to the whole in point of size'. It is a commonly held view that the starting point of scale should be the size of the average human being. Once the scale has been set, and in most cases it will be related to the human figure, it should be consistently applied throughout the building. There is also the matter of neighbourliness to be considered. Wherever possible, buildings should adopt the same scale as adjoining buildings. Figure 7.4 provides an illustration where this has not been done. It is also best to relate to the main horizontal lines of adjoining buildings – i.e. the eaves, string corses and window heads.

Fig. 7.4 Neighbourliness: a house in Grovesnor Square, London, where the scale is not matched to neighbouring buildings

Contrast
Another requirement is that the composition should include contrast and avoid monotony. This can include: contrasts in form and mass, for example use of the cube, cylinder, and hemisphere, as shown in Figure 7.5; contrast in size between primary form of the same shape, for example, use of cylinders, as shown in Figure 7.6; contrast in colour, for example between black and white; contrast in texture, for example between smooth and rough surfaces; contrast between solids and voids; and contrast between light and shade.

Solids and voids
The right handling of solids (mass) and voids (spaces) is essential. For example, on the elevations the voids formed by the windows and door openings should be of pleasing proportions and also present an appropriate contrast to the solids of the wall surface. This means that either the solids or the voids must dominate. If they are equal the effect presented will be one of indecision.

Regulating lines
These are the lines which appear on, and divide up, the surface of the building and give character to the mass.

Fig. 7.5 Contrasts in form and mass: the Church of the Miacoli, Venice

Fig. 7.6 Contrasts in sizes of primary forms: the Chiesa del Santo, Padua

Harmony
When the designer has completed his work he should have achieved harmony – an accord between all the elements that make up the building; something which Le Corbusier expressed as a pure creation of the spirit.

Plan arrangement
Finally, in this limited consideration of architectural composition, mention should be made of the importance of the plan. Le Corbusier described the plan as the generator, and stated that, 'mass and surface are determined by the plan. The plan determines everything. The plan proceeds from within to without; the exterior is the result of the interior.'

7.4 User requirements

The designer has to ensure that the building is designed to meet the needs of the people who will occupy and use it. This necessitates studies to establish user requirements. There has to be a detailed analysis as to the function of the building and the activities which will take place within it. The required environmental conditions will have to be decided and matters as diverse as appearance and toilet requirements agreed.

An example of a factory is used below to list the sort of questions the designer will need to ask before finalising his studies and design.

- What type of processes take place in the factory?
- If there are a number of processes, do they have to be separated?
- What plant and machinery will be installed?
- Are line layouts (illustrating the manufacturing process) and a plant layout (illustrating the plant and equipment) available?
- Does the factory have to be single-storey, or would a multi-storey building be acceptable?
- Does the need for a continuous production line dictate the length of the building?
- Is there a need for a continuous uninterrupted space across the width which will dictate the bay spacing?
- Is there a minimum clear height requirement?
- How many people will occupy the factory, and what hours will they be working? What is the likely proportion of men to women?
- What are the requirements for meals, toilet facilities, medical facilities, etc.?
- What level of lighting is required? Is daylighting essential in any areas?
- What level of heating is required? Is there a need for air conditioning in any area?
- What will the noise levels be from the machines?
- Are there any environmental factors, for example fumes or dust?
- What loadings are expected from the machinery, etc.?
- What degree of security is required?
- What services are required to serve the manufacturing process?
- Is there a requirement for future expansion?

The above list is by no means exhaustive, but is merely meant to give an indication of the type of questions the architect or architectural technologist will have to ask. This will entail a detailed study to establish user requirements, and the results will clearly act as a constraint on the design.

7.5 Anthropometrics and ergonomics

In section 7.3 it was stated that the scale of a building will in most cases be related to the size of the average human being. This is a logical approach because most buildings, the notable exception being agricultural buildings, are constructed to be occupied and used by human beings. Once it is decided to develop buildings to suit their needs, it is sensible to consider the sciences of anthropometrics and ergonomics. The data from these two sciences can, when included in the design process, be regarded as useful constraints.

Anthropometrics is defined in *Chambers* dictionary as 'the measurements of the human body'. Some measuring units, such as the foot, are derived from measurements of the human body, and should alert us to the importance of body measurements. People's weight, height, width, eye height, arm reach, hand size, stride length, and other body measurements and shapes influence decisions such as corridor widths, stair and ramp dimensions, door and window sizes and positions, and a host of other factors relevant to the design of a building. The data obtained from anthropometrics are used in the science of ergonomics as a means of producing 'user-friendly' buildings.

Ergonomics is the study of humans in relation to work. It includes studies on factors such as illumination, colour, temperature, noise, vibration, dust, and fumes. When used in conjunction with data obtained from anthropometrics they can provide valuable information for building designers. A consideration of the science of anthropometrics and ergonomics at the design stage is important. As has been stated, it means taking into account the effect of human dimensions and proportions on many things, including the sizes, proportions, and arrangements of rooms, spaces, furniture, and equipment, and the coordination needed between them.

There are other less basic matters that come within the scope of ergonomics and anthropometrics which the designer needs to consider, and some simple examples are given below.

In a work situation people need to have a suitable level of lighting in order to perform a wide variety of tasks. The Illuminating Engineering Society publishes recommendations for various situations, for example drawing offices require a level of 750 lux.

Ill-lit and badly maintained stairs cause many industrial accidents. Painting the tread nosings in a light colour makes for greater safety.

The reaction of human sight to colour should influence the designer's choice of colours. Red, orange, and yellow suggest warmth and are stimulating, and surfaces of this colour appear to advance. Green and blue suggest cold and are less stimulating than red, and surfaces of these colours appear to recede. White makes an object appear large. Black suggests gloom and boredom. Cool colours on side walls and warm colours on end walls make a long narrow room seem wider.

Noise is a source of irritation to many people. Heavy equipment in factories and other buildings transmits vibration and should be avoided by careful foundation design. Air-borne noises are also troublesome, and measures to reduce the noise level should be considered, for example using heavier construction, making everything as airtight as possible, or providing double glazing with a 100 mm space between the glazing.

People need temperature and humidity levels appropriate to the activity in which they are engaged and which is neither too hot nor too cold.

Dust and fumes are a source of discomfort and can be a health hazard to humans. Exhaust systems should be installed to overcome the problem.

Every attempt should be made to make manual lifting and manipulation of loads as easy as possible, for example by avoiding the need to lift above eye level or to push and pull at a low level.

7.6 Disability

Although several pieces of legislation, including the Building Regulations 1991, take account of the needs of disabled people, they are not always considered by the building designer. There are exceptions, such as old people's homes and hospitals.

Also, special toilets for the disabled are often available in buildings used by the public. Furthermore, most social housing provided by housing associations are designed with disability in mind. The concept of 'Life Time Homes' is an example of houses designed with a number of features which will allow families to stay in the same house should any of its members become disabled. However, frequently the problems of the disabled are largely ignored. This is perhaps surprising in view of the fact that there are over 6 million people in the United Kingdom with a disability. In addition there are millions of elderly folk with mobility and other problems who would welcome some consideration. This suggests there is a case, when the designer is formulating his design, for the needs of the disabled to be added to the lsit of welcome constraints.

The reason why this is not generally done in practice is probably mainly because of the extra cost involved. This will often override any ambition to provide a building which can be given a 'disability-friendly' seal. The other disincentives to action are the profusion and diversity of the disabilities.

Nevertheless, there are needs, problems, and solutions common to considerable numbers of people:

- Extra space should be provided for wheelchair users and for the walking disabled;
- Barriers and obstacles and raised thresholds should be avoided and, even, walls should be omitted where feasible.
- The structure needs to be stronger to make it suitable for the extra loading from support rails, lifting aids, etc.
- Support rails are invaluable to many disabled people who need to steady, stabilise, and pull themselves along when walking. Rails are a great help in bathrooms and WCs. Lifting aids may also be required in bathrooms and where people need to move from a horizontal to vertical position.
- Take account of the weakness of disabled people and the difficulty they have with manipulative movements. It is therefore important not to make self-closing door devices too strong, doors too heavy, or windows difficult to open. Ensure that stopcocks, heating, and other controls are easy to operate, that lever action taps are provided, and that light switches work by rocker action.
- Take account of the reaching limitations of wheelchair users and other disabled people and of the need to consider the views available to people sitting in wheelchairs. This means placing door handles, window controls, plumbing and heating controls, and electrical switches at suitable heights for disabled people. Consideration should be given to fixing cill and transom lines at levels which will not interfere with views outside the building and continuing some windows down to floor level.
- Avoid open riser staircases, winders, and splayed steps. Provide a gradient of 38°. Make sure the staircase is well lit, with light coming towards and not down the staircase. Provide handrails on both sides of the staircase. Ensure that the design and construction of the staircase is suitable for the installation of a stair lift at a later date.

Improvements in facilities for the disabled and the elderly should take place in 1999 when an extension to Part M of the Building Regulations come into operation. Measures include the provision of entrance doors in new homes wide enough to allow for wheelchair entry, and the provision of switches and socket outlets at an appropriate height from floor levels. These provisions are in line with the intentions of the Disability Discrimination Act 1995.

7.7 The site

In the initial stages of the design of a building the architect or architectural technologist needs to investigate the site to decide its suitability for the building required by the client. This investigation is related to the environment, which includes all the things surrounding the site, and the climate. The site investigation will incorporate the site accesses, boundary features, topography, subsoil, services, and underground hazards. All of these items act as constraints in the design of the building.

Sometimes the architect or architectural technologist will be involved in the selection of the site. This is the best arrangement, as a properly trained and experienced architectural practitioner should be better placed than the layperson to select a site most suitable for the building required by the client. This is particularly true nowadays when the ideal building site, even if there were ever such a thing, is very hard to find. Difficult sites, such as those of awkward shapes, or on steeply sloping ground, or having poor subsoil, or uninviting surroundings, will often be developed, whereas in the past they would not be used for building purposes. Unusual sites such as these need expert assessment.

If there is a choice of sites it is obviously important to select the best possible site the client can afford. This is particularly vital when the building is a speculative venture. The biggest single factor likely to encourage people to buy a new speculative built house is that it is located in an area which the prospective purchaser finds attractive. This is clearly linked with the environment, for houseowners, and owners of other types of buildings, are concerned with ease of access, local amenities, views, climate, and all the other environmental factors. These will be considered in more detail in the next section.

The first constraint exercised by the site is its area and plan shape. The area is the most obvious constraint, as the area of buildings which can be built on the site clearly cannot exceed the site area and in practice will be considerably less. This is because it is seldom possible to build over the whole of the site. Instead, the available space has to be apportioned between the buildings, roads, circulation and parking areas, and landscaped and open areas. The site area may also be relevant to statutory rulings regarding the density of developments allowed in a particular area. For example, traditionally, areas zoned for housing have been restricted to a density of so many houses per acre or hectare.

The shape of the site is a less obvious constraint but may influence the size, shape, and proportions of the buildings. If the site is long and narrow it will probably mean that the buildings have to be elongated. A triangular site may present problems to the designer, but could lead to an unusual and more interesting layout.

The next constraint is the site contours. A flat site would at first seem advantageous, but could mean it is suceptible to flooding, particularly if it is low lying. This could affect the decision as to whether or not to include a basement or semi-basement in the building. A steeply sloping site will influence the cost of the building because of the effect on the type and levels of the foundations. It could also affect the levels of the ground floor and possibly result in a split-level solution. If the contours are pronounced it is almost certain to influence the position of the building on the site and might affect the building in other ways such as the location of the entrances.

The orientation of the site, relative to the north point, will also affect the position of accesses, entrances, and windows, because the aspect governs the quantity of sun the various elevations receive. There is an obvious advantage in ensuring that the rooms in which people spend most of the daylight hours have the most sun. This may mean, for example, that a house on a north-facing site may be designed so that the main living rooms are at the back rather than at the front of the house.

The subsoil under the site will influence the type of structure and possibly the height of the building. Foundations are one of the major factors in the cost of a building, and if because of a poor subsoil the foundation costs are excessive it will mean that there is less money available for other elements of the building. This in turn could affect the overall design of the building. It is advisable – many would say essential – to carry out a soil investigation before proceeding too far with the design, and this is achieved by means of trial holes and boreholes. Information on the type of subsoil and safe bearing capacity is necessary in order to design a safe and economic building.

The level of the water-table – that is the level at which water appears naturally in the ground – needs to be established. A high water-table may mean that a subsoil drainage system needs to be incorporated into the design if flooding is to be avoided. It will also affect the floor levels, as there is a strong case for keeping all floors above the expected water-table level.

Consideration should be given to any existing physical features on the site which could enhance the setting of the proposed building. There could be a lake, or some attractive mature trees which need to be retained. This could mean siting the building outside these physical features, or even incorporating them within an internal courtyard around which the building is designed. Either way the siting and design of the buildings is likely to be affected. There may also be some existing buildings on the site which need to be retained, or incorporated within the new buildings. If so, these will also act as a constraint on the design.

If existing buildings surround certain parts of the site the designer may plan his building to avoid looking out onto the existing structure in order to ensure the maximum privacy for the building's occupiers. It can be seen therefore that the existing landscape and buildings surrounding a site are likely to influence the juxtaposition of the building and the position of the windows.

Again, existing services, ether below or above ground level, can influence the location of the buildings on the site, and in some cases can restrict the size of the building.

7.8 Environment

As has already been stated in section 7.7, the environment, by which is meant the things surrounding the site, is often of particular importance to the prospective occupier of a building and is likely to influence, and act as a constraint on, the design of a building.

Climate is an important factor which acts as a constraint on building design and which affects the siting and appearance of buildings. In the tropics, for example, where the sun is too hot and too bright for people, the aim is more likely to be in keeping the sunlight out of the building rather than letting it in. In the dry tropics this has resulted in the traditional house having thick walls and small windows, whilst in the humid tropics the buildings will tend to incorporate devices such as canopies, overhangs, and louvres so as to shade the walls without restricting the flow of air.

Traditionally, in the UK windows are likely to be of various shapes and sizes, depending on the use of the rooms, their aspect, and views. The designer has to decide on the purpose of the windows (e.g. lighting, ventilation, views) before he can decide the best shapes and sizes.

The aspect of the site is obviously of considerable importance, because it will govern the total number of hours of sunshine a building will receive and at what time of the day. There is no legal requirement which states that a habitable room must have sunlight, although there is a code of practice which recommends that every living room should have at least one hour of sunshine a day during at least 10 months a year.

There is also a recommended daylight factor for various types of buildings, which is represented as a percentage of the illumination for a point indoors as compared with a point outdoors. For example, an entrance hall needs 1%, and a bank needs 2%. The need for daylight will influence the shape of the rooms and buildings. Various charts and other aids are available to give the conditions for different rooms and skies, but as a generalisation a rectangular room with windows in the long wall will be better lit than if the same areas of windows are in one of the short walls.

Whilst the aspect will be the main factor governing the amount of sunlight entering a building, other factors, such as the slope of the ground and the shape, size, and position of surrounding buildings, will also have a part to play.

There will be some situations, even in the UK, where sunlight needs to be controlled. Examples are art galleries, museums, and libraries containing valuable books, where direct sunlight could damage the contents, and also exits from garage areas where sun dazzle could adversely affect the car drivers.

The designer also needs to consider the expected rainfall on a building, both to design the drainage system correctly and to make the right decisions to prevent rain penetration. It is the author's personal view that the use of flat roofs need to be considered with care in order to ensure that they are watertight. However, it should be stated that where a flat roof is not watertight the fault is likely to be traced back to incorrect design or workmanship. If doubts remain about the wisdom of using flat roofs in areas of heavy rainfall, the designer can use a steeply sloping roof. Obviously such a decision will affect the appearance of the building.

Sometimes, however, a flat roof will be a logical choice. In the Middle East, for example, where there is a low rainfall and where, because of the hot weather, the inhabitants may wish to sleep on the roof, the roof is more likely to be flat. Admittedly, the rain, when it comes, may fall in quite large amounts, but the people of these areas often have a more enlightened attitude to roof maintenance than do inhabitants of the UK, so that flat roofs create fewer problems.

The problem of rain penetration is linked to wind pressure, as wind can often drive rain into buildings, particularly through places such as window openings. The prevailing winds in the UK are from the west. The direction of the wind will affect decisions such as the location of walkways and entrances. The designer will also take account of other factors such as the fact that conditions tend to be uncomfortable for pedestrians when the wind is blowing and they are walking in a gap between high and low buildings.

The wind effect will also be affected by the surrounding landscape. Again, the shape of the buildings will affect their strength in certain directions and their ability to resist wind pressure. If the expected wind force on a wall is considerable it will have to be strong enough to resist such pressures, and this will influence the construction and materials used. The lifting of lightweight roofs by suction also needs to be considered in areas of high wind pressure, with particular care taken with regard to problems from roof overhangs.

Snow is less likely to be a difficulty in the UK than in other countries, but the designer will need to consider the weight of snow on the roof. He will bear in mind the possibility of snow finding its way into the building if there is a defect in roof and consider if this is more likely to happen with a flat roof rather than a pitched one.

It will be readily appreciated that climate varies considerably from country to country, but it is also true that there are variations between various parts of the UK. Records kept by the Meteorological Office indicate that, generally, the northern and eastern parts of the country are colder than the south and that the west is the wettest part of the country. Designers and contractors often make use of the meteorologist to mitigate the worst effects of the climate.

The amount of dust, salt, sand, and man-made additions to the air, such as waste from chimneys, will affect the degree of pollution surrounding the building. The resulting pollution may damage people's health and adversely affect building materials. This will inevitably influence the choice of building materials and hence the appearance of the building.

Noise, originating from places such as airfields, railways, motor traffic routes, industry, and public playgrounds is another factor the designer should consider. This will affect the siting of the building with regard to keeping it as far away as possible from noise sources. Particular care will be taken with the location of rooms requiring quiet conditions, including the positioning and sizes of windows and other openings.

7.9 Cost limits

Cost limits are an important constraint on the design of a building because the amount of money the client is able and willing to spend will control its size and quality. It is often said that you get what you pay for, and this is certainly true of buildings. There are very few cases when an architect or architectural technologist is told by the client to proceed with the design regardless of costs. Generally, there is a limit to what the client can afford, so the designer, with the aid of the quantity surveyor, has the responsibility of ensuring that the design and construction of the building is subject to cost limits, cost planning, and cost control.

Cost limits

Cost limits dictate the total amount of money the client is able to spend on a project. The design team ensures by means of cost planning and cost control that the cost limit figure is not exceeded.

Cost planning

Cost planning means allocating the available money between the different parts of the building, generally in respect of elements such as substructure, floors, roof, walls, doors and windows, stairs, finishes, services, etc. As the amount of money the client has to spend is generally limited, it means that in practice if a disproportionate sum is spent on one item there will be less money available for the other items. A factory owner may be less concerned about the appearance of the building than with the annual running costs. He may therefore want the designer to economise on the cladding so that more money is available for insulation and an efficient heating system. Again, a speculative builder may decide to spend money on luxury kitchens and bathrooms in his houses because he believes this will make them easier to sell. This may lead him to save money on things that the purchasers are less likely to notice, such as the roof construction and drainage.

It can be seen therefore that cost planning is part of the design process, because decisions on the allocation of money have to be made at the design stage and will obviously influence the appearance of the building. These decisions may also affect the size of the building because there will often be a choice between a smaller building with high standards of construction and finishes, or a larger building constructed to minimal standards.

Cost control

Cost control starts at the design stage and continues throughout the job. It means checking costs at all stages to ensure that the client's cost limits are not exceeded. If more money is spent on one element than was planned, money will have to be saved elsewhere to avoid exceeding the cost limits.

Project duration

The duration of the project, in respect of both design and construction time, also has an effect on costs and could act as a constraint on the design of the building. This is a result of the fact that costs are continually escalating, because of inflation and increases in the cost of labour and materials during the life of the project. The designer may make a decision to simplify the design and construction of the building as much as possible so as to reduce the programme time and minimise the effect of inflation. This will affect the appearance of the building.

Maintenance costs and cost in use

The designer also needs to consider the cost of maintenance as part of the design process. Maintenance costs are often related to correct design and to decisions as to whether it is worthwhile paying for better, more robust materials and the best available workmanship so as to reduce future maintenance costs.

The subject of maintenance is connected to cost in use of a building. This consists of the annual equivalent worth of initial expenditure on the building plus the average recurring costs (i.e. items such as maintenance, replacement, decorations, running costs of services, etc.).

It may be that over a period of, say, 60 years a poor-quality building which only just meets the requirements of the building and other regulations costs more on average every year than a good-quality building. This is because in the poor-quality building there are extra costs for maintenance, replacements, decorations, and running costs which do not occur on a good-quality building with the best work-manship and materials, self-finished surfaces, high standards of insulation, and an efficient heating system.

In working out the cost for a 60-year period the accumulated costs (total of initial expenditure plus recurring costs for 60 years) must be divided by 60 to give the annual cost. Allowance must be made for interest on money not used for the initial expenditure and for the cost of borrowing extra money to finance a more expensive building initially.

Cost value

When the designer presents the proposed design to the client the design will need to be accompanied by an estimate of the cost. Clients will often view the cost aspect with regard to the following:

- the total cost of the building,
- the cost value,
- the effect of the building market on the cost.

In looking at the total cost of the project the client will need to satisfy himself that an equivalent building could not be obtained at less cost from some other source. It is possible, for example, that a person wanting a bungalow built on his site may discover a timber-system-built bungalow which would meet all his needs, available at a much cheaper price than the traditional design offered by the designer.

Again, an industrialist may be disappointed by the high cost of an architectural practitioner's design and turn to a design-and-build contractor to provide a new factory.

The client will also consider the cost value, or how valuable the completed building will be, to him. Above all he will want to assure himself that the building is economically viable. There is clearly little value, for example, in an industrialist having a factory built, equipping it, starting production, and then discovering that the profit is less than he would have obtained from putting his money in a deposit account at the bank.

Economic factors

The third factor to consider will be the economic factors at the time the building operations are about to begin. It could happen that, because of a lot of people wanting work undertaken at a particular time, and a shortage of labour and materials, that building costs are escalating. If, as would probably be the case, a fluctuation clause is included in the contract, the client may decide that these additional costs mean that the project is no longer viable. In such circumstances the client may either cancel the project or else wait until the building market is more favourable to clients.

All the above factors will act as a considerable constraint on the design.

7.10 Legal requirements

The law is concerned with rules which society agrees to obey in order to follow an acceptable way of life. There are two main groups of laws. Common law is unwritten, and follows custom and precedent, relying on the binding decision of judges. Legislative law is law made or approved by parliament, and includes orders in Council, statutory instruments, and byelaws. Sanctions are imposed as an aid to enforcing the law, and these may take the form of fines, imprisonment, or the awarding of damages.

The law affecting construction work is complicated and extensive and acts as a considerable constraint on the design of the building. It includes the law of property and land, environmental powers (including statutory consents and planning law), copyright law, and laws relating to building contracts.

Whilst the architectural practitioner is not expected to have the legal knowledge of a lawyer, he is expected to have a reasonable understanding of the law for all matters which in any way affect his role as the client's agent. In addition he is expected to have a detailed knowledge of those matters, such as the building regulations and building contracts, which are his direct concern.

Property law

The law of property and land use may influence the design of a building in respect of matters such as trespass, nuisance, boundaries, party walls, and easements, including ancient lights. These subjects are dealt with under separate section headings later in this chapter.

Restrictive covenants

Restrictive covenants are another possible design constraint. They are restrictions on the use of one piece of land to the benefit of the owner of other land. Sometimes, such covenants dramatically affect the design of a building. An example is that of a man who sells off part of his garden as building land. In order to protect the enjoyment of his own house he may include a restrictive covenant in the conveyance that only a bungalow may be built on the land and that the appearance must be in character with the surrounding properties.

Landlord and tenant covenants may affect the architectural practitioner undertaking work in buildings which the client leases rather than owns. For example, care must be taken to ensure that parts which are regarded as landlord's fixtures are not altered or removed.

Environmental laws

There is a wide range of legislation which can be loosely linked together under the heading of environmental laws. One example is pollution laws, which are intended to prevent people's health being endangered. They include clean air acts to avoid air pollution, public health acts to prevent water pollution, noise abatement acts to minimise noise nuisances, and other acts affecting the storage of refuse.

Highway acts

The various highways acts can also affect the building designer. An example is the powers under which the highway authorities can prescribe an improvement line – that is to say, a proposed widening of a street. This means that land will be taken off the adjacent sites and should therefore be taken into account by the designer when he sites his proposed building.

Housing Grants, Construction and Regeneration Act 1996

This act is of importance to architectural practitioners involved in work to existing housing. It makes provision for grants and other assistance for housing purposes and deals with action to be taken in relation to unfit housing. It also deals with the provision of grants and other assistance for regeneration and development. Other parts of the Act amend the provisions relating to home energy efficiency schemes, the dissolution of urban development corporations, housing action trusts, and the Commission for the New Towns. Further parts of the Act are concerned with The Architects' Registration Board, which is covered in section 2.6 of this book, and construction contracts, which are covered in section 8.4.

Account must be taken of the various housing acts. This means ensuring that when work is completed to renovated houses they are fit for human habitation, that drains and WCs have been properly repaired, that provision has been made for the removal of refuse, that bathrooms or shower rooms are provided, and, in the case of multiple-occupied housing, that suitable means of escape in the event of fire has been arranged.

There are two other major constraints: building regulations, which are covered in the next section, and town planning acts, which are covered in section 7.12.

Copyright

The legal aspects of copyright laws were introduced in section 4.17. It is important that the designer takes account of copyright law. One would normally expect the designer to produce an original design for a building. There may be occasions, however, when the project consists of extending an existing building by another designer. In such a case the client might insist that the extension should copy the style of the original building. Again, the client may give his designer a sketch of a building designed by another designer, and ask that certain features shown on the sketch be incorporated in his proposed building. In such cases the designer must make sure he does not infringe another designer's copyright. This has a constraining effect on the designer.

Safety, health, and welfare legislation is covered in sections 4.15 and 4.16. Other legislation is listed under section 4.18.

7.11 Building regulations

Building regulations are concerned with the construction of buildings, rather than their appearance. They are intended to ensure that the design and construction will be such as to ensure public health and safety. These also act as a considerable constraint on the designer. Most building work in England and Wales operates under the Building Regulations 1991 (note: Scotland has its own regulations). The Building Regulations (Amendment) Regulation 1994 introduced new approved documents for part F (ventilation) and part L (conservation of fuel and power); see below.

There are two ways of complying with the regulations. The common method is to follow the means for meeting the requirements of the Regulations described in the set of Approved Documents. The alternative is to devise your own solution for meeting the requirements.

The regulations are set out in the parts and Approved Documents listed below. Examples are given as to how they exercise constraints on the design and construction of buildings.

- Approved Document to support Regulation 7: materials and workmanship.
- Approved Document A: structure. This will affect the size and spacing of columns and beams, the thickness of walls, and the number, size, and positions of openings.
- Approved Document B: fire safety. This will affect the arrangement of corridors and staircases and the construction of elements of structure.
- Approved Document C: site preparation and resistance to moisture. This will affect the construction, and hence the appearance, of floors, walls, and roofs.
- Approved Document D: toxic substances. This will affect the types of insulating

materials used in the cavities of the cavity walls, with a marginal effect on the cost and construction.

- Approved Document E: resistance to the passage of sound. This will affect the construction, and hence the appearance, of walls and floors, because of the need to provide sound resistance.
- Approved Document F: ventilation. This will marginally affect the appearance because of the measures needed to provide room ventilation.
- Approved Document G: Hygiene. This will marginally affect the planning and appearance of parts of the building because of the need to provide an acceptable standard of hygiene with respect to food storage, bathrooms, hot water, and sanitary conveniences.
- Approved Document H: drainage and waste disposal. This will marginally affect the planning of the building because of the need to provide a satisfactory drainage system.
- Approved Document J: heat-producing appliances. This will affect the appearance of the building in the vicinity of fireplaces, stoves, etc., because of the requirement to design and construct these areas so that they will not constitute a fire hazard.
- Approved Document K: stairs, ramps, and guards. This will affect the appearance of staircases and ramps, as they have to be constructed to ensure that people using them are afforded a safe passage.
- Approved Document L: conservation of fuel and power. This will affect the appearance of the building as a result of the necessary choice of materials, and limited window areas, so as to achieve the prescribed standards of thermal insulation.
- Approved Document M: access and facilities for disabled people. This will marginally affect the planning and appearance of buildings, because of the necessary provision of acceptable standards of access, and, where appropriate, wheelchair space for disabled people.
- Approved Document N: glazing.

Other aspects of the Building Regulations are covered in section 8.24.

7.12 Town planning acts

The town and country planning acts give local authorities a wide range of powers to control development in their area. The main legislation providing this control are as follows:

- Use Classes Order 1985,
- Town and Country Planning General Development Order 1988,
- Town and Country Planning Act 1990,
- The Planning (Listed Buildings and Conservation Areas) Act 1990,
- The Planning (Hazardous Substances) Act 1990,
- The Planning (Consequential Provisions) Act 1990,
- Planning and Compensation Act 1991,
- Town and Country Planning (General Development Procedure) Order 1995,

- The Town and Country Planning (Fees for Applications Amendment) Regulations 1997.

Development plans are prepared with the dual aim of protecting the natural and built environments and achieving a balanced allocation of available land to meet various needs (i.e. housing, industrial, recreational, etc.). There are two types of development plans: structure plans and local plans.

Structure plans are generally prepared by county councils, and they control the class of building allowed in a particular area (i.e. domestic, office, factory, etc.). This zoning of particular areas for different purposes, including land allocated as part of the green belt, acts as a considerable constraint.

Local plans are generally prepared by district councils and they provide detailed treatment of the development in all areas, resulting in further constraints.

The exception to the system of dual control of development plans, outlined above, are the London boroughs and metropolitan districts, which are responsible both for structure plans and for local plans.

As well as the power to control the class of building allowed in a particular area, various councils also exercise the additional constraint of controlling the density of a proposed development; for example in the case of a housing development the council might stipulate a maximum number of dwellings per hectare. It could limit the size of a building on a particular plot, or the height, either in metres or the number of storeys.

The actual appearance of the building will often be controlled. This is virtually certain with areas designated as Conservation Areas, which are considered to include a natural and built environment of special interest. Developments in such places will have to be in accord with the special visual quality of the area. However, even in other areas the appearance of proposed buildings will generally be expected to be in sympathy with existing buildings.

Another constraint on building, engineering, and other operations, carried out on, under, or over land is that permission has to be obtained for a change of use of a building (e.g. using a house as a shop, or a shop as a factory). There is also the power to place a preservation order on a tree, and it then becomes an offence to cut down or lop the tree without first obtaining permission from the local planning authority. The planning authority also controls advertisements, including those on buildings.

Other aspects of the town planning acts are covered in section 8.25.

7.13 Trespass

Trespass in relation to land is the unlawful or unwarrantable invasion upon another person's land. As far as the law is concerned 'land' means anything which is on the land (e.g. a building) and anything which is below the land (e.g. the subsoil) or above the land (e.g. a crane jib) as well as the surface of the land. Trespass may concern the designer and other members of the building team in a number of ways, and act as a constraint.

First, if any of the building team need to enter someone else's land in order to undertake their work it is important that they obtain permission from the owner before doing so. This includes obtaining agreement to swing a crane jib over the land adjoining the building site.

Second, if people are walking across the building-owner's land without permission, the architectural practitioner, in his role as the client's agent, would be expected to alert his client and check that no right of way has been established which could interfere with the building operations.

Third, it is important to check before starting a building project that all the work can be completed without the need to enter the neighbouring owner's land. Even entering a neighbour's land and placing a ladder against a wall means that trespass has occurred. Action can be brought for trespass even if no damage has been done.

The important point to remember with regard to building projects is that permission should be sought for any action which could result in trespass taking place, and this happens when entry is made to land without the owner's consent.

7.14 Nuisance

A nuisance is an action which interferes with another person's use or enjoyment of his property. In law, there are four classes of nuisance: private, public, statutory, and bye-law.

Private nuisances

This is a nuisance that affects a person in his own home, or on his own land. Examples are when the roots of a neighbour's tree undermine the foundations of one's building or when people park their lorries outside one's building and cause a disturbance leaving noisily in the middle of the night.

Public nuisance

This is a nuisance which affects many people, or occurs and annoys people in a public place, such as a highway. Examples are obstructing a public highway or polluting a public water supply.

Statutory nuisance

This is a nuisance which affects the general public and which parliament has sought to prevent by passing specific laws. Examples are the nuisance of obnoxious fumes being discharged into the atmosphere and for which the preventive measures are the Control of Pollution Act 1974 and the Clean Air Act 1969.

Bye-law nuisance

This is also a nuisance which affects the general public but is dealt with by the local authority under powers delegated to them by parliament. Examples are the dumping of rubbish, and the creation of noise and smells from manufacturing or other operations.

Summary

In respect of all the above nuisances, the building team can be either the offender or the victim. In any event, the nuisance is likely to act as a constraint on a building project.

7.15 Boundaries

Boundaries may be marked by fences, hedges, ditches, walls, roads, rivers, or streams. The architect or architectural technologist needs to establish the exact position of the boundaries, not only to ensure that all building work is carried out on land which the client actually owns, but also because exact distances from building faces to boundary lines are relevant to conformity with certain building regulations. It is necessary for this confirmation of the boundary positions to be done in the initial stages of the project, generally as part of the site investigation (section 9.3). This will generally mean consulting with the client's solicitor, studying and making copies of the plans that are normally attached to the deeds, and making a site inspection to compare the information obtained from the deed plans with the apparent boundary positions defined on the site by fences, hedges, and so on.

If after studying the title deed documents and plans and making a careful site inspection there is still uncertainty about the precise position of the boundaries, a meeting should be held with the adjoining owners and agreement reached on their location.

7.16 Party walls

Definitions

A party wall is a wall forming part of a building and separating two adjoining buildings which are under different ownership. The party wall can be located entirely on one building owner's land, or partly on the land of two different owners.

A party floor is a floor forming part of a building and separating two adjoining properties (e.g. two flats).

Party structures are structures (walls, floors, and ceilings) separating properties which have different owners and which are approached by separate staircases and lobbies.

The Party Wall etc. Act 1996

Until 1 July 1997 when the above Act came into force there was no legislation governing work to party walls, except for properties in inner London, which were covered by the London Building Act (Amendment) Acts 1939. The 1996 Party Wall etc. Act brings to the rest of the country the benefits which London has enjoyed for over 60 years. Work to building elements, in which more than one person has an interest, is likely to act as a constraint, but in cases where the procedures are clearly set out, and both owners are protected, there should be less chance of delays and disputes arising.

Extent of Act

The main items covered by the Act are:

- construction of new walls on boundary lines;
- repairs and modifications to existing party walls, including raising or reducing the height and modifying the thickness;
- underpinning existing walls;
- excavations adjacent to neighbouring properties;
- inserting flashings, damp-proof courses or other waterproofing into existing party walls;
- removal of chimney breasts, chimneys, flues, or other projections or overhangs;
- insertion of ties to stabilise existing party walls;
- weatherproofing of walls exposed by demolition of adjoining properties.

Procedures

At least one month before commencing any building work, the building owner must notify all the adjoining owners affected by his intended work of what work is proposed.

If the adjoining owner agrees to the proposals he must serve a consents notice on the building owner. If he does not agree there is a disputes procedure in which each owner is entitled to appoint a surveyor to represent him. These two surveyors appoint a third surveyor who, if the other two surveyors are unable to come to an agreement, will resolve the dispute by making an award.

7.17 Easements

An easement is a right benefiting the owner of one piece of land over the owner of another piece of land. These easements are transferred with the land if it is sold.

Rights of way

A right of way is the right to pass over someone else's land. If such an easement is granted it may affect the siting of the building because of the need to avoid the position of the right of way.

A public right of way can be established if the owner of a piece of land allows members of the public to use a path over his land for more than 20 years without interruption.

Rights of drainage

A right of drainage is the right to lay drains under someone else's land. As with the previous case, it can restrict the siting of the building.

Rights of light

A right to light, which is traditionally termed an 'ancient light', may have been acquired by the adjoining owner. The general rule is that if a window has had uninterrupted light for more than 20 years it is entitled to continue to enjoy that benefit, and nobody can materially reduce the light by erecting a building or screen in front of it.

Existing buildings with rights of light, which are located on land adjoining the building site, exercise a considerable constraint on the site development.

Right of support

The architect or architectural technologist will need to remember that owners of adjoining land may have a right of support from the client's land. In designing the building the designer must ensure it does not include excavations which will mean the withdrawal of support to the adjacent land.

7.18 Building services

Building services are generally assumed to include hot and cold water supplies; above-ground and below-ground drainage, including sanitary appliances; refuse disposal; heating; ventilation; air-conditioning; electrical installations, including lighting and telecommunications; gas installations; fire protection; mechanical conveyors; and security systems.

The total cost of these services, including plant, ducts, pipes, and cables, together with the space allocated in the building to accommodate the services, is a major cost factor in most buildings. The figure may vary beween 20% and 60% of the total cost of the building.

Building services are used as a device to vary the environment within a building and create acceptable conditions inside when conditions outside are totally unacceptable. In practice people can only exist within a limited range of temperatures without taking special steps to mitigate the effects of the climate.

The extent to which building services will influence the overall design of the building will depend on the use and complexity of the building.

In some buildings special environmental conditions need to be created and this will affect the whole form of the building. An example is a factory manufacturing items such as computer tapes which need to be produced under clean-room conditions. In such a building the conditioned air needs to be absolutely clean. One solution is for the plant-rooms to be placed on the roof of the clean-room and to have the air flowing from holes in a filtered ceiling downwards through the room into a perforated floor and then back up to the high-level plant-room via vertical ducts at the sides of the room.

In another building the manufacturing process might involve extensive services and controlled light and heating conditions. The client might require a windowless box with artificial lighting and a sophisticated heating system involving a high standard of insulation. The form and appearance of such a factory will be largely influenced by the building services needs. Even in buildings where the services are less complicated and restrictive, there will be about 10% of the floor area allocated to plant items and vertical ducts. There will also be the need for floor ducts and voids in the ceiling space to house services. The location of these items will have an influence on the overall design.

Consideration of building services are less critical in conventional houses, but space still has to be allocated, generally in the roof, for water tanks, pipes, and cables, and there will be a need to provide at least some wall chases and accommodation for cables and small pipes.

It is important to consider building services during the initial design stage. Space for major plant items such as boilers, air-conditioning equipment, and substation equipment has to be selected and allocated to suit the most efficient operation of the building services.

Apart from occupying space and influencing the overall layout, plant provision tends to affect the elevations, as plant-rooms generally need to be provided with louvres, grilles, and special accesses and may be of different heights from other parts of the building. Sometimes, the plant-rooms may be located on the roof or even in separate buildings. The decision as to the exact routes of the ducts or the service distribution will clearly have an effect on the overall planning. The type of heat emitters, grilles, and other terminal devices will affect the inside appearance of the building. Consideration of heating and air-conditioning is linked to insulation, the size and positions of the windows, as well as to the orientation of the building. It can be seen therefore that the building services will affect the overall cost, shape, size, appearance, and orientation of the building.

They will also have a considerable effect on the construction programme. As the services content of most buildings is relatively high they will have to be carefully integrated into the overall programme so that they can be completed as quickly as possible, to achieve continuity of work. The incorporation of builder's ducts within the design to accommodate the distribution of all services will assist in this aim. It will also be helpful in effectively maintaining the completed building.

The ducts provide a space through which services pass – either conditioned air fed directly into the duct, or services such as gas, water, and drainage pipes, and electrical cables.

Ducts have many functions. The most obvious one is to conceal the services, thus improving the appearance of the building. They also prevent services becoming a nuisance to the occupiers of the building, for example noise from pipes or ducts, danger from hot pipes, and reduction of dust-catching ledges. The ducts themselves also give protection from physical and other damage. Further advantages are to allow easy installation, independent of the remaining construction operations; easy inspection, maintenance, and replacement; and facilitation of alterations and additions; they also tend to discipline the services designers and installers as to where they locate the pipes, cables, etc.

The following are the main types of ducts which the designer needs to incorporate into the design:

- main horizontal ducts, which are commonly at ground level, but may be at roof level, particularly in respect of air ducts;
- main vertical ducts which link services to each floor;
- lateral subsidiary ducts which provide local horizontal distribution and may be in ceiling voids.

In terms of size, there are walk ducts with a minimum height of 2 metres; crawl ducts with a minimum height of 1 metre; and recessed ducts and casings which have space for the services, but no working space inside the duct.

The ducts may be prefabricated and supplied by the services subcontractor, but generally some, if not all of them, will be constructed by the main contractor in materials such as brickwork, blockwork, and reinforced concrete.

The availability and location of the public services can also act as a constraint on the design. If services are not availabile it will mean, for example, that electricity will have to be privately generated, and sewage treated within the site, which clearly has cost and other implications.

There could be restrictions on the use of public services. An industrialist, for example, might need to use large quantities of water in the manufacturing process, and the authority responsible for the sewers might not permit this volume of water to discharge into the system during the daytime, as it would overload the sewers. This could mean storing the waste water in large tanks so that it can be discharged into the public sewers in the evenings when the volume of water in the sewers is much less.

Public service authorities may have other special requirements as a condition of supplying their service. For example, electricity boards commonly require large users of electricity (such as industrialists) to provide transformer chambers within their premises.

Even if public services are available when required their actual position may influence the siting of the building if an economical arrangement of building services is to be achieved.

7.19 The contractor

During the design process the architect and architectural technologist should spare a thought for the contractor. In the interest of everyone, including the client, designers should design their buildings in such a way that the contractor's job is made as easy as it can be. Whilst it is true that virtually anything is possible, if an architect or architectural technologist has a reputation for unusually complicated detailing which makes the buildings difficult to construct the contractor is likely to take account of this fact when preparing the tender, and the client will pay extra for the designer's bad reputation.

This does not mean that the designer must necessarily abandon aesthetics for the practicalities of building, but he should keep the method of construction as simple as possible. As a general rule, if something is easy to draw it is likely to be easy to build.

Sometimes it will be possible to build to suit a rationalised system of construction. This means, for example, ensuring as far as possible that items of construction are not interdependent on each other, the use of integrated components where feasible, and having the minimum number of different components.

Care should also be taken to design elements which are easy to fix and which suit the contractor's plant, for example care should be taken to relate the size and weight of units to the cranage likely to be available. It is helpful if the structure can be designed in a way that facilitates stability during the construction process. Concrete work is often an expensive and time-consuming part of the construction, and for *in situ* work the formwork is the major element. The designer can assist in this area by producing a design where the formwork is as uncomplicated as possible, with simple profiles, bold splays, and no square arises. It should be recognised that construction joints are difficult to hide and that large uninterrupted areas of exposed smooth concrete are best avoided. Where acceptable, dry techniques, particularly in respect of finishes, can help the contractor to achieve a fast programme.

With regard to services, it is an advantage if, as far as possible, these can be installed independently of the structure and finishes, for example by the maximum use of ducts, which are designed with the building and not added as an afterthought.

It is also obviously vital that the architect prepares his production information in a manner and order to suit the contractor's programme. It is not suggested that the architect and architectural technologist should know as much about the practicalities of building as the experienced contractor, or do anything likely to prejudice the quality of his design or the client's interest. He should, however, be sympathetic and knowledgeable about the contractor's problems, and, where possible, specify methods which will assist the contractor to do his work quickly and efficiently.

8

General design procedures

8.1 Introduction

There are some aspects of the procedures that the designer follows, which are of interest and relevance at all stages of a project. They include the RIBA Plan of Work, the contract, production information, and various statutory regulations. These matters are discussed in this chapter.

8.2 Royal Institute of British Architects' plan of work

In order to fulfil his role effectively as a client's agent the architect has to organise his business in a logical way. It is easier to do this if he adopts a series of routine procedures for every contract. The Royal Institute of British Architects (RIBA) publishes the *Architects Job Book* for the use of architects, which outlines the way they should administer a building project both at the pre-contract stage and at the contract stage. The *Architect's Job Book* details the various stages of the RIBA plan of work. Although it is comprehensive and describes all the activities the architect needs to undertake, it is flexible enough to suit the requirements of any project. It is no doubt also widely used by other 'non-architect' designers. The various stages are as follows:

stage A: inception; ⎫ The RIBA standard appointing documents generally
stage B: feasibility; ⎭ refer to stages A and B as being a combined stage
stage C: outline proposals;
stage D: scheme design;
stage E: detail design;
stage F: production information; ⎫ The RIBA standard appointing
stage G: bills of quantities; ⎭ documents generally refer to stages F
stage H: tender action; and G as being a combined stage
stage J: project planning;
stage K: operations on-site;
stage L: completion;
stage M: feedback.

There are some items of work which will be repeated at most stages. These are as follows:

- prepare office resources for each stage of the job;
- keep records and files up to date;
- keep client in the picture, particularly in respect of matters affecting programme or costs;
- circulate relevant information to all members of the design team;
- confirm everything in writing, using an agreed form of communication;
- check that the project is proceeding in accordance with the agreed programme and cost limits;
- check that design office costs and staff resources are not being exceeded;
- make sure that nothing is done contrary to statutory requirements;
- ensure that all fees and other charges are paid as they become due;
- on completion of one stage prepare for the next stage.

8.3 British Institute of Architectural Technology's plan of work

The British Institute of Architectural Technology's (BIAT's) documentation refers to eight work stages. They are:

> stage O: survey;
> stage A: inception;
> stage B: feasibility studies;
> stage C: final scheme drawings;
> stage D: detail design;
> stage E: production information;
> stage F: contract preparation and administration.

A summary of the contents of the various work stages is given in BIAT's Confirmation of Instructions form, which is shown in Figure 11.40.

8.4 Contracts

Reasons for drawing up building contracts
The main reasons for drawing up a building contract are:

- to identify the parties involved in the project, and to state the basic details, such as what the project is, how much it will cost, and how long it will take to complete the work;
- to define the rights and responsibilities of the parties on issues that could be a source of trouble and expense; examples are variations and extension of time (see chapter 10).

Essentials of a contract
A contract is a legally binding agreement between the parties to it. Contracts are commonly made in writing, and, although not essential, this is recommended. There are certain conditions which must apply, including the following:

- a contract is only valid when an offer has been accepted; in other words both parties must have accepted an agreement;
- both parties must be able to enter legally into a contract; for example, they must be at least 18 years old and of sound mind;
- the contract must be legal and possible to adhere to;
- both parties must derive benefit from the contract; for example, one party may have a building built and the other party may receive money for undertaking the work.

Parties to a contract

Building contracts are mainly between the client, known as the employer, and the builder, known as the contractor. Each of these parties may be a single person or a group of persons. A corporate entity can enter into a contract, but, if so, someone has to sign the contract on behalf of the company.

Standard forms of contract

In the construction industry it is common practice to use standard forms of contract prepared by a body known as the Joint Contracts Tribunal (JCT). The JCT forms of contract are prepared by representatives of various bodies, such as the RIBA, Royal Institution of Chartered Surveyors (RICS), Building Employers Confederation (BEC) [formerly the National Federation of Building Trade Employers (NFBTE)], and local authorities. The main subdivisions are by the type of employer and the form of pricing. This results in the following standard 1980 JCT forms of contract:

- Private With Quantities;
- Private With Approximate Quantities;
- Private Without Quantities;
- Local Authorities With Quantities;
- Local Authorities With Approximate Quantities;
- Local Authorities Without Quantities.

There is also the Form of Agreement for Minor Works 1980. This is a very abbreviated form of the standard edition.

The Intermediate Form of Building Contract 1984 was devised because a contract was needed which was less complicated than the 1980 JCT standard forms but not as simplified as the 1980 Minor Works Form. The Intermediate Form of Building Contract 1984 is produced in a single edition for use by private individuals, companies, and local authorities.

The Prime Cost Contract 1992 is available for use where prior estimating is impractical and the contractor is paid for the costs incurred by him (prime costs) plus a fixed or percentage fee.

The Management Contract 1987 provides for contracts in which the contractor manages the works.

All the above JCT standard contracts have been amended since they were first introduced.

There are also special Scottish forms of contract, which are necessary because the Scottish legal system is different from the English system. Other forms of standard contracts include a subcontract form for use between the main contractor and subcontractor.

In addition to standard JCT contracts there are contracts issued by the Association of Consultant Architects (ACA), the Institution of Civil Engineers (ICE), and a wide range of government works, bearing a GW prefix (e.g. GW/Works 1).

The type of standard contract used will depend on the type of job. Clearly, the JCT private edition contract will be used for private employers, whether a single individual or a large company. The JCT local authority contract will be used for local authority work.

The differences between the private edition and the local authority edition are relatively small. For example, the term 'architect' is used in the private edition, and the term 'supervising officer' in the local authority edition. Other examples are that the local authority edition has provision regarding payment of fair wages and avoidance of corruption.

The edition with quantities is used for most large jobs; the edition without quantities, for small jobs, such as a single house; and the edition with approximate quantities for jobs where the bills of quantities are not precise and there needs to be special provision for measurement at the end of the contract.

The Minor Works Form is used for very small projects, such as a house extension or maintenance contracts where no specialist work is involved.

The Intermediate Form of Building Contract is used where the work is straightforward, both in the private sector and the public sector, and with or without quantities.

Prime cost contracts are generally used in conditions of uncertainty but where once the contract has been signed there will be no alterations to the nature, or scope, of the works.

Reasons for standard contracts

From the contracts listed above (which is not an exhaustive list) it can be seen that there are a considerable number of standard forms of contract. Such forms are prepared and used because they are considered to have the following advantages:

- it saves time to use a contract which is immediately available rather than having to prepare a new contract for each project;
- the contract is detailed and fair to all parties as it is the result of much time, effort, and expertise;
- people become familiar with the documents by constant use.

Contract documents

The 1980 standard forms of contract consist of a number of parts, as described below.

Articles of agreement
This is where the parties sign the contract, and the architect and quantity surveyor are named. The articles of agreement also provide details of the type of work and define the basic obligations of all parties involved in the contract.

Part 1: general conditions
This part contains a wide range of clauses, including the contractor's obligations, the architect's instructions, variations, extension of time, certificates, and payments. Some of the items are mentioned elsewhere in this book, but, for more detailed coverage, the reader is advised to refer to the excellent books on the subject of building contacts, including those listed in the bibliography of this book.

Part 2: nominated subcontractors and nominated suppliers
This consists of two clauses, one of which deals with subcontractors and the other with suppliers.

Part 3: fluctuations
This part deals with the ways in which fluctuations in the price of labour and materials will be dealt with.

Appendix
This part, together with the articles of agreement, give the contract its individuality. It states the contract particulars, including the start and finishing dates.

Other items
In addition to the contract itself, the contract document consists of the contract drawings and a priced copy of the bill of quantities. If the form of contract is a 'without quantities' edition, a specification will be used instead.

When the contract has been signed the contractor is entitled to a certified copy of the bills of quantities, a contract, a further unpriced copy of the bills, and two copies of the contract drawings. One copy of the contract drawings should be kept on-site.

Law relating to construction contracts

The most important legislation relating to construction contracts is contained in part II of the Housing Grants, Construction and Regeneration Act 1996 (commonly referred to as 'the Construction Act'). Among the matters covered are adjudication and payments.

The Act gives a party to a construction contract the right to refer a dispute arising under the contract to an adjudicator. There is a time-scale for the appointment of the adjudicator – generally within seven days of serving a notice – and for the time required for the adjudicator to reach a decision – generally within 28 days. The decision of the adjudicator is binding until the dispute is finally settled by other means, that is, by legal proceedigns, by arbitration, by mediation, or by agreement. Alternatively, the parties may agree to accept the decision of the adjudicator as finally determining the dispute. The subject of arbitration is referred to in section 10.15, and the subject of mediation in section 10.16.

With regard to payments, the Act states that a party to a construction contract is entitled to payment by instalments, and that the contract must provide an adequate mechanism for determining what payments become due under the contract and when.

Projects without contracts

Construction projects sometimes proceed without the parties entering into a contract. In such cases the common law will apply. This means, for example, that if a contractor does work for a client, with the client's approval, he is, according to the law, entitled to expect payment, even though there is no binding agreement between the two parties.

8.5 Determination

Most standard building contracts, such as the JCT contracts, make provision for the 'determination' or ending of the contractor's appointment by either party. Strictly speaking, it is not the ending of the contract, because the contract must continue after determination to provide a framework for resolving the situation. Determination is likely to be a final act, unlike suspension, which generally means the temporary suspension of work on-site.

In the case of most building projects the contract comes to an end when both parties have completed what they promised, that is, the contractor has completed the work and the employer has paid for it.

Breach of contract

A breach of contract is an unwarranted failure to discharge contractual requirements. If the breach is a serious one it may allow the other party to act as though the contract has been terminated. Some examples of where this could be the case are:

- the contractor stops work, and leaves the site;
- the contractor fails to complete the work;
- the contractor fails to rectify defective work;
- the employer fails to pay the sums due on the dates stated in the contract.

Frustration

Another reason for determination is what is termed 'frustration'. This is when something happens, such as a serious fire or explosion in the building, which makes it impossible to comply with the terms of the contract, that is, to construct the building by a specified date.

Agreement
It is also possible for determination to take place by agreement between the parties to the contract. It is usual in such circumstances to record the agreement in writing.

Procedure and effect of determination
The contract will state the procedures to be followed in the event of determination, and these should be strictly adhered to. Determination does not mean that the contract has ended. Any relevant conditions will continue to apply.

8.6 Production information

Production information is the total information the design team produces in order to facilitate the erection of a building. In the widest sense it will consist of more than just drawings. There are generally, in all but the smallest jobs, four ways in which the contractor and others receive information – drawings, schedules, specifications, and bills of quantities.

8.7 Importance of accuracy

It is vital that both production information and information prepared in the earlier stages is accurate and absolutely clear and easy to understand. Care must be taken to avoid errors and conflicting and incomplete information. Such errors will at best lead to indecision and delays on-site and elsewhere and will at worst lead to mistakes in the finished building. They may also confuse the client, which is something well worth avoiding.

Accuracy should be the constant aim from the earliest stages of the project, that is, at the feasibility studies and sketch design stages. There may sometimes be a temptation to create false impressions in the initial presentation sketches in order to 'sell' the scheme to the client. Such inaccuracy can, however, be embarrassing at later stages when it is found to be impossible to convert an approved sketch proposal into reality at the working drawing stage.

8.8 Drawings

This is the main medium the designer uses to convey his requirements to everyone involved in the building project.

Information requirements

The architect and architectural technologist will need to remember that, to some extent, each person requires different information. The building control officer, for example, is concerned mainly that the drawings comply with the building regulations. The primary interest of the structural engineers will be with the architectural practitioner's intentions regarding overall dimensions, beam and column sizes and spacings, use of buildings, loadings, and exposure. The building services engineer is mainly concerned with duct spaces, acceptable positions of hole sizes in the structure, fixing positions, and allocation of plant areas. The contractor, of course, needs detailed information about everything, as he is involved in obtaining materials and components and employing labour and plant to erect the building.

Standard sheet sizes

Construction drawings are usually produced on standard sheets known as A sizes. These conform to the recommendations of the International Standards Organization (ISO). Figure 8.1 illustrates these sizes.

Organisation and management of drawing work

As projects become larger and more complicated it is necessary to adopt correct techniques for organising and managing the drawing work. However, even on small, simple projects many of the general principles outlined below will apply.

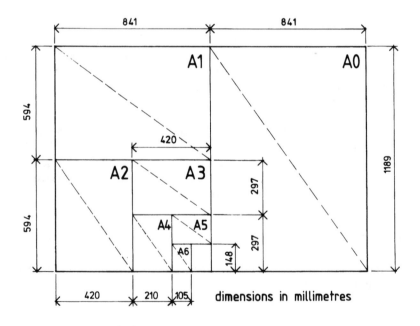

Fig. 8.1 Drawing paper: standard sizes recommended by the International Standards Organization

Whenever possible the following decisions should be taken before work on the production information drawings begins.

Drawings
- Prepare a list giving the title of each drawing required.
- Decide the content of each drawing.
- Choose scales for each drawing.
- Decide the size of the standard drawing sheets.
- Determine the reference techniques to be followed, including the grid.
- Decide the tolerances to be allowed.
- Agree the style and content of the title panel.

Outstanding information
- List all outstanding information.
- Record who is to supply this information.
- Agree dates when the information will be provided.

Programme
- Agree a programme showing the dates each drawing is to be provided.

Drawing registers
A drawing register is an important part of management procedures. It can provide the following information about each drawing:

- number (e.g. 359A/12a)
- title (e.g. electronics factory Epsom for Henry Electronics Limited);
- discipline (e.g. architectural);
- type (e.g. location drawing, floor plan);
- scale (e.g. 1:100);
- sheet size (e.g. A1);
- revision suffix (e.g. a);
- names of people who have been sent a copy (e.g. quantity surveyor, etc.).

Drawing numbers
Various numbering systems are used by construction design staff. A typical system will consist of the following components, in order:

1. a project number or letters;
2. a discipline letter, for example

A architectural,	S structural engineering,
D drainage,	W water services,
H heating,	C air-conditioning,
E electrical,	L landscaping;

3. an identifying number within each discipline;
4. a revision siffix.

A drawing with the number 399A/12a would mean that the project had been given the number 399; that it is an architectural drawing, and the twelfth such drawing to be prepared for the project, with the revision 'a' denoting there has been one revision since the drawing was first issued.

Checking drawings
In order to reduce the risk of errors and omissions it is important to check each drawing before it is issued. The draughtsperson responsible for the drawing should make their own check, but whenever possible a further check should be made by someone else sufficiently experienced to be able to recognise the accuracy and completeness of the drawing. The procedure is to check that the drawing is:

• technically correct and complies with all the regulations;
• dimensional accurately, arithmetically correct, and drawn to scale;
• of an acceptable quality with regards to lines, legibility, and general appearance;
• provided with the correct symbols and uses standard conventions;
• annotated correctly;
• supplied with a correct title panel.

Checklists
Checklists are useful tools during both the preliminary stage of organising the drawing work and the actual drawing stage. They help to ensure that a systematic approach is adopted in directing the drawing work and are a means of highlighting decisions which have to be noticed and of avoiding errors and omissions. Examples of two such checklists are given in Figures 11.12 and 11.13.

8.9 Drawing structures

The designer has the choice of structuring the drawings by type of information, trade arrangement, operational arrangement, or by some hybrid system.

Type of information
This is the commonest method. The drawings are divided into location drawings, assembly drawings, and component drawings.

Location drawings
These show where the work will be but may not show how the work will be performed. Location drawings give an overall impression of the building and provide key dimensions to set out the whole building, they locate spaces and parts such as doors and windows, and they give a key as to where more detailed

information can be obtained. Location drawings include site plans, floor plans, sections, and elevations.

Site plans These locate the buildings, roads, landscaping, etc. on the site and often provide information regarding levels. They are commonly drawn to a scale of 1:200 or 1:500.

Floor plans These locate spaces such as rooms, and parts such as doors and windows. The most useful scale is probably 1:100 but 1:200 and 1:50 are also used and occasionally 1:20 and 1:25 are used. Figure 8.2 is an example of a location floor plan, originally drawn on an A4 sheet.

Sections These give a vertical view of the building, including information on overall vertical dimensions and levels. They are drawn to the same scale as the floor plans.

Elevations These show the external faces of the buildings. They are drawn to the same scale as the floor plans.

Assembly drawings
These show how the building is put together on-site and generally provide more detailed information as to the construction of the building. They commonly consist of sectional plans and vertical sections. Examples are details of window openings, details of the junction between a floor and wall and between a column and a wall. Common scales are 1:5; 1:10, and 1:20. Figure 8.3 is an example of an assembly drawing, originally drawn on an A4 sheet.

Component drawings
These show details of items manufactured on-site and off-site and give full information about components such as doors and windows. Elevations are generally drawn to a scale of 1:100; 1:10, or 1:5. Figure 8.4 is an example of a component drawing, originally drawn on an A4 sheet.

Sheet arrangements
The arrangement of the various drawing parts on the sheets will vary, according to the size of the building and the preferences of the designer or draughtsperson. In the case of a small project, such as the small bungalow shown in Figure 8.2, all the drawings can be prepared on A4 sheets. This is not a very common arrangement, but the compact file of A4 drawings produced is very easy to handle.

A commoner arrangement for a project consisting of a small house or bungalow is to arrange all the location drawings – site plan, floor plans, sections, and elevations – on a single A2 or A1 sheet of paper, with assembly drawings and component drawings being produced on separate sheets, preferably of the same size. With a

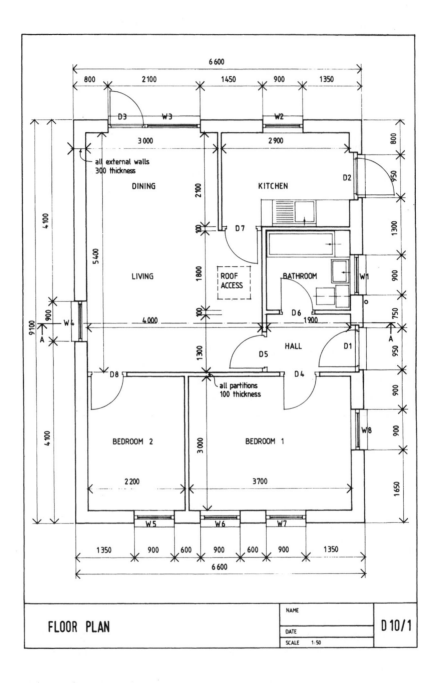

Fig. 8.2 Location drawing

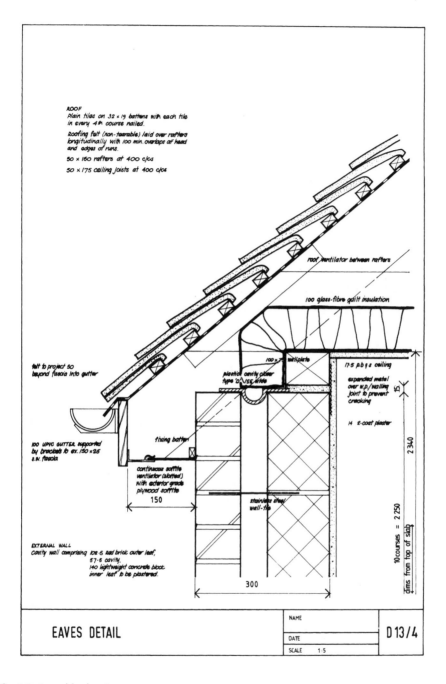

ROOF
Plain tiles on 32 × 19 battens with each tile
in every 4th course nailed.

Roofing felt (non-tearable) laid over rafters
longitudinally with 100 min. overlaps at head
and edges of runs.

50 × 150 rafters at 400 c/cs

50 × 175 ceiling joists at 400 c/cs

roof ventilator between rafters

100 glass-fibre quilt insulation

felt to project 50
beyond fascia into gutter

100 × 75 wallplate

17·5 p b & s ceiling

plastics cavity closer
type 'b' 150 wide

expanded metal
over w.p./walling
joint to prevent
cracking

14 2-coat plaster

100 UPVC GUTTER supported
by brackets to ex.150 × 25
s.w. fascia

fixing batten

continuous soffite
ventilator (slotted)
with exterior grade
plywood soffite

150

stainless steel
wall-tie

2 340

EXTERNAL WALL
Cavity wall comprising 102·5 red brick outer leaf,
57·5 cavity,
140 lightweight concrete block
inner leaf to be plastered.

300

10 courses = 2 250
dims from top of slab

EAVES DETAIL

NAME

DATE

SCALE   1:5

D 13/4

Fig. 8.3 Assembly drawing

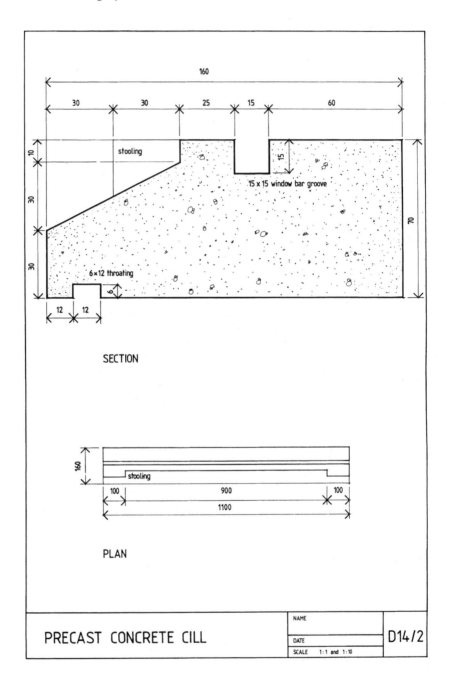

160

30   30   25   15   60

10

stooling

15

15 x 15 window bar groove

30

70

30

6×12 throating

6

12   12

SECTION

160

stooling

100   900   100

1100

PLAN

PRECAST CONCRETE CILL

NAME

DATE

SCALE   1:1 and 1:10

D14/2

Fig. 8.4 Component drawing

larger project, the same arrangement can be used, but with an A0 sheet for the location drawings.

As the project increases in size it will not be possible to include all the location drawings on a single sheet, so one or more sheets will be used for each type of location drawing – that is, a site plan, floor plans, sections, and elevations.

Trade arrangement

This system owes its origin to the days when there were no main contractors, and each trade had a separate contract and set of drawings. Nowadays each trade is not so clearly defined, and projects are often complicated, so the system is less frequently employed.

Operational arrangement

This method was devised by the Building Research Establishment (BRE), based on operational bills. The drawings are arranged to illustrate site operations performed by one person, or a gang, between definite breaks in activities. For example, the brickwork from damp-proof course to first floor level.

Hybrid system

In this system, drawings relate to specific parts of the building, for example elements such as the building frame.

8.10 Dimensions

It is important that all drawings are fully dimensioned so that the contractor and others know the required size of every part of the building. It is sensible, however, not to duplicate dimensions, as this makes the drawings unnecesarily crowded.

Horizontal dimensions

Horizontal dimensions should, where possible, be indicated on plans rather than on elevations. Where feasible dimension lines should be located outside the building or object rather than inside it.

Overall dimensions of every side of the building are essential information for the site engineer or whoever is responsible for setting out the building. They are equally important to the quantity surveyor to enable him to 'take off' items such as foundation lengths. In addition to the overall dimension of buildings, the site engineer will also require dimensions relating the building to fixed points, such as an existing road or building. Site boundaries also need to be defined.

Lengths must be given of all walls or parts of walls, as must the widths of all windows and door openings and their lateral positions in the walls.

Internal dimensions of every room and space must also be provided. These are needed by the person responsible for setting out the internal walls and partitions and also by the quantity surveyor for calculating the areas of floor and ceiling finishes and for the runs of items such as plaster finishes.

Dimensions should be taken to structural surfaces, for example to the face of a brick wall rather than the face of the plaster finish.

Vertical dimensions

Vertical dimensions should, where possible, be indicated on sections rather than on elevations. All vertical dimensions of a building should relate to a site datum. The site datum is a fixed vertical level on the site and for convenience is often set at the ground floor level of the building under construction.

Different members of the building team tend to follow different practices regarding the measuring points for vertical dimensions. The client is concerned with clear storey heights, that is, the dimensions between the finished floor level and the finished ceiling levels. Architects and architectural technologists will invariably give the finished floor level (FFL) on their drawings. Site staff work initially to the structural floor level (SFL). Carpenters working on a building having a timber roof will be interested in the level of the underside of the ceiling joists rather than the level of the ceiling finish. Structural engineers need to know the SFL, and their vertical dimensions will generally be measured from SFL to SFL.

Final point

The final point about dimensions is an obvious one. Mistakes in dimensioning can be expensive both in terms of time and money, so it is worth checking and double checking that there are no errors. If any dimension is not drawn to scale, the letters 'NTS' (not to scale) should be written after the dimension.

8.11 Computer-aided design and draughting

Computer-aided design and draughting (CAD) systems are now extensively used in architectural offices and elsewhere. Integrated design and drawing systems are available with powerful hardware and a wide range of peripherals, such as plotters and colour printers.

Plotters are in effect automated drawing boards and are available in A3, A2, A1, and A0 sizes, with multipens which enable the plotter to draw lines of varying thicknesses without the need to change pens (Figure 8.5). Printers provide copies in paper form of the drawing the computer produces.

Originally, CAD systems produced working drawings in two dimensions only, but in addition to traditional plans, elevations, and sections they are now able to provide perspectives, wire-frame and solid models, simulated walk-throughs, and animation. A further benefit of a CAD system is that the data produced by the computer can be sent electronically down the telephone line to some other office, such as the quantity surveyor's or the contractor's office, in a matter of minutes.

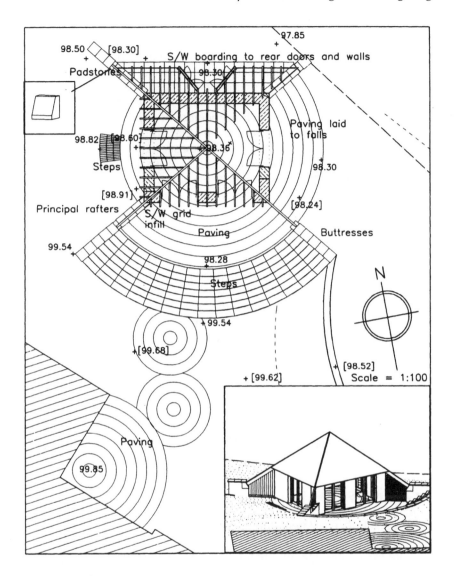

Fig. 8.5 Computer drawing of a summerhouse, Radstock (Barry Christian, Architect)

The range of software available has dramatically increased since CAD was first introduced to architectural offices, when the software was limited to drawing straight and curved lines. Computers can now be linked to external databases and can automatically produce elevations, schedules, perspectives, and calculations. A CAD system is able to quickly add texts and dimensions to drawings, and there are now few jobs which the architectural draughtsperson can undertake quicker or cheaper without use of a computer. The one exception is probably a very small job.

Once an architectural practice has decided to use a CAD system a decision has to be made as to the method of operation. It may not be feasible to treat it as a resource, like a photocopier, which anyone can use as and when required. It is more likely that the computer equipment will be housed in a separate room, with one or more computer operators working under the direction of a CAD section head or manager. These staff should not be isolated from other staff members. Often a CAD operator will be considered to be a member of a specific group in the office and produce all the computer work needed by that group.

Increasingly, architects, architectural technologists, and other technical staff in architectural practices will hand over the production of drawings to the computer operator, but they will still need to have a sound knowledge of construction detailing.

8.12 Storage of drawings

However drawings are produced they will need to be stored for easy access during the course of the project. Drawings should be filed flat and not folded or rolled. Traditionally, this is achieved by use of plan chests, but specially designed cabinets are also available which permit drawings to be stored vertically.

Separate drawers will generally be allocated for the various types of drawings produced by the architect or architectural technologist, as well as those produced by other members of the design team, for example consulting engineers and subcontractors. Negatives should be kept separate from prints.

Drawings which are out of date, owing to the issue of revised drawings, should either be destroyed or, if they need to be retained for record purposes, they should be clearly marked with the word 'superseded'. Information on the storage of record drawings for completed projects, including microfilming, is given in section 5.14.

8.13 Schedules

Schedules are tabulated statements of information. In their simplest form they consist of a list of items, as in the case of schedules of work (see section 8.14 below). More frequently, the information is contained within a network of boxes.

Schedules have the merit of providing information in a form which can be easily checked. They are also useful for easy ordering of components and materials. Schedules are commonly used to record information on items such as doors, windows, lintels, ironmongery, finishes, colour schemes, manholes, and inspection chambers.

8.14 Schedules of work

As was stated in the previous section, a schedule of work is simply a list of items – that is, a list of items of work which have to be undertaken. Its use is generally restricted to alterations, refurbishment, and maintenance work as opposed to the construction of new buildings.

Schedules of work are often used in conjunction with plans and other location drawings and can prevent the drawings being overloaded with notes. For example, the schedule can list the walls which have to be replastered or redecorated, instead of this information being written on the drawings.

A schedule of work should not include details of the materials or workmanship – this is the job of the specification (section 8.15–8.18). Neither should it contain quantities – this is the job of the bills of quantities (section 8.19).

8.15 Specifications

A specification is a written document which describes all the work which is to be carried out, including the quality of work and the standard of workmanship. It gives a good general view of the work but is also able to set out some things in a more detailed way than is possible with notes on drawings. It should not, however, give information on quantities, except in the case quoted below, where the specification and bills of quantities are combined in a single document.

In the case of new buildings the specification is frequently incorporated into the bills of quantities as a preamble to the bill. Where there is no bill of quantities the specifications will be a separate document. The contractual implication of this is that if there are no bills of quantities the specification becomes a contract document.

8.16 Traditional specification

This type of specification gives the full details as to what is required, including the exact method of construction. The specification is generally divided into sections, starting with preliminaries, followed by the various trades, such as excavations, concrete work, and brickwork and blockwork. Information about the materials and workmanship is given under the same section.

8.17 National Building Specification

The National Building Specification (NBS) uses the CI/SfB (Construction Industry/ Samarbetshommitten for Byggnadsfragor) coding system. It provides details of the materials under the heading 'Commodities', with the workmanship items grouped together under a separate heading. A collection of standard clauses are provided which can be used for any specification.

The idea behind the CI/SfB coding system is to facilitate cross-referencing between all project documents as well as with general trade literature. The NBS was originally published by the National Economic Council and is now published by the RIBA. The arrangement of the various sections follows the *Standard Method of Measurement* (SMM) system (see section 8.20).

8.18 Performance specification

This method of specification writing is more likely to be used for sending to a supplier of components (e.g. doors). It consists of a detailed statement of requirements defined by the level of achievement required. In other words, it states what is needed in terms of performance rather than in terms of how the need is to be met, as with a traditional specification. Take a door as an example: a traditional specification would not only give the size of the door but would also give a full description of the construction and the type of materials to be used both for the core and for the facings. A performance specification would give the size and requirements in terms of appearance but would then go on to define what is required in terms of strength, sound insulation, fire resistance, spread of flame, etc.

8.19 Bills of quantities

The bills of quantities (BQ) is a document containing all the items of materials and labour necessary to construct the building. A full description is given of the quality of materials and the standard of workmanship required. The general conditions under which the work is to be done is stated, together with all preliminaries.

Each building trade has an individual bill, which is given a number (e.g. bill 1, preliminaries and trade preambles; bill 2, excavator; bill 3, concretor). The set of individual bills forms a document which is known as the bills of quantities (or BQ or BOQ). Note the use of the plurals *bills* and *quantities* for the complete document.

The bills of quantities are generally prepared by quantity surveyors and quantity surveying technicians. They are used by contractors to price the work shown on drawings and are described in specifications.

The value of the BQ is generally considered to be as follows:

- all contractors tender under identical conditions, which is a fairer arrangement;
- there is less chance of misunderstandings during the course of the work;
- if changes are necessary there is likely to be an agreed rate for pricing the variation;
- it assists in agreed payments by stages;
- it saves the expense of each contractor preparing his own BQ.

A sample page for a typical BQ is shown in Figure 8.6.

8.20 Method of measurement

The method of measurement generally used (e.g. whether concrete is described as metres cubed, or metres squared of a certain thickness) is given in the *Standard Method of Measurement* (SMM). The current edition is the 7th edition and it is referred to as SMM7. The JCT forms of contract (section 8.4) assume that bills of quantities have been prepared using SMM7, unless otherwise stated. The SMM7 is issued by the RICS and, being a standard and widely accepted and used document,

SUPERSTRUCTURE   BILL NO   MASONRY
                                                                £

Blockwork; as specification ref:
      concrete common blockwork –
Tarmac Topblock Hemelite;
including forming weep holes; as
specification ref:

Walls
  100 mm thick   1022 m^2

Closing cavities
  100 mm wide; blockwork 100 mm
  thick; vertical   29 m
  100 mm wide; blockwork 100 mm thick;
  horizontal   42 m

Blockwork; as specification ref:
      concrete common blockwork
Tarmac Topblock Topcrete SPW

Walls
  195 mm thick; facework one side;
  bonding to other work   82 m^2

Blockwork; as specification ref:
      concrete common blockwork

Walls
  50 mm thick   20 m^2

Blockwork; as specification ref:
      concrete common blockwork;
Tarmac Topblock Topcrete

Walls
  100 mm thick   7 m^2
  215 mm thick   103 m^2
  100 mm thick; bonding to other work   1 m^2
  140 mm thick; bonding to other work 86 m^2

                              TO COLLECTION   £

Fig. 8.6 A sample from a typical bills of quantities

enables the contractor to price the work in accordance with recognised conventions. It is prepared by the RICS and BEC with the blessing of the RIBA.

It means that bills of quantities are nearly always set out in a standard way – that is to say, the general format is the same for every job. It also ensures that the work is set out in accordance with the JCT standard forms of building contracts.

8.21 Preparation of the bills of quantities

Traditionally, bills of quantities are prepared in a number of stages. First, measurements are 'taken off' from the drawings and entered on dimensional paper. Then, the dimensions are 'squared' to provide, for example, the number of metres squared, of brickwork and metres squared of concrete. These are transferred to abstract paper, and like dimensions are aded, or 'cast', together. The final stage is to 'bill' the information into the familiar form of bills of quantities.

However, with the advent of computers it is becoming common practice to feed the descriptions into a computer, which undertakes all the calculations and produces a complete printout of the bills.

8.22 Nominated subcontractors

Reason for existence
Architects and architectural technologists need to make decisions on key elements of the building, such as the structural frame, in the early stages of a project. This fact has led to the emergence of nominated subcontractors.

Definition
A nominated subcontractor is a person or company named by the architect or architectural technologist to be responsible for carrying out part of the work (e.g. the structural steelwork).

Significance
This nomination puts them in a special relationship with the architect or technologist. In the case of structural steelwork, for example, it could mean that the nominated subcontractor could undertake some, or even all, of the steelwork design. However, once the contractor has accepted the architectural practitioner's nomination, and the subcontract is signed, the relationship is the usual one of contractor and subcontractor.

The fact that nominated subcontractors are appointed at an early stage will generally mean that the client will need to be involved. The architect or technologist will need to analyse the information on the quotations received from the subcontractors so that he can make a recommendation to the client as to why a particular quotation should be accepted.

Checks on suitability

There are various questions the architect or technologist can ask to help him decide which subcontractor to recommend. They are as follows:

- Has the subcontractor been used before and was he reliable?
- Do the materials and workmanship meet the architect's or architectural technologist's precise requirements?
- Do the materials and workmanship meet all statutory requirements, British Standard Specifications, codes of practice, and other national and international standards?
- Are the programme dates which are offered acceptable?
- Is the quoted price acceptable?
- Is the quoted price unambiguous? What, if any, discounts are offered?
- What are the terms of payment?

Documents used

The current procedures and forms used for nominated subcontractors, were introduced in 1991. They simplified the previously used method, particularly in respect of avoiding the 'to-ing and fro-ing' of documents between the parties involved.

The documents are as follows:

- NSC/T part 1: the architectural practitioner's invitation to a subcontractor to tender;
- NSC/T part 2: the subcontractor's tender;
- NSC/T part 3: the conditions which have to be agreed by the contractor and the subcontractor nominated by the architectural practitioner;
- NSC/A: the articles in the agreement between the contractor and nominated subcontractor;
- NSC/N: the standard form of nomination instruction for a subcontractor.

8.23 Nominated suppliers

Reason for existence

Nominated suppliers exist for the same reason as nominated subcontractors; namely, that often architects and architectural technologists need to make early decisions on the choice of certain components and materials because they affect the early design stages. In such cases they will arrange for the early nomination of a suitable supplier.

Documents used

The following documents are used for nominated suppliers:

- TNS/1, Tender: issued by the architect or architectural technologist inviting tenders, which may subsequently be accepted by an order from the main contractor to the nominated supplier;

- TNS/2, Warranty: an optional warranty from the nominated supplier to the employer.

8.24 Building regulations

The current building regulations in force in England and Wales are the 1998 edition of the Building Regulations 1991, made under the Building Act 1984. The parts of the Regulations are listed in section 7.11.

Purpose
The main purpose of the Building Regulations is to ensure a minimum standard of health and safety for all people who are in or about buildings. They also deal with the conservation of fuel and power and facilities for disabled people in public and commercial buildings, including offices and shops.

Exemptions
Although the majority of buildings and building work require permission under the Building Regulations, there are many exemptions. The following do not need Building Regulations approval:

- educational buildings (not including houses, offices and showrooms) erected to plans approved by the Secretary of State for Education;
- prison buildings and buildings for the detention of criminals;
- buildings (not including dwellings, offices, and canteens) on a licensed site under the Nuclear Installations Act 1965;
- buildings subject to the Explosive Act of 1875 and of 1923;
- buildings subject to the Ancient Monuments and Archaeological Areas Act 1979;
- any other building controlled under other legislation;
- buildings owned and used by statutory undertakers (e.g. a water company);
- buildings (not included dwellings, offices, and showrooms) used in connection with a mine or quarry;
- buildings not frequented by people (e.g. a detached building housing fixed plant or machinery);
- greenhouses and agricultural buildings, provided they are located a minimum specified distance from buildings containing sleeping accommodation;
- temporary buildings and mobile homes;
- ancillary buildings (e.g. a building used only by people engaged in construction during the course of the work or in the sale of buildings);
- small, detached buildings with a total floor area of not more than 30 square metres and with no sleeping accommodation;
- a garden wall or boundary wall;
- replacement windows;
- repairs of a minor nature to houses, shops, and offices;

- conversion of house to shops and offices;
- installation of fittings, other than an extension of the drainage or plumbing, within a house, shop, or office;
- electrical wiring.

Work subject to control
Work which does need Building Regulations approval includes the following:

- installation, extention, or alterations of fittings such as drains, heat-producing appliances, washing and sanitary facilities, and unvented hot-water systems;
- extension to a house, except a porch or conservatory built at ground floor level and less than 30 square metres in floor area;
- garage extension to a house, shop, or office, except a car-port extension built at ground level, open on at least two sides, and less than 30 square metres in floor area;
- detached garage, except where the garage is a minimum distance of 1 metre from the house or built of non-combustible materials and with a floor area of under 30 square metres;
- loft conversion;
- internal structural alterations to houses, shops, and offices;
- installation, replacement, or alterations to a shop front;
- conversion of houses into flats;
- conversion of shops and offices into houses or flats;
- installation of cavity wall insulation.

Cautionary note
In cases where approval is not required under the Building Regulations it should be remembered that the work may be subject to other statutory consents or approvals, such as approval under town planning acts, fire regulations, the Party Wall Act and water bye-laws.

There are some 'grey' areas where it is advisable to check with the local authority. Examples are work to a party wall (see section 7.16), underpinning, removal of a tree close to a wall, the addition of a floor screed which reduces the height of a safety barrier and the building of parapets which may increase snow accumulation and consequently the roof loading. The Building Regulations also apply to certain changes of use.

Obtaining approval
There are two alternative systems of building control, and a choice has to be made as to whether to apply to the local authority or to a private approved inspector. At the present time, possibly because of problems with obtaining suitable professional indemnity insurance, private approved inspectors do not appear to be widely used.

Approval from the local authority
The application should be sent to the Borough Planning and Engineering Department, or a similarly named department of the local authority, and will normally be dealt with by the building control department. Every local authority has a building control department which checks and appraises all applications for Building Regulations approval. Building control officers also have the job of visiting the sites where building work is in progress and checking that the work is being done in accordance with the approved drawings and the requirements of the Building Regulations. The site inspections are made at specific stages of the construction, for example when the excavations are completed and when the foundations are competed but before they are covered up.

When approval is sought from the local authority as opposed to a private approved inspector, application may be made either by the deposit of full plans or the giving of a building notice.

The deposit of full plans Two sets of detailed plans for domestic buildings, and four sets for shops, offices, factories, hotels, boarding houses, and other buildings to which the Fire Precautions Act 1971 applies should be submitted with duplicate copies of the completed application form supplied by the local authority (see Figure 11.8). The plans should consist of:

- a site plan and/or block plan drawn to a scale large enough to indicate the position of all proposed and existing buildings; drainage lines, sizes, gradients, outfall, and sewer connection; boundary positions; and site access and positions of adjoining roads;
- plans of each floor, and enough sections drawn to a scale (commonly 1: 100) large enough and detailed enough to provide full constructional details, incuding foundations, walls, floors, roof, insulation, ventilation, windows, doors, etc.

Note that in practice 1:100 elevations are often submitted with the plans for Building Regulations approval, but this is not essential. The application form and drawings submitted, should, however, be accompanied by any relevant structural calculations.

A prescribed fee has to be paid, in two stages. A plan fee must be included with the submission, and an inspection fee is due following the first inspection on-site. The amount of fee payable depends on the size and type of building (i.e. depending on whether it is a small domestic building, alterations work, etc.). Currently, the fee for a new house of up to 250 square metres is £260.

On receiving the application forms, drawings, and so on, the local authority will check them and take one of the following actions:

- It may send a notice to the applicant stating that the plans have been passed. Work can then commence on-site, provided at least 48 hours notice has been given to the local authority. The approval notice will be issued within five weeks.
- It may send a notice to the applicant stating that the plans have not been passed. It may ask for certain amendments to be made to the drawings, or request more information.
- It may send a notice of conditional approval that is, state that the scheme is

approved subject to certain changes being made, or specific conditions being complied with.

The main advantage of initially submitting a 'full plans' application is that once they are approved the building can be constructed in accordance with these plans, with the confidence that the local authority will be satisfied with the result.

The giving of a building notice   Copies of a site plan should be submitted, similar to the one used for a full plans application. No other drawings are required at the time of submission, although the local authority may ask for more drawings to help them with their inspection role.

No fee is payable on giving a building notice, but a fee is charged when the local authority make their first site inspection of work, amounting to the same as the total sum paid for a full plans application.

The local authority will not notify the applicant as to whether or not his application has been passed or rejected. They will, however, visit the site once the work commences and will inform the applicant if they find anything which does not comply with the Building Regulations. Further information, such as structural calculations, may be required by the local authority as the building work proceeds.

Approval from an approved inspector
If the application is made to a private approved inspector, the inspector and applicant must jointly give the local authority an 'initial notice', a site plan, description of the works, including drainage details, together with evidence that an approved scheme of insurance applies to the work.

Work cannot start until the initial notice has been accepted, or 10 days have passed without it being rejected. The work then has to be done to the satisfaction of the inspector. If the applicant wishes he can submit detailed plans to the inspector and ask him to provide a Plans Certificate certifying that the plans comply with the Building Regulations. On completion of the work the inspector will ussue a Final Certificate.

The private approved inspector must generally be independent of the builder, but there is an exception to this general rule in the case of extension or alterations work to one-storey or two-storey houses.

The need for structural and 'U' value calculations can be dispensed with by submitting a certificate from an approved qualified engineer or designer.

Responsibility for ensuring adequate drainage provision and building work over sewers is under the control of the local authority.

Relaxation
There is provision for dispensing and relaxing the regulations in appropriate cases. A relaxation can be given by the local authority in respect of part B1 ('Means of Escape'); parts L2 and L3 ('Conservation of Fuel and Power'); and schedule 2 ('Facilities for Disabled People'). Lower standards of performance will be accepted in each case.

Dispensation

A Dispensation can be given by the local authority in respect of Regulation 7 ('Materials and Workmanship'); part A ('Structure'); parts B2, B3, and B4 ('Fire Protection'); part C ('Site Protection and Resistance to Moisture'); part D ('Toxic Substances'); part E ('Sound Resistance'); part F ('Ventilation'); part G ('Hygiene'); part H ('Drainage'); part J ('Heat Producing Appliances'); and part K ('Staircases and Ramps'). In such cases the local authority may agree that a particular regulation does not need to apply to all.

Determination

If the local authority rejects the plans submitted to them under the Building Regulations, an application can be made to the Secretary of State for a ruling on the specific requirements of the local authority. This is known as a determination. A fee is payable, the amount depending on the size of the project. If a determination is sought, it must be made before construction begins.

A determination may also be sought if the applicant acknowledges that his application does not meet specific requirements of the regulations but considers they are too severe in his particular case. The appeal to the Secretary of State must be made within a month of the rejection notice being issued.

An approval or rejection notice is not given for a building notice, and there is no procedure for seeking a determination.

Building work which does not conform

If the local authority considers a building has been erected which does not conform to the Regulations, they can serve a notice requiring it to be altered or pulled down.

Penalties for contravention

The local authority can prosecute anyone who builds without notifying them or for carrying out work which does not comply. Anyone convicted is liable to pay penalties and costs, with the final penalty for a breach of the building regulations on a built property being the dismantling of that building.

8.25 Town planning acts

Purpose

The purpose of town planning acts is to ensure that all buildings are of an acceptable appearance, are appropriate to their surroundings, and, in town planning parlance, will not be 'detrimental to the amenities of the area', or 'against the public interest'.

A list of the relevant town planning acts, information on development plans, including the power of the county councils, district councils, and London boroughs and metropolitan councils to control development, and the constraints that town planning acts impose on designers are dealt with in section 7.12.

Exemptions

Some projects are exempt from having to apply for approval because they do not involve development or may be permitted by the General Development Procedure Order. The following do not need planning permission:

- small developments, including extensions to semi-detached and detached houses of not more than 70 metres cubed or 15%, whichever is the greater, up to 115 metres cubed; and extensions to industrial buildings by 25% of volume and up to 1000 metres squared of floor space;
- buildings on agricultural land for agricultural use;
- temporary buildings (e.g. contractor's site huts);
- certain developments undertaken by local authorities and statutory undertakings;
- erection of garden walls, fences, and gates.

Change of use

Planning permission will generally be required when there is a change of use (e.g. conversion of a house into a factory) although some changes are permitted by the General Development Procedure Order.

Preliminary action

To obtain planning permission, application must be made to the planning department of the district council. The architect or architectural technologist normally acts as the employer's (client's) agent. The usual procedure is to have an initial discussion with the town planning officer (or borough development officer) and to look at the structure plan and zoning for the area to decide whether planning permission is likely to be given.

Dependent on these preliminary enquiries, a decision can be made as to whether to apply for outline planning permission (i.e. permission in principle to erect the building) or full planning permission. In most cases a detailed application from the outset is probably the best way to proceed.

Outline planning permission

If outline permission is to be sought, the following information is required:

- four copies of the application forms, generally consisting of part 1 for all applicants, plus part 2 for industrial, office, and shop developments, giving additional details of traffic, parking, etc.;
- one copy of a certificate (from a choice of four, see immediately below) confirming the situation regarding ownership of the land on which the development will take place

- certificate A is used when the applicant is the owner of the land,
- certificate B is used when notice has been given to any person who was an owner or part owner of the land during the 28 days prior to the application being made,
- certificate C is used when certificates A and B are not applicable,
- certificate D is used when the owner of the land is not known;
- one copy of a site plan or block plan indicating the position of the development.

Full planning permission

If full planning permission is sought, information is required as for outline permission, plus the following:

- four copies of every floor plan;
- four copies of every elevation.

The drawings should show the features of the site, including any trees; the location of all existing and proposed buildings; and external finishes, including colours.

The information required by the planning authority can be deduced from looking at a town planning application form. A completed form is shown in Figure 11.8.

Fees

Under the Fees for Applications and Deemed Applications (Amendment) Rgulations 1997 fees are payable to the planning authority when planning applications are made.

The amount varies according to the type of application and the type of development. For example, for an outline application the fee is £180 per 0.1 hectares of site area; for the enlargement of an existing house, £90; and for the erection of a non-residential building larger than 75 square metres, the fee is £180 per 75 square metres, up to a maximum of £9000. The above amounts are the fees which became valid on the 4 February 1997.

Decisions

The decision on the application rests with the local authority planning committee, with guidance from professional planning officers. They generally meet once a month throughout the year. Minor developments (e.g. house extensions) may be determined by the local authority planning officers. These decisions are called 'delegated decisions'. Once the planning authority have reached a decision they will send a 'decision note' to the applicant.

Planning conditions

Sometimes planning permission is only granted subject to planning conditions. A planning condition is a requirement which can be properly imposed to meet the objectives of planning policies relevant to the proposed development. The planning condition must be fair, reasonable, and relevant to the proposals concerned. For example while it would be considered reasonable for a developer to include enough car parking spaces for people occupying the new buildings, it would be unreasonable to expect him to provide sufficient spaces to meet the needs of a nearby local authority recreational facility.

Time limits
The planning authority must give a decision on the planning application within eight weeks of the application being made unless the applicant and the planning authority agree to extend this period.

If outline permission is obtained, full permission has then to be obtained within three years. If full permission is obtained, work on-site must start within five years.

Appeals
If planning permission is refused, on either an outline or a full application, an appeal can be made to the Secretary of State for the Environment.

Applicants can also appeal against a planning condition which a local authority is seeking to impose. The appeal is made initially to the local authority, but if this is refused an appeal can then be made to the Secretary of State and ultimately to the courts on a point of law.

Listed buildings consent and conservation area consent
Consent is required for any proposal which involves the demolition of part or all of a building listed as being of special architectural or historic interest, or demolition of any building within the curtilage of a listed building.

Consent is also needed for proposals which involve alterations to a listed building, or the demolition of part or all of any listed building with a conservation area.

Trees
Tree preservation and planting comes under the control of town planning legislation, and specific action with regard to the planting or preservation of trees on a building site may be a condition of granting planning permission.

Trees should not be cut down, or lopped, without the agreement of the planning authority, unless the trees are dead or dangerous.

8.26 Fire Precautions Act 1971

A fire certificate needs to be obtained from the local fire authority for certain classes of non-domestic buildings, for example places of amusement, educational establishments and residential establishments such as hotels, hostels, and old people's homes.

The main emphasis is directed towards the safety of the occupants in case of fire, including a safe means of escape.

It is sensible for the designer to have an informal meeting with the local fire officer at the design stage of the project to ascertain the officer's requirements and to incorporate them into his design and then into the building. This should mean that when the building is completed, and the fire officer makes his inspection of the building, everything will be to his liking, and he will issue a fire certificate.

It is necessary for a fire certificate to be issued before a building can be put to its intended use, for example a hotel cannot accept any guests until a fire certificate has been issued for the building.

If after his inspection the fire officer is dissatisfied with the fire precautions provided, he will serve a notice on the building owner stating what needs to be done and giving a time-scale for the work.

The fire certificate, when it is issued, will provide certain information, such as the use of the building, the means of escape in case of fire, the method of ensuring a safe means of escape, the type and positions of all fire-fighting equipment, and information on the fire alarm system.

If the building owner is aggrieved at the refusal to grant a fire certificate, or at the contents of the certificate, he can appeal to the magistrate's court, but he must do so within 21 days.

8.27 Insurance

Insurance of a building is not a statutory requirement, but the architect and architectural technologist need to remember that the client will almost certainly want to insure the building. This may not be possible unless the insurers are satisfied that the building does not constitute an undue fire risk. In the case of a large complex building, the designer will often meet with the insurers, who may consist of a consortium of insurance companies, to agree his scheme before it is finalised.

The interests of the insurers will often be different from those of the statutory authorities. The principal concern of the building control officer and the fire officer will be the safety, particularly the means of escape in the case of fire, of the building's occupants. The insurers, on the other hand, will be more concerned with restricting the extent of the damage to the building and contents. This may lead the insurers to demand a higher standard of provision (e.g. in the case of fire walls) than is required by the Building Regulations and the Fire Precautions Act. Failure to include this extra provision may mean that when the building is completed the client may have difficulty in insuring his building or be asked to pay excessive rates for his insurance cover.

When advising his client on building insurance, the architectural practitioner may wish to draw the client's attention to the Building Users Insurance Against Latent Defects (BUILD). This type of insurance provides cover against latent defects for a period of 10 years after the building is completed. Cover is restricted to the main structure and weatherproof envelope. The policy is agreed at the design stage and a single premium is paid.

Although there are benefits to the client, there are even more to the designer, as his liability for latent defects is reduced.

9

Pre-contract procedures

9.1 Introduction

The first main part of a building project is the pre-contract period, from the moment a client first approaches the architect with his requirements to the time when the main contract and subcontracts have been signed.

This is covered by stages A to J of the Royal Institute of British Architects' (RIBA's) Plan of Work, and the full procedure is explained in the RIBA *Architect's Job Book*. This documentation has been prepared specifically to provide guidance for architects as to the proper procedures which should be followed during the course of a project, and the text throughout refers to architects. Other architectural practitioners, notably architectural technologists, will in practice follow similar procedures, but as chapters 9 and 10 are mainly concerned with RIBA documents the term architect will be used throughout.

The nine stages included in the RIBA Plan of Work, which take place before operations commence on site, are as follows:

stage A	inception,
stage B	feasibility,
stage C	outline proposals,
stage D	scheme design,
stage E	detail design,
stage F	production information,
stage G	bills of quantities,
stage H	tender action,
stage J	project planning.

Although the RIBA Plan of Work is used as the basis for the order in which architects undertake their various tasks, both during the pre-contract stages (discussed in this chapter) and during the contract stages (discussed in chapter 10), it is only used as a framework. It is not important whether listed items are always rigidly included in their suggested stage. Sometimes tasks will be done at a different stage from that listed, or a number of tasks will be combined together, or there will be an overlapping of stages. The main thing to remember is that the architect must work in a logical and systematic way and make sure that all decisions and instructions are properly recorded. The RIBA Plan of Work is an invaluable guide to the way the architect arranges his work, but it is a flexible not rigid pattern of operations.

Detailed bills of quantities will always be prepared during the pre-contract stage, as these are required for tendering purposes. Detailed specifications are also required for the same purpose. The exact extent of the drawings prepared will vary from contract to contract. Ideally, every drawing the contractor needs to complete for the contract will also be produced at the pre-contract stage, but on large, complicated jobs this is seldom practicable. The amount of information provided will depend to a great extent on the contractual form used, but an indication on the information provided for tendering is given later in this chapter (section 9.12).

During the pre-contract stages various letters will be written and agendas for meetings and other documents prepared. Some example of these are included in chapter 11. They relate to a project for a factory, for the assembly of electronic components, together with a two-storey office block.

9.2 Stage A: inception

At this stage the client approaches the architect for his professional assistance. The architect agrees to help him and establishes the terms of his appointment and the client's requirements.

The architect has to undertake the following tasks:

- check it is possible to accept the job, including satisfying himself the client is genuine and has the resources to finance the project, making sure that no other architects are involved, and that he has the resources to meet the client's needs;
- agree the terms of the appointment, including responsibilities, fees, employment of the quantity surveyor and other consultants, and channels of communication;
- obtain initial details of the client's requirements;
- initiate office procedures, including opening files, a job book, fees, and other records and deciding how he will organise his part of the job and who will be involved.

A job directory will be prepared in which the names, addresses, and telephone numbers of the client, his representatives, the various consultants, and any other interested parties will be entered.

At least one meeting with the client will be necessary. The architect will probably avoid seeking too much detail from the client at this stage but will aim to establish the general nature of his requirements, together with the location of the site and some detail. The information obtained can be recorded on a briefing checklist (see Figure 11.1).

Agreement will need to be obtained on the terms of the architect's appointment, together with details of the fees. Traditionally these are charged at a percentage of the cost of the project, with the exact percentage dependent on the type of job. A schedule of fees will normally be prepared ready for completing during the various stages of the job. A chart, recording resources to be allocated to the job, with performance targets, will also generally be prepared. It is important for the architect to plan his part of the work in such a way that he completes it within the total amount of his fees.

At this stage the main financial concern of the architect will be to establish cost limitations. The architect may mention typical costs per square metre of floor area, but all figures should be quoted with reservations and it is best, if possible, to leave this matter until the feasibility stage (stage B).

The tender procedure will also need to be discussed, together with the form of contract to be used and decisions regarding the appointment of nominated sub-contractors and suppliers.

The architect will inform the client of approvals required under planning, building, and other regulations, giving him details as to how this will affect the pre-contract programme and what fees are payable.

Agreement will have to be made as to who will be acting for the client. If the project is anything more complicated than a simple building, such as a house, with only the intending owner or owner-occupier involved, a decision will need to be made as to which members of the client's staff will have power to act for him. Similarly, there is a need to know which members of the architect's staff will be involved in the project and what authority each of them will have.

It is clearly important that satisfactory methods of communication be established during the initial stages of the job. The architect will often advise the client on the best way of setting up communications with the design team, including defining individual responsibilities and methods of giving and receiving instructions.

The procedures for the next stage of the project will generally be discussed with the client, and in particular his agreement will be obtained for meeting any charges likely to be incurred, such as trial holes or boreholes dug as part of the site investigation.

Everything which is agreed at the initial meeting should be confirmed in writing. A typical letter sent to the client after such an initial meeting is shown in Figure 11.2. This will generally be followed by the signing of an appropriate 'memorandum of agreement'.

9.3 Stage B: feasibility

At this stage the architect will establish whether it is technically possible to construct the building the client requires on the available site. In undertaking this appraisal the architect will have to obtain the following details:

- additional information on the client's requirements to that provided at the inception stage (stage A);
- detailed information on the site;
- information from third parties who may be involved with the proposed building;
- information on costs.

The way in which the architect obtains the detailed information from the client will vary according to the particular job. In the case of a house it will probably entail a meeting with the client during which the client will provide details as to who will occupy the house, detailing the life-style of the occupants, and confirming how much money it is possible to spend on the project. In some cases the client may spell out in detail the size, location, and appearance of all the rooms required, and even take the architect around houses containing features he would like incorporated in the proposed house.

In the case of an industrialist requiring a factory, the architect will need to obtain details of the manufacturing process, which may involve visits to the client's other factories, and detailed meetings with the industrialist's staff.

Certainly, a job of any complexity will require more information than the outline details obtained at the previous stage and illustrated in the typical briefing checklist (see Figure 11.1). Part of the detailed briefing document is shown in Figure 11.3. This more detailed brief will include information such as sizes, function, and spatial relationships of all rooms and areas, including details of services, and finishes to walls, floors, and ceilings.

In order to obtain information about the site there will need to be a site investigation. As an aid to this task, architects will often use standard site investigation report forms (see Figure 11.4). A standard checklist (see Figure 11.5) is also used by architects for surveying sites and buildings which are part of a building project. As well as looking at the site and writing down what he sees, the architect will need to survey the site to establish the plan size, details, and contours. He will also need to arrange for trial holes to be dug or boreholes to be drilled to establish the nature of the subsoil.

One of the most important third parties involved in the scheme will be the local authority planning department. The architect will normally have an informal meeting with the responsible planning officer to establish whether planning permission is likely to be given. If at this meeting, for example, the planning officer states it is most unlikely permission will be given to build a house, as that particular site is in an area zoned for industrial use, the architect may decide it is not worthwhile proceeding with the scheme. A standard briefing checklist is often used to record information obtained from the local authority (see Figure 11.6).

Meetings may also take place with the highway authority to check there are no problems relating to access into the site, and confirmation will be obtained from the statutory undertakings, such as water, gas, and electricity companies, that all the services the client requires for his building are available.

At the conclusion of all his investigations and enquiries the architect will then be able to report back to the client to state whether or not it is a feasible proposition to build a building of the type the client requires on the site in question. Sometimes the answer will be a straight 'yes'. At other times the architect will report that is is possible to build a building to meet the client's needs but that it would have to be in a different form from that originally envisaged.

In any event the architect will also include a preliminary cost appraisal to check on the feasibility of providing the type of building the client wants for the amount of money he has to spend. It should be emphasised that any estimates given will be very approximate, based possibly on a square-metre price, linked to a schedule of accommodation and room areas. The topic of 'approximate estimates' is considered in the next section. Often cost studies of alternative solutions to the one originally discussed with the client may be prepared if this is thought to be in the client's interest.

The form of the feasibility report will depend on the size, type, and importance of the project. On a very small job it may consist of little more than a long letter. On a large important job it will include drawings, perhaps a model, details of people involved, information on the site, design constraints, cost appraisals, the anticipated programme, together with schedules of the accommodation and room areas.

At stage B the architect will also need to confirm the appointment of the quantity surveyor, engineer, and other consultants, and prepare for the next stage of the project.

The design team needs to be organised, with the roles of the members clearly defined and relationships between the design team and client's representatives established.

9.4 Approximate estimates

As the cost of any job is so important, particularly to the client, approximate estimates are expected to be provided at the various pre-contract stages of the project. They are generally an essential part of the feasibility stage (stage B) discussed in the previous section. Unfortunately, these approximate estimates are often a 'bone of contention', especially when events prove them to be inaccurate. Nevertheless, they are the basis on which the client will instruct the architect to proceed with work.

When presenting an estimate it is important to clarify the date to which it is linked, for example does it refer to the date it is given to the client, the date the job is expected to start, or is it the actual cost of the completed building? Clearly, with inflation to be contended with, the three estimates based on these three dates, perhaps separated by several years, are likely to be significantly different.

It is also important to state clearly what is included in an estimate, and what is excluded.

The architect will, of course, generally remind his client that, until the detailed drawings have been prepared and priced, the estimate can of necessity only be approximate. Nevertheless, if the tender price is dramatically more than the first approximate estimate the client is likely to lose confidence in the architect and may even consider abandoning the project.

There are various types of approximate estimates and some of the more common ones are listed below.

Cost per unit of accommodation

Such costs are, for example, the price per bed for a hospital: per scholar for a school per seat for a church, theatre, or cinema: or per room for a block of flats. These unit costs provide an almost immediate method of putting a 'price tag' on a larger building. However, unless the figures are based on similar buildings they can only be taken as very approximate. To produce the approximate cost using this method, all that is required is for the client to state how many beds, scholars, seats, or rooms are needed, so that the architect or quantity surveyor, using a unit cost derived from previous, similar jobs can prepare an estimate by making a simple calculation.

Cost per square metre of floor area

This is a quick and easily adjustable method but it takes no account of heights, complexity, or plan shape of the building. Again, with this method an approximate cost can be produced without the need for any drawings. The client will have to supply a schedule of room areas to which the architect will add areas the client may have omitted, such as circulation spaces, toilets, etc. This will give an overall floor area, which can be multiplied by a price per square metre, derived from previous jobs. However, if the project is sufficiently advanced for sketch plans to have been prepared, the floor area, and hence the estimate, can be calculated with greater accuracy.

Cost per metre cubed of building

This is also a fairly quick method, but as it is generally used to produce an overall figure for the volume of the building it takes no account of the different room heights and uses within different parts of the building. Again, it is theoretically possible to produce an estimate before any drawings have been prepared, by calculating the total floor area, as described above and then multiplying it by an assumed average height, to arrive at the cubic capacity of the building. However, in practice this method is more likely to be used when plans and sections are both available, so that the cubic capacity can be calculated with a greater degree of accuracy.

Cost per element of building

When information on elements such as floors, walls, roof, etc. are available this method provides a more accurate estimate but takes longer to prepare, and sketch plans, elevations, and sections are required. Each element, including finishes, is priced according to a unit rate per square metre.

In addition to the above methods, at the later stages of the design process the quantity surveyor may take off approximate quantities to arrive at a more accurate estimate.

9.5 Stage C: outline proposals

At this stage the architect, with help from other members of the design team, will carefully analyse the client's requirements. He will relate these requirements to the information obtained in stage B, on feasibility, from the site investigation and other sources. Any further information needed from members of the client's organisation will be obtained, and studies will be made of circulation and other problems, and alternative design solutions considered.

Expert advice will be obtained from the various consultants on the structural, building engineering services, and cost aspects. Account will be taken of all the constraints disclosed during this stage and previous ones.

Having collected together all the relevant information, and having considered the various alternatives, the architect, with other members of the design team, will decide in outline the best design solution and prepare the outline scheme drawings.

The quantity surveyor will consider the cost limits of the project, and the architect will help him in this assessment as required. The quantity surveyor will probably translate the cost limits into a price of so much a square metre for each building included in the project. The architect will discuss with the quantity surveyor what standard of building can be provided within these limits.

An outline pre-contract programme will be prepared so as to give the client an indication as to when the building work will commence on-site and how long it will take to complete. It is important that the client realises that between the time he instructs the architect to act for him and the time when building work commences on-site there are a number of processes which have to be undertaken. If any of these processes take longer than anticipated this will delay the starting date for building work. For example, if the client says he will give a decision to proceed within a week of receiving the scheme design from the architect, but actually takes a month to make up his mind, this will delay the job by three weeks. If an architect just gives the client a date when the job will start, without the back-up of a programme, it is likely the client will assume the date will remain fixed in spite of anything that happens in the intervening period. Figure 9.1 shows a typical pre-contract programme.

There is not necessarily a clear demarcation between the various design and drawing stages. For example, detailed design drawings, such as 1: 100 location plans, elevations, and sections, may be used for obtaining the statutory approvals and will then have some additional information added to them so that they can become part of the production drawings issued to the contract for use on the site. The stage at which some, or all, of the applications for statutory approvals are made will also vary from project to project.

A report will be prepared for consideration by the client. The drawings submitted with this report will, as the name implies, be in outline only. They may consist of little more than a block layout showing the relationship between the different types of accommodation for each floor, with main dimensions. In other words, individual rooms would not be shown. A site plan would normally be provided, showing the position of the buildings on the site, with the location of the services. The written part of the report would indicate the type of structure envisaged, the scope of intended building engineering services, and information on the programme and cost.

At this stage 15% of the fees will typically become due, so the architect will submit his account to the client, asking for payment.

9.6 Communicating design outcomes

The architect has the task of producing a design which will, in his professional judgement, completely satisfy his client's brief. Having done this, he has the task of

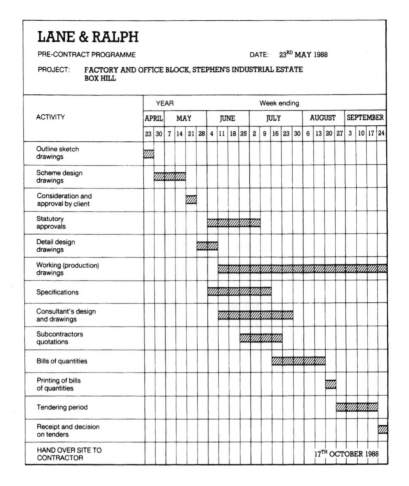

LANE & RALPH

PRE-CONTRACT PROGRAMME   DATE: 23ᴿᴰ MAY 1988

PROJECT: FACTORY AND OFFICE BLOCK, STEPHEN'S INDUSTRIAL ESTATE
            BOX HILL

ACTIVITY	YEAR															Week ending						
	APRIL	MAY				JUNE			JULY				AUGUST				SEPTEMBER			
	23	30	7	14	21	28	4	11	18	25	2	9	16	23	30	6	13	20	27	3	10	17	24
Outline sketch drawings	▨																						
Scheme design drawings		▨▨▨																					
Consideration and approval by client				▨																			
Statutory approvals								▨▨▨▨															
Detail design drawings						▨																	
Working (production) drawings										▨▨▨▨▨▨▨▨▨▨▨▨												
Specifications								▨▨▨▨															
Consultant's design and drawings									▨▨▨▨													
Subcontractors quotations										▨▨▨												
Bills of quantities											▨▨▨											
Printing of bills of quantities															▨							
Tendering period																▨▨▨						
Receipt and decision on tenders																						▨
HAND OVER SITE TO CONTRACTOR																	17ᵀᴴ OCTOBER 1988						

Fig. 9.1 Pre-contract bar chart programme

presenting his design solution to the client. This will generally happen at stage C (outline proposals, discussed in the previous section) and generally a more detailed submission will follow in the next stage to be considered (namely stage D, scheme design).

Perspectives

There are a variety of methods that can be used to present the design solution, and the choice will be influenced by the type, size, and value of the project. The architect will generally aim to achieve a good standard of presentation, both as a matter of professional pride and also as an attempt to impress the client and others such as the planning authority of the attractiveness of the design. The architect should remember that many laypeople have great difficulty understanding drawings, so a perspective is most helpful in portraying the appearance of the building. Laypeople may comprehend plans, but to many people of a non-technical background, sections tend to be something of a mystery. On a small project, such as a house, a useful way of presenting the design solution is to provide floor plans and a perspective. On a larger project, such as a factory, it will be helpful to show the general massing and the relationship between the main areas, and this can often be achieved by looking over the roofs of the buildings and providing a bird's-eye view. It is also helpful to indicate the nature of the area adjoining the site.

Perspective drawings and photographs
When a building is to be erected on a site between existing buildings the perspective should show the surrounding buildings or site (Figure 9.2). One method is to produce a perspective which is a combination of a drawing of the proposal, arranged with photographs of the existing buildings. It can then be rephotographed to give a realistic impression as to how the proposed buildings will relate to the existing buildings.

Models
Models are especially useful and are a good way to explain and 'sell' the project. On an industrial complex a model showing the interrelationship of new and existing buildings is very helpful. The model does not have to be expensive, as often a simple 'block' model, without a lot of detail, will be adequate. Models are also an effective way of depicting constructional methods, particularly when novel techniques are intended. Figure 9.3 shows a model used to illustrate the constructional system used for a prefabricated building.

Full presentation
On the larger, more costly projects, it is worth spending time and money on a more elaborate presentation. A detailed model will be expected, perhaps showing part of the internal layout. If a formal presentation is required (e.g. to a board of directors) it is worth preparing photographic slides of all models, internal and external perspectives, views of the site plans, and other drawings so that the scheme may be presented in an orderly fashion, with an appropriate commentary (Figure 9.4).

Use may also be made of computers in the presentation of design outcomes. In addition to producing perspectives they can be used for simulated walk-throughs and animation.

Communicating the design to the design team
The architect also needs to communicate his intentions to specialist members of the design team, and others. As was stated in section 8.8, he needs to remember that each person, to some extent, requires different information, but they all use drawings as the normal means of communication. The architect will generally use this

Fig. 9.2 Pseudo-perspective drawing of council offices, Tewkesbury. Building Partnership (Bristol) Ltd; drawn by W. Spencer Tart

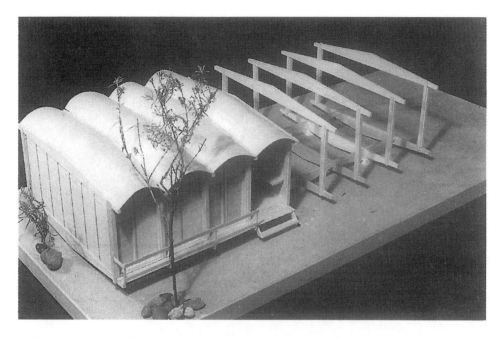

Fig. 9.3 Model used to illustrate constructional system. OEDS Ltd., Kuwait

means of relaying his design intentions but will tailor his drawings to suit the needs of individual members of the building team. This will often be achieved by making negative copies of the basic drawings and adding information specifically to suit different people.

9.7 Stage D: scheme design

At this stage the design team will prepare a sufficiently detailed scheme design to show the spatial arrangements of the various parts of the building, as well as the appearance of the building, and an indication of the materials used.

In order to do this the architect will need to complete his studies to establish 'user requirements'. If necessary, additional visits and investigations will be made to achieve this. The client will be asked to provide any additional information required by the architect. The architect will also check that the client has acquired the site.

In order to organise the design, meetings at which solutions will be discussed and developed will be necessary. Decisions will be made regarding design aspects, materials, finishes, services, contributions by specialist firms, and various other matters.

It is likely that at this stage application will be made to the local authority for full planning permission and Building Regulations approval. There is, however, no hard and fast rule as to the exact stage when approval is sought. For example, sometimes

Fig. 9.4 Carefully drawn design of a hotel interior (Malcolm Read, MCSN, FSAI)

applications may be delayed until stage E (detail design). Generally, the same drawings will be used in support of both the planning application and the Building Regulations application, although, strictly speaking, sections are not required for planning approvals and elevations are not needed for Building Regulations applications.

The information required in support of the planning application was discussed in section 8.25. It will generally be sensible before depositing the application to have a further informal discussion with the local planning officer so as to arrive at a solution which has his support. At such a meeting he may suggest that it is likely permission will only be given subject to planning conditions. As has been previously stated, such planning conditions must be fair, reasonable, and relevant to the development concerned (section 8.25).

The information required in support of the Building Regulations application was discussed in section 8.24. Certain work, listed in that section, is exempted from building controls, and if this appears to be the case for a particular project the local authority should be approached for their confirmation.

The appropriate fees for the town planning and Building Regulations applications will have to be sent to the local authority, along with the relevant forms and drawings.

When considering the application the local authority will check that bodies responsible for matters such as highways, drainage, and safety in respect of fire are happy with the proposals. This is another reason why it is advisable to consult informally with the local authority before making a submission. They will often be able to advise the architect of other approvals required at this stage. In any event it is sensible to approach everyone likely to be affected. For example, if a fire certificate will be required for the completed building it is advisable to discover the fire officer's requirements at a stage when they can be incorporated in the drawings submitted for planning and Building Regulations approvals.

An example of part of a planning application form is given in Figure 11.8, and an example of a Building Regulation application form is given in Figure 11.10.

The quantity surveyor will prepare a cost plan and the architect will help him as required. This cost plan will indicate to the client the approximate cost, so that he is aware of his financial commitment, and will show how the total cost is allocated among the various parts of the project. Figure 9.5 shows part of the cost plan for a project. There will also be a separate sheet for the factory building, again sub-divided into the various elements, and a sheet for the external works. These three parts of the project will be added together, with a further addition for preliminaries, to give the total cost of the job.

The design team's proposals need to be submitted to the client in an attractive form. As in previous stages the content will depend on the size and importance of the project but will normally include plans, basic sections, and elevations or perspectives. Sometimes, models and photographs will be used. The written part of the submission will generally include an outline specification, an explanation as to how the client's requirements have been met, outline information on the build-ing engineering services, programme details, and estimated costs.

The scheme design is expected to summarise the client's requirements in respect of accommodation and the general arrangement of the buildings, and he needs to be advised that once he has approved the scheme he should not make any changes unless he is prepared to risk incurring additional costs.

A further 20% of the architect's fees are now due, so the architect will generally submit his account for this amount. Preparations will be made for the next stage of the project so that the work can proceed in a smooth and orderly manner as soon as the client has approved the scheme design and authorised proceeding to stage E, detail design.

9.8 Stage E: detail design

At the end of the previous stage, the client should have given approval for the pre-contract work on the project to proceed on the basis of the scheme design draw-ings. It is important that he is aware that any modifications from now on may lead to him incurring extra costs and to a possible delay in the start and completion of the project on-site. The client should be politely informed of this fact in writing. A typical letter is shown in Figure 11.11.

COST PLAN	SHEET NO. 2
PROJECT FACTORY & OFFICE BLOCK, STEPHEN'S INDUSTRIAL ESTATE, BOX HILL	
PART OF PROJECT OFFICE BLOCK	

ELEMENT	£	COST
Substructure incl. grnd slab	16,000	
Frame	23,000	
Upper floors	8,000	
Stairs	6,000	
Roof	13,000	
External walls	38,000	
External doors / windows	37,000	
Internal walls / partitions	4,000	
Floor finishes	13,000	
Wall finishes	10,000	
Ceiling finishes	11,000	
Fittings	6,000	
Furniture	6,000	
Sanitary appliances	6,000	
Services equipment	—	
External drainage	3,000	
Refuse disposal	—	
Discharge pipework	3,000	
Cold water services	3,000	
Hot water services	7,000	
Heating services	32,000	
Air conditioning services	—	
Gas services	3,000	
Special services	—	
Electrical services	26,000	
Lifts / hoists / conveyors	—	
Fire protection	7,000	
Lightning protection	3,000	
Burglar protection	3,000	
Audio systems	3,000	
Special installations	—	
TOTAL COST (taken to summary)	£290,000	
TOTAL FLOOR AREA	600 SQUARE METRES	
PRICE / SQUARE METRE	£483	
DATE PREPARED	6TH MAY 1988	

Fig. 9.5 Cost plan

At stage E the design is developed in a more finished form, including more detailed drawings and specifications and incorporating the specialist contributions of the various consultants. The drawings and specifications will form the basis of the production drawings prepared at the next stage.

Once again meetings will take place between the various members of the design team and, where necessary, further information will be obtained from the client, mainly on a matter of detail.

The precise extent of the work done at this stage, and during the preceding stages, will vary to some extent from project to project but will include most design details, coordination of the work of all the consultants, including the structural design and building engineering services, and finalisation of details of the standard of equipment, materials, and finishes to be incorporated in the buildings. Any consents relevant to this stage will be applied for.

Discussions will take place, and agreement be reached, as to the tendering procedures for the main contract and subcontracts and the advance ordering of any materials critical to achieving the required programme.

If it was not done at the previous stage it will now be necessary to 'freeze' the design, or in other words to refuse to allow any futher variations in the design. This is essential because variations which particularly to the client may seem of a minor nature can have significant implications on building engineering services, structural design, and the construction programme. An example of this is that the client might decide to exchange an area of office space originally located on the top floor with a library housing rare books originally located on the ground floor. The client might consider this change quite insignificant, requiring little more than a change of name, but in fact it is likely to have important implications with regards to floor loadings and environmental conditions. As has already been stated, it is important that everyone, client and design team, is made aware that any changes at all can result in abortive work, delay, and additional costs.

At this stage, as at all other stages, the quantity surveyor will check that the design is being kept within the cost limits. At the completion of this stage the design team will report back to the client and supply him with copies of relevant drawings and specifications. Subject to the fee arrangement agreed with the client, the architect is entitled to another 20% of his fees.

9.9 Stage F: production information

At this stage the detailed drawings and specifications are completed, incorporating the specialist design work done by the consultants and nominated subcontractors and suppliers. It is an important stage as it involves most of the production information which will be used by the contractor to construct the building accurately, economically, and efficiently. Particular care therefore needs to be taken. Failure to do so will inevitably lead to increased costs, either initially because the contractor is not sure what is required and covers the worst possible case when preparing his tender, or at a later stage when missing items form the basis of a claim for extra money.

Coordination is required between the work of the various members of the design team, and meetings will take place to ensure that harmony is achieved. A checklist may be used to ensure that the production information is properly organised. An example of such a standard checklist is shown in Figure 11.12.

Drawings required will include location drawings, such as site layouts, and general arrangement drawings. When these are ready, negative copies will be prepared and distributed to the various consultants. This will, for example, enable the building engineering services consultant to plot the services on the floor plans. Other drawings required are assembly drawings and component drawings. Schedules will also be needed. It is vital to ensure that all drawings are accurate, comprehensive, and complete. A drawing checklist is a valuable aid in this respect. A typical example of such a document is given in Figure 11.13.

Work will be done on the specification. This, in theory, used to be provided by the architect, but increasingly nowadays the quantity surveyor takes responsibility for it and it becomes an integral part of the bills of quantities.

The production information produced by the architect is also used by the quantity surveyor to prepare the bills of quantities. The bills are produced mainly at stage G, but there will often be an overlap between the stages. The architect will need to liaise closely with the quantity surveyor at stage F to ensure that the overall cost is kept within the cost limits.

In order to ensure that the work continues to be coordinated, it will be necessary at this stage for all members of the design team to have meetings. The work needs to be planned properly, information from the client and other sources distributed, and responsibilities established.

Specialist quotations are likely to be obtained at this stage and, if the proposed programme warrants such action, client agreement may be obtained to place advance orders for certain materials and work. Applications for any outstanding statutory approvals will have to be made.

This is generally the stage at which preliminary work will take place on tendering and contract arrangements. Agreement needs to be reached with the client as to the names of the contractors who will be invited to tender for the job and a check made as to their suitability.

If consideration is being given to including on the list the names of contractors who are unknown to the architects, they will generally be sent a standard letter asking them to supply information about their organisation and previous jobs they have undertaken. An example of such a letter is shown in Figure 11.14. Sometimes it will be necessary to obtain references from architects or clients they have worked for previously. An example is shown in Figure 11.15. Figure 11.16 shows an assessment form to help decide the suitability of a prospective tenderer.

The tender programme will also have to be decided. Certain information needs to be gathered together in readiness for the preparation of the tender documents. This particularly refers to information which will be included in the 'preliminaries' section of the bills of quantities, such as arrangements for visiting the site, trial or borehole details, site restrictions, etc. Often, decisions as to the form of contract will be made at this stage.

Stage F is also an appropriate time to consider, and discuss with the client, the appointment of the clerk of works and resident engineer, assuming that the size of the project warrants such appointments.

9.10 Stage G: bills of quantities

At this stage the most important thing the architect does is to hand over to the quantity surveyor a full set of his, and the various consultants', drawings and other documents so that the bills of quantities can be prepared. This does not mean that every drawing required for the project will necessarily be completed. However, it does mean that all drawings, schedules, specification notes, sketches, and other information which the quantity surveyor requires in order to prepare accurate bills of quantities must be handed over to him.

The architect's work does not end there, however. As the quantity surveyor begins to prepare the bills of quantities there will probably be a steady stream of queries. Some of these will be made and answered by telephone, and others by fax or e-mail. Perhaps the quantity surveyor will sketch details on A4 paper to record what has been agreed between him and the architect. The architect may also visit the quantity surveyor's office to resolve some queries. It is also common practice for question-and-answer sheets to pass to and fro between the architect and quantity surveyor.

Everyone, for example the consultants, must be informed of the changes and decisions resulting from the day-to-day discussions between the architect and the quantity surveyor. The architect will, of course, ensure that his drawings, schedules, and other documents are corrected and updated as necessary.

Meetings will be held by the design team at this stage. They will include meetings of all team members. A typical agenda for such a meeting is shown in Figure 11.17. There will also be less-formal meetings between individual members to discuss matters of detail.

As has been previously stated, the bills of quantities document is prepared in stages, so, initially, changes and additions to drawings can be made without too much trouble or inconvenience to the quantity surveyor and others. However, as the time to 'abstract and cast' is reached, and certainly by the time of billing, it is too late for any more revisions or additions. This is another stage of the 'freezing' process discussed in section 9.8 on stage E. Changes which are required after this point are too late to be billed and are recorded as draft architect's instructions.

Any work which is not possible for the quantity surveyor to detail fully when the work is billed needs to be entered as a prime cost or provisional sum. This will normally include major subcontracted items, such as building engineering services. This means that before stage G has ended it will be essential for the architect to have obtained quotations for all items which will be undertaken by nominated subcontractors and suppliers.

Stage G is a busy time, particularly for quantity surveyors, but also for the architect and other members of the design team. In order to ensure that nothing is forgotten, a standard checklist for stage G may be used. An example is shown in Figure 11.18.

If it has not been done at the previous stage, the architect will discuss the appointment of the site staff. In addition to the clerk of works, on a large job with a high building engineering content, there may also be a specialist clerk of works to take responsibility for this part of the project. There will also be a resident engineer to look after the structural aspects. As the client will pay their salaries and expenses he will obviously have to agree the terms of their appointments. The people involved in making the appointments will probably meet to discuss the matter, including the role of each of the site staff. A typical agenda for such a meeting is shown in Figure 11.19.

The architect will also want to be sure that as soon as the bills of quantities document has been completed, the next stage (stage H, tender action), can commence. Sets of drawings will therefore be assembled to issue the bills of quantities and other contract documents, and anything else which needs to be done in order to proceed to the next stage will be done.

If the final list of tenderers has not already been agreed with the client and quantity surveyor it should be prepared at this stage. It is common practice at stage G to send preliminary invitations to all tenderers on the list, in readiness for sending the formal documents when stage H (tender action) is reached. A typical letter is shown in Figure 11.20. The progress from inception to tender is a lengthy one, so it is important not to delay this progress by indecision at the point where one stage finishes and another starts.

At this stage, as at all others, it is important that the client is kept fully in the picture. If there is a risk of anything going wrong the client must be told. For example, it is possible that all approvals have not been received, or that the insurance company has not agreed the design and construction. Whatever the possible problem the client must be informed. Honesty and straightforward approach at all times is truly the best policy. In particular, if the client insists on proceeding before all necessary approvals have been received it must be made quite clear to him that he is going ahead at his own risk.

At this stage 15% of the fees will typically be due, so if this is the agreed arrangement the architect will present the client with his account for this amount. This is a convenient point to state that the architect must make sure that the client pays all outstanding bills. He needs to ensure that bills are submitted and paid promptly.

Having completed the work for this stage the architect should check that his records are in order and up to date. He should file away sets of documents, clearly stamped as follows:

- drawings and documents supplied to the quantity surveyor;
- drawings and documents supplied to nominated subcontractors and suppliers;
- architect's draft instructions to be issued when the contract is let;
- drawings and documents to be supplied as contract documents.

9.11 Stage H: tender action

At this stage the architect is involved with obtaining tenders and making decisions on the contract. He is in contact with the client and advises on the appointment of the successful contractor.

A meeting with the client is particularly important at this stage, not only to get confirmation to proceed further but also to settle any outstanding matters in relation to the obtaining of tenders. These could include finalising the choice of contractors who will be invited to tender for the project, agreeing the form of contract, and confirming tender procedures. This will also be a convenient time to check that the client fully understands his own roles and responsibilities and those of the architect during the contract period, as well as giving a further warning of the financial effects of any late changes.

If a preliminary letter to the selected tenderers, confirming their willingness to tender for the job, was not sent at the previous stage, it will be done at this stage.

The documents required for tendering will now be assembled into sets, consisting of two copies of the bill of quantities and specification, a set of drawings and schedules, two copies of the form of tender (see the typical example in Figure 11.21), an addressed envelope for the return of the tender, an addressed envelope for the return of one copy of the priced bills, together with a covering letter (see the typical example in Figure 11.22).

Sometimes a pre-tender meeting will be held with the contractors, either collectively or individually. At this meeting the critical aspects of the project will be explained to the contractors, such as the way the job will be organised and controlled, the client's requirements, the programme, the general design, and construction, with particular reference to any unusual features such as special construction techniques and services requirements. The aim should be to draw the attention of the contractors to anything in the documents which is not obvious at 'first sight' but which will have a significant effect on the contractor's costs or programme. It is in everyone's interest that all contractors tender for the job with a full knowledge of the facts. There will be opportunities at such a meeting for the contractors to ask questions.

The letter of invitation to tender can then be issued, together with the documents listed previously. Copies of the letters of invitation to tender will be sent to the client, quantity surveyor, and consultants.

If there are other drawings available but which were not included in the tender documents an opportunity will be given for contractors to view them, generally at the architect's office. Sometimes the arrangement will have been mentioned in the bills of quantities or in the covering letter sent with the tender documents.

At this stage the contractors will visit the site and the architect will have to make any necessary arrangements to facilitate these visits.

It is likely that as the contractors price the work they will have queries which they will raise with the architect, and which he will answer. It is important that the architect informs all tenderers of any additional information arising from these queries.

Once the tenders have been prepared, arrangements have to be made for their opening. This may be done informally, or at a meeting with, or without, the client. Although at one time it was common practice for all contractors to be present at the opening of the tenders, this is not now the normal procedure.

A check will need to be made that all documents have been received and are in order. An initial comparison will be made of the tenders, and they may be entered on a standard form, as shown in Figure 11.24. The lowest tender will then be examined in more detail. If this is in order the tenderer can expect ultimately to receive the contract. If there are any errors in the tender, there are three possible alternatives:

- the error is corrected, but with an adjustment at the end, so that the contractor stands by his original figure;
- the error is adjusted, but the tender still remains the lowest;
- the tenderer withdraws, in this case the quantity surveyor will examine the next-lowest tender.

Having thoroughly checked the tenders and made an 'in-depth' comparison the quantity surveyor will report back to the architect, and a tender report, with a recommendation stating which tender should be accepted, will be sent to the client. Depending on the size of the project, this report may be a fairly short letter, or quite a lengthy report which includes a breakdown of the contractor's prices.

Once the client has formally accepted the tender, all the tenderers can be notified of the results. Typical letters are shown in Figures 11.25 and 11.26.

Also at this stage the architect should check there are no outstanding problems – for example statutory approvals, insurances, or rights of way – and advise the client accordingly. He will also check that there are no fees or other costs due from the client.

9.12 Concept of tendering

The concept of traditional competitive tendering is to present the client (employer) with comparable prices obtained from a number of different contractors. This is achieved by the design team, acting on behalf of the client, sending all competing contractors identical information – that is, bills of quantities, specifications, drawings, schedules – on which they can base their tenders.

A system of open tendering may be used in which any firm wishing to compete is allowed to submit a tender. The open tender system has its disadvantages. As far as the contractors are concerned it involves them in a large amount of work, with only a limited chance of success, as they are likely to be in competition with a large number of firms. The danger to the client is that if everyone is allowed to join the competition it is less likely they will all be of equal standing and reliability.

A system of selected, or closed tendering, is often preferred, and in this system the architect, generally with the help of the quantity surveyor and the agreement of the client, prepares a list of contractors who will be invited to tender. As a rule, the invited firms are known to the architect or quantity surveyor, but sometimes they are selected from contractors who respond to an advertisement in the local or technical press.

The number of firms who should be invited to tender is a matter of opinion, but some architects and quantity surveyors set the figure at between four and eight, depending on the size and type of the job. In preparing the list of tenderers it is important to ensure, as far as possible, that they are all capable of undertaking the work to the required standard and time-scale.

The architect will, on a project of any importance, prepare his list of tenderers about three months before the work is due to start on-site. This is because a number of processes are involved, and they each take time to complete. The client has to be consulted, a check has to be made that all the firms on the list wish to tender, the documents have to be assembled and dispatched, the contractors need time to prepare their tenders, the submitted tenders have to be analysed, and the successful contractor will require time to prepare to start work on-site (i.e. the contractor will need a 'lead-in' time).

Sufficient time must be allowed for contractors to prepare their tenders – generally at least four weeks, unless the project is a very small, uncomplicated one. It is worth mentioning that, particularly with selected tendering, it is good practice to award the contract to the firm who submits the lowest tender. Clearly, an architect who acts otherwise will soon lose credibility with contractors whose prices were the lowest but who were not given the jobs. The legal position is discussed in section 9.14.

Although selective tendering is a well established system, offering the client reliable information on the cost of the project and the satisfaction that the selected price is competitive, it is not the only available method. A strong case can be made for involving the contractor in the project at the design stage, mainly on the grounds that the design cannot be divorced from the construction process. If the contractor's expertise is utilised in respect of economic constructional techniques, the best use of proprietary components, and the appropriate utilisation of subcontracting skills the architect is more likely to design a building which can be built more easily, quickly, and at less cost. It is often true that if a building is easier to build the workmanship is likely to be better. Certainly, it is fair comment to say that if the design team produce details which require the craftspeople to have three pairs of hands to construct them the quality of the work is likely to suffer.

Early involvement of the contractor often leads to an early start by the contractor, particularly if the work on-site commences before all the drawings are completed. This should mean that the project will also be completed earlier, and the client will gain an earlier financial benefit from his investment.

The adoption of a system of nominating a single contractor at an early stage places an additional responsibility on both the architect and the quantity surveyor. The architect must take care to select a thoroughly reliable contractor who can make a positive contribution to the project if brought in at the design stage. The quantity surveyor will play a major role in ensuring that an effective system of cost control is established and that the nominated contractor does not overcharge the client for the work.

Standard forms and letters which may be used for the tendering procedures are shown in chapter 11.

9.13 Information for tendering

The following information will normally be sent to contractors who are invited to tender for a project:

- bills of quantities (two copies);
- specification, if not an integral part of the bill of quantities (one copy);
- one set of drawings, typically containing the following:
  - block plan, locating the site,
  - site plan, locating the position and extent of buildings, roads and pavings, services, fences etc.,
  - floor plans, sections, and elevations, showing the location of all spaces, elements, and materials, including the following:
    - demolitions,
    - excavations and earthworks,
    - foundation arrangement, including piling and underpinning work,

- concrete work, including positions and general profiles of all slabs, beams, walls, columns, and staircases,
- steel frames, including positions of beams and columns,
- brickwork and blockwork, including positions of all openings, piers, special features, etc.,
- wall panels,
- finishes to all walls, floors, ceilings, and roofs, clearly defining the positions and extent of each finish,
- tanking to basements and other areas, and other special waterproofing treatments,
- glazing,
- painting,
- services, with routes of ducts, pipes, and cables;
- assembly drawings to clarify unusual details, or items which cannot be adequately described in the bills of quantities or specification;
- component drawings, including the following:
  - windows and curtain walling,
  - doors and shutters,
  - rooflights,
  - pre-formed staircases, ladders, and balustrades,
  - duct covers,
  - built-in fittings;
- information, on, for example, loadings (required for the contractor's temporary works items, such as formwork and craneage);
- forms of tender (two copies);
- addressed envelope for the return of the tender,
- covering letter sent out with the documents and containing the following information:
  - list of enclosures,
  - time, date, and place for the return of tenders,
  - details of when, how, and where additional drawings to those sent to the tenderers can be inspected,
  - arrangements for inspecting the site,
  - time, date, and place where the tenders will be opened and whether contractors may be present (note that generally this will not be permitted),
  - a request for contractors to acknowledge the safe receipt of all the documents.

9.14 Architect's responsibility towards tenderers

It is a long-established practice when inviting contractors to tender to state that no guarantee is given to accept the lowest tender, or any of the tenders, submitted. At the 'invitation to tender' stage the architect is therefore under no legal obligation to any of the contractors who are tendering.

An obligation arises when a contract situation occurs, as a result of both parties accepting an agreement, that is, when an offer made by one party (the contractor) is accepted by the other party (the employer).

When a contractor submits a tender he is deemed to have made a firm offer to build a specific building, for a stated price, in a stated period of time. The contractor may, when submitting his tender, add conditions on the form of tender sent to him, and they will become part of his tender offer. If the architect, acting on behalf of the employer, accepts this tender offer, a binding contract takes place. If the architect objects to the conditions which the contractor has added to his tender offer, there is no binding contract. This is in accord with one of the principles of a binding contract – that the parties to the contract must reach an agreement.

The translating of the contract into a written agreement should be a matter of form, once the architect, acting for the employer, has given an unqualified acceptance of the contractor's tender offer.

After the tenders have been received the architect, generally with the help of the quantity surveyor, will check that the contractor has not made any errors in pricing the bills of quantities. If a serious mistake has been made, the architect is under an obligation to draw the contractor's attention to the error and give him the opportunity to remedy the situation.

If the architect fails to draw the contractor's attention to errors he may find himself sued by the contractor. This situation arose in a case which came before the courts in 1955 – *Dutton* vs *Louth Corporation*. The contractor claimed that the architect misled him into signing a contract, because he (the architect) had noticed an error of £100,000 in the contractor's priced bills of quantities but had not drawn the contractor's attention to it. At the original hearing the contractor won his action against the architect and the Corporation, but the judgement was subsequently reversed by the Court of Appeal. The grounds for this reversal was that although the architect had not drawn the contractor's attention to this particular error of £100,000 he had given a general warning to the contractor that there were serious errors in his bills of quantities.

9.15 Stage J: project planning

At this stage the contract documents are prepared and signed. As a preliminary to this the architect will generally meet with the client, and probably also with the contractor, and settle any outstanding contractual matters.

At the meeting with the client, if he has not previously done so the architect needs to explain clearly the detailed workings of the contract, particularly the role of the client, as the employer, and the role of the architect, as the employer's agent. It has to be remembered that each of these parties has responsibilities and rights. It is also important to explain the method of payment, including the use and meaning of interim certificates, architect's instructions, variations, and retention. It is particularly important that the client be told tactfully, but firmly, that if the contract is to run smoothly everyone must understand and honour their rights, responsibilities, and limitations. A checklist is a useful aid to ensure that nothing is forgotten. An example is shown in Figure 11.27.

At the meeting with the contractor the architect will confirm the content of the contract documents and agree any outstanding contractual points, including the appointment of any nominated subcontractors. The architect will present the contractor with a list of firms he is considering using in addition to those already selected and named at the tender stage. He will check that the contractor has no objection to any of the names on the list. Letters will be sent both to the successful and to the unsuccessful subcontractors and suppliers. Examples of typical letters are shown in Figures 11.25 and 11.26. Official instructions will also be sent to the contractor telling him to accept the subcontractor's quotations. The full procedure for placing orders formalising the subcontract work with the nominated subcontractors, which was described in section 8.22 will then be set in motion.

The architect will also remind the contractor to obtain his written agreement on the domestic subcontractors he wishes to use. This is to ensure, for example, that the contractor does not employ a subcontractor who has recently provided the architect with a poor service on one of his other recent projects.

Critical programme dates will need to be agreed, including dates for the possession of the site. He will probably also inform the contractor of the date of the initial project meeting between the design staff and the contractor. Project meetings are those which take place before work starts on-site, at which stage they are termed 'site meetings'.

Following the meeting with the contractor the contract documents need to be prepared, including the completion of the agreement and appendix and the deletion of clauses from the conditions as appropriate.

There are a number of operations involved in the signing of the contract, and these are, in summary, as follows:

- preparation of sets of contract documents;
- despatch of the contract to the contractor for checking and signature;
- sending of the contract to the employer for signature;
- checking that all documents are in order;
- sending the contractor a copy of the contract;
- retaining the client's set of the contract documents, with his agreement;
- checking the contractor's insurances;
- informing the client of his insurance responsibilities.

It is now necessary to assemble the production information in readiness for the project meeting. This will consist of two copies of the drawings, schedules, bills of quantities and specification, as well as the architect's instructions already issued. Copies will also be required of statutory approvals, any additional decisions on nominated subcontractors and suppliers, and a copy of the architect's and contractor's programmes.

Prior to the project meeting the architect will often hold a meeting to brief the site supervisory staff. Typical agenda notes for such a meeting are as follows:

- introduction of employer, architectural staff, quantity surveyor, consultants, clerk of works, and resident engineer;
- outline of the main features of the contract with regard to the design, construction, and programme;
- handing over of relevant documents (e.g. copy of contract, drawings, bills of

quantities and specification, drawing register, site diary, report forms, and checklists);
- procedure regarding on-site instructions, including architect's instructions and clerk of works' instructions;
- procedures on communications (e.g. site meetings);
- methods of checking work and maintaining quality control (e.g. site tests, conformity with British Standard Specifications and codes of practice), visits to contractor's and subcontractors' workshops);
- keeping of site records;
- clarification of limitation of site staff's power (e.g. to do nothing which may incur extra costs or delay the job, without first refering to the architect).

One or two project meetings will be necessary before work actually starts on-site. Notes on typical agenda items for these meetings are given as follows:

- introduction of participants, who, typically, but not always, will consist of the employer, architect partner, job architect, quantity surveyor, consultants, clerk of works, resident engineer, contracts manager, and site manager;
- handing over to the contractor of production information previously assembled;
- site arrangements, such as possession date, site access, services diversions, security arrangements, location of huts, temporary services, and sign boards;
- decisions on site meetings, including venue, chairperson, participants, agendas, and minutes;
- procedures for communications;
- procedures for issuing instructions and information;
- queries on subcontractors and suppliers;
- financial arrangements, particularly method of payment, variations, and day-works.

10

Contract procedures

10.1 Introduction

The second main part of a building contract commences when the work starts on the site, and ends when an analysis is done of the completed building, to decide whether or not the project has been a success.

The following three stages are included in this part – all of them take place after the contract has been signed:

> stage K   operations on-site,
> stage L   completion,
> stage M   feedback.

10.2 Stage K: operations on-site

At this stage the site is handed over to the contractor and the actual building process commences. Throughout this period, regular site meetings are held, and the architect, with the help of other members of the design team, will carry out overall supervision and arrange for payment for the work.

From the point when the site is handed over to the contractor, until the finished building is handed over to the client, the site becomes the total responsibility of the contractor. In handing over the site, the architect should remind the contractor of his obligations in respect of security and site safety. The contractor should be informed of any special conditions applying to the site, such as rights of way, preservation of existing trees, and protection of neighbouring properties. The handing over of the site should normally be done by means of a letter sent by the architect to the contractor, which records both the date and conditions which apply to the site. A typical letter is shown in Figure 11.30.

Now that the work is about to start on-site the architect will check that the contractor has copies of all the drawings and other information he requires, including the full details for setting out. He will remind the contractor of the importance of keeping one set of contract drawings and one copy of the bills of quantities on the site.

Generally, the contractor and architect will meet on-site to resolve all outstanding items relating to the setting out of the work which were not settled at the project meeting held during the previous stage. These items could include some of the following:

- siting of temporary huts, storage areas, mixing areas, temporary roads and pavings, and spoil heaps;
- position of fences, hoardings, and access into the site;
- position of the main sign board, to the architect's design;
- protection to existing properties, trees, etc.;
- position of site datum and bench marks;
- problems relating to setting out.

If necessary, the architect will check the setting out and levels, or authorise the clerk of works or resident engineer to do so on his behalf.

During the whole period that building operations are taking place on the site, the architect has responsibility for general supervision. Regular inspections will take place and liaison will be maintained with the clerk of works, resident engineer, and the consultants to ensure that specified materials and constructional techniques are employed and that adequate quality control is provided. A site inspection checklist is a useful aid to ensure that the inspection and supervision is carried out in a methodical and thorough way. Typical checklists are shown in Figures 11.31 and 11.32.

The clerk of works will be carrying out a continuous check to ensure that all work is done in accordance with the latest drawings and specifications, and will inform the architect immediately he notices any discrepancies. He will issue a weekly report to the architect summarising the current position on the site. A typical example of such a report is shown in Figure 11.33.

It is important that records, including the clerk of works' daily site diary, are kept up to date. Progress photographs should be taken, generally in conjunction with the contractor. All drawings must be updated, particularly where they relate to items which will be 'hidden' on completion of the work – for example the precise position of the underground drains. On most projects, changes, even if they are of a very minor nature, take place during the course of site operations. It is important that such changes are noted and a full set of record drawings maintained.

Architect's instructions and variations will be issued as necessary, and both the client and the quantity surveyor will be kept informed. All instructions should be issued to the contractor, including those for subcontractors and suppliers. Verbal instructions should be confirmed in writing within seven days, and the clerk of works' instructions within two days. Written confirmation of architect's instructions will generally be achieved by use of standard forms. A typical example is shown in Figure 11.35.

If there are still subcontractors or suppliers who have not been nominated, the architect will have to do so sufficiently early so as not to prejudice the contractor's agreed programme. Instructions will be issued to the contractor, and the unsuccessful subcontractors and suppliers will be notified.

Particular attention will be paid to any circumstances which could lead to dealys. Preventive action will be taken where possible, but if delays are unavoidable it is necessary to establish who is responsible, as there are contractual obligations. All claims for an extension of time will be considered, and the architect will issue a Notification of an Extension of Time where applicable, generally by issue of a standard form.

Interim certificates, based on the quantity surveyor's valuation, will be issued at regular intervals, generally every month, and day works will be authorised as necessary. The architect, under the guidance of the quantity surveyor, will direct the contractor as to the amount included in an interim certificate for each sub-contractor and will also inform the subcontractor of this fact, generally by means of a standard form. The contractor has the right to expect that the certificates, including those for nominated subcontractors, will be issued by the architect strictly in accordance with the terms of the contract, and the architect has a responsibility to ensure that this happens. Standard forms will generally be used for certificates, and a typical form is shown in Figure 11.36.

The architect will hold regular meetings at the site, generally every month, although on some contracts they may take place more frequently. These meetings will be attended by the design staff, including the clerk of works and resident engineer, the contractor, and also the subcontractors and suppliers, as and when required. It is important to insist that everyone attending has the power to act for their respective companies, so that firm decisions can be made at the meetings. It is also important that the minutes are circulated soon after the meeting – within 24 hours is a reasonable period – and that the minutes clearly state what action is required and by whom. Agreement should be reached with those attending the meetings that any disagreements with the recorded minutes must be notified to the architect within seven days of receiving the minutes. A typical agenda for an architect's site meeting is shown in Figure 11.34.

The contractor will normally hold his own production meeting prior to the architect's progress meeting. This will be arranged and chaired by the contractor, but the architect will be expected to attend if invited by the contractor.

Contact must also be kept with all members of the design team regarding matters of design. On large projects there will probably be regular meetings, but on smaller projects the contact may be more informal. The main aim is to ensure that everyone is fully aware of their responsibilities and knows precisely who is supposed to do what – and when. Particular care needs to be taken to ensure that all drawings and other information required by the contractor are available to suit his agreed programme.

Regular contact will be maintained with the client. He will be particularly concerned with anything relating to progress, costs, and the finished building. The client should be sent copies of the minutes of site meetings, even if he does not attend them. He should also be sent a financial statement each month with the total cost forecast. Care should be taken to ensure that the client's approval is received for any additional costs arising from changes in the design, from additional items of work, and from adjustments to the provisional sums.

As this stage draws to a close it is necessary for the architect to prepare for completion. He will need to collect 'as built' record drawings together with all the information needed for the building owner's manual.

It will also be necessary to initiate action for the commissioning and testing of the services installation. The procedure for this will have to be agreed with the other parties who are involved but typically will be as follows:

- agree programme;
- subcontractors test their services;
- system is charged with water, air, etc.;
- system is regulated and balanced.

10.3 Site supervision

Site inspections and site supervision both take place during stage K of a building project. These two terms can be defined as follows. A *site inspection* is an examination by means of a visual inspection of the construction work by a suitably qualified person (e.g. an architect, architectural technologist, building inspector, or clerk of works) to check that all completed work has been done to an acceptable standard. Inspections are made at specific stages during operations on-site and before the work is covered up. For example, to state an obvious case, the foundations are inspected before the trenches are filled in. When inspections are made as part of the process of obtaining local authority approval, the inspector may issue a certificate of inspection. The British Institute of Architectural Technology's standard certificate of inspection is reproduced in Figure 11.49.

Site supervision is the direction of site operatives by a suitably qualified person (e.g. a trade foreman or charge hand) during the progress of building work. The supervisor will check that the work is being done to an acceptable standard, for example that the brickwork matches the sample panel.

It can be seen that site inspections and site supervision are two different things, but the supervision is often helped by the inspections. In addition to being helped by regular site inspections, site supervision is also supported by samples and testing and is formalised by means of site meetings. The purpose of site supervision is to ensure that the contractor constructs the building in accordance with the production information produced by the design team and within the terms of the contract between the employer and the contractor.

Under the terms of the contract, the contractor has a duty to comply with the specified standards of materials and workmanship and to keep a competent person on-site to take charge of the work. On projects of any significance a site manager will be in overall control and will have foremen and assistants to help him.

Supervision by the design staff will be divided between the architect and consultants, who will make regular visits to the site, the clerk of works, and possibly a resident engineer, who will generally be based on-site.

As a matter of courtesy, the architect should always notify his presence to the site manager when he arrives on-site. He must realise that the site manager is in control and must not give instructions direct to the contractor's workers. When the architect makes his site inspection, he will generally be accompanied by the clerk of works and possibly by the site manager or one of his staff.

Architects often use a standard checklist for site inspections (see Figure 11.32). This can be arranged on a trade basis, to make sure everything is properly checked, and in accordance with the production information. A check also needs to be made that the contractor's own supervision is adequate, in respect of matters such as materials and components delivered to the site, including their storage, protection, and security. It is also important to ensure that the requirements of health and safety legislation are being met. In addition to keeping a close watch on materials, workmanship, and safety, the architect will also expect the contractor to check regularly that the project is on programme.

10.4 Samples and testing

The architect will request samples of various materials and components, such as bricks, tiles, pre-cast concrete units, doors, windows, ironmongery, electrical fittings, and sanitary fittings. This is to satisfy him that the architect's and employer's requirements are being met and also, in the case of items showing on the outside of the building, that the planning authority's conditions are complied with.

In certain cases, for example external facing brickwork, the architect may request that a sample panel of the work be erected. This will be used as a standard for the whole job.

The architect may also make visits to the workshops of the contractor and sub-contractors to ensure that the components (e.g. pre-cast concrete panels) are of an acceptable standard and appearance. Concrete will be regularly tested on-site (e.g. by means of a slump test to check workability). The testing of hardened concrete will be achieved by sending cubes of concrete to an approved laboratory so that the strength of the concrete can be checked.

Other materials, such as bricks, blocks, and floor tiles, may occasionally be sent to the laboratory for testing. In all other cases the architect will expect the British and European standards to be complied with (see sections 5.4 and 5.5).

10.5 Site meetings

Site meetings are often used to formalise decisions made, and things observed, during the architect's inspections. They are generally divided into two parts, namely, policy and production.

Policy meetings

A policy meeting is likely to be chaired by the architect, working to a standard agenda, and confirming everything discussed, by issue of minutes. The aim will always be to arrive at clear and unambiguous decisions, and typically there will be a ruling that any dissent must be notified within seven days of receiving the minutes. Typical items on the agenda will be as follows:

- weather report, including working days lost since the previous meeting;
- labour force on-site, by trade;

- programme situation (note: under the terms of the contract the architect has a right to two copies of the contractor's master programme);
- architect's instructions and variations;
- daywork sheets;
- reports from the contractor, clerk of works, consultants, quantity surveyor, and subcontractors.

Production meetings

A production meeting is the contractor's meeting with the purpose of planning and organising the work, and will be chaired by the contractor. The architect or clerk of works will generally attend part or all of the meeting if requested, and other attenders will consist of key members of the contractor's staff, subcontractors, and suppliers.

10.6 Architect's instructions

However carefully the design team have prepared the production information, almost inevitably there will be a need to issue further instructions, drawings, and schedules after the contract has been signed. These additional detailed requirements and items of information are known as 'architect's instructions'. The Royal Institute of British Architects issues a standard form called Architect's Instruction which is used to record any instruction given by the architect. This is reproduced in Figure 11.35.

Architect's instructions cover a wide range of items but they are restricted to matters specifically mentioned in the contract. They include the following:

- compliance with statutory requirements;
- discrepancies in documents;
- levelling and setting out of the work;
- variations;
- making good any faults;
- removal of work or materials not in accordance with the contract;
- expenditure of provisional sums;
- subcontractor's work.

10.7 Variations

Variations are orders, issued during the course of the contract, to alter the originally specified work. They are brought about as a result of one of the following reasons:

- alterations are needed because of statutory requirements;
- alterations, additions, and omissions are required because either the employer or the architect changes their mind;
- errors or omissions have occurred in the bills of quantities.

The architect can only issue a variation within the terms of the contract. He cannot issue a variation which would radically change the whole contract, for example which would turn an office block into a hospital.

Variation orders generally mean a variation in the amount of the contract. This is achieved either by using prices for a similar item in the bills of quantities or by using daywork sheets.

A variation is an architect's instruction, but not every architect's instruction is a variation, as some merely amplify previously given information.

10.8 Daywork sheets

When variations are necessary and work is difficult to measure or value (e.g. repair work, and forming openings in work already built) there is provision in the Joint Contracts Tribunal (JCT) Form of Contract to price through daywork sheets. The daywork sheet will list the following:

- labour, given in hours, under the name of individual workers;
- materials, stating quantity and description;
- plant used;
- transport used;
- overheads, such as insurance and holidays with pay;
- percentage addition, corresponding to the amount in the bills of quantities.

There is a national schedule of daywork rates, issued by the Royal Institution of Chartered Surveyors (RICS) and the Building Employers Confederation (BEC), which will govern the rates charged.

Daywork sheets must be submitted to the architect or his representative, usually the clerk of works, within a week of the work being carried out. They must relate to an architect's instruction. The architect or clerk of works will sign the daywork sheets as accurately recording the work carried out. They will be checked by the quantity surveyor who will satisfy himself that the hours and materials are reasonable for the work undertaken, that the rates are fair, and that the arithmetic is correct.

10.9 Delays

It is an unfortunate fact of building life that building projects often run behind programme and are not completed by the date stated in the contract. These delays may be the fault of the contractor, the employer, the design team, or sometimes of outside circumstances for which nobody is really responsible.

The contract includes an agreed date when all work will be completed. Also within the contract is a provision under which the contractor can claim for an extension of time. The circumstances under which the contractor may do this are given in the next section.

The contractor must give the architect written notification of any delays and the involvement of any nominated subcontractors. The effect of the delay must be stated so that a revised completion date can be fixed.

If the delay is due to the inefficiency or incompetence of the contractor, and this results in the contractor failing to complete the building by the date stated in the contract, the contractor is liable to pay the employer what is known as 'liquid and ascertained damages'. The amount of these damages are stated in the appendix to the contract and is usually fixed at so much money per day or week.

10.10 Extension of time

An extension can be granted to the contractor if delay is due to the following:

- the actions of the architect or employer, such as
  - variations,
  - architect's instructions which delay work,
  - late issue of drawings, etc.,
  - delay by employer's directly employed staff affecting the work,
  - the opening up of completed work later found to be correct;
- actions outside the control of parties to the contract, such as
  - *force majeure* (eventualities over which the contractor has no control, such as a strike),
  - exceptional inclement weather,
  - fire, flood, storm, etc.,
  - civil disturbance.

The architect is expected to act as an independent professional in the matter of granting an extension of time. He will be aware of the fact that if he certifies an extension of time which is too short the contractor may suffer a loss, whereas if the period is too long the client will be the one to suffer.

10.11 Death of architect

If an architect dies during the course of a contract the employer will have to reach agreement with the contractor regarding the appointment of another architect. If necessary the matter will have to be referred to arbitration (see section 10.15). The matter cannot be dealt with by the deceased person's (i.e. the architect's) executors, because the architect's appointment is a personal contract between the architect and his client.

10.12 Death of employer

The situation is considered to be different if the employer (client) dies. In this case the employer's executors are expected to take over the role of employer and discharge his responsibilities and liabilities under the terms of the contract.

10.13 Bankruptcy

If during the course of the contract the contractor becomes bankrupt the employer is entitled to employ another contractor to complete the building work. In the words of the JCT Form of Contract the employment of the contractor under the contract is automatically determined, that is, brought to an end. It is generally assumed that any materials on the building site are the property of the employer. The onus is on the trustees in bankruptcy to prove otherwise.

10.14 Disputes

It is a regrettable fact of life that in all areas of human activity disputes between the parties involved do sometimes occur. In the construction industry the disagreement will be between the employer (client) and the contractor (builder) or between the contractor and subcontractor, or subcontractor and subcontractor.

The best way is obviously to avoid disputes. There are ways of promoting this approach, for example as was suggested in the Latham Report (see section 3.7 and section 11.16), by improving procedures relating to procurement and tendering. Regrettably, however, disputes will still arise despite all efforts to avoid them. In such circumstances there is a choice to be made as to whether settlement is to be by litigation or by an alternative method, such as arbitration or adjudication.

The JCT and other forms of contract have been prepared with great care and should cover most eventualities. Many disputes which arise will be settled amicably by the parties involved, and the architect will have a special part to play in this respect. Although it is the client who employs him, and pays his fees, he has a responsibility to ensure that both the employer (client) and the contractor (builder) are fairly treated under the terms of the contract. The architect is expected to act impartially in this respect, and in effect becomes an arbitrator – a person who settles disputes.

In cases which cannot be settled by the parties to the contract, even with the honest efforts of the architect, the contract contains a provision for the matter to be referred to arbitration. This avoids using the traditional alternative of bringing a lawsuit against the other party, which is invariably a longer and more expensive method of settling a dispute.

Arbitration is particularly appropriate when the dispute is technical rather than legal. It has the further advantage that the parties involved in the dispute have some control over the choice of judge if the matter is referred to a court. There are also disadvantages with arbitration compared with newer alternatives which have become available in recent years.

10.15 Arbitration

Definition
Arbitration means the settlement of a dispute between two or more parties by appointing a person called an arbitrator to whom both parties have agreed to submit their differences, and whose decision is binding on both parties.

Situation prior to 1996
Prior to 1996, when new legislation designed to improve contractual relationships was placed on the statute books, the arbitration law was piecemeal and did not provide an all-embracing code of practice. The relevant legislation at that time were the Arbitration Acts of 1950, 1975, and 1979 and the Consumer Arbitration Agreement Act 1988.

Guidance as regards arbitration was, and still is, given in the JCT standard contracts. Their Arbitration Rules were published in 1988 and lay down standard procedures for every instance where the parties to a building contract are referred to arbitration.

Arbitrators
If the parties cannot agree on the choice of an arbitrator, a suitable person will be selected by the President or Vice-President of the RIBA.

Generally, the person appointed as arbitrator will be either an architect or surveyor with a thorough knowledge of arbitration procedures, or a lawyer with some knowledge of building. His fees are paid jointly by the parties to the dispute.

Matters appropriate for arbitration
Matters which, according to the JCT contracts, can be referred to arbitration during the progress of the work are:

- appointment of a new architect or quantity surveyor, for example where the previous architect or quantity surveyor has died;
- validity of an architect's instruction;
- withholding or incorrect preparation of certificates;
- dispute in connection with the employment by the employer of others to carry out the work when the contractor has failed to comply with the architect's instructions;
- dispute in connection with an extension of time;
- result of the outbreak of war.

Other matters can generally be dealt with by arbitration after the practical completion of the contract.

JCT arbitration rules

The rules allow for a document of arbitration, a full procedure with an oral hearing, and a short procedure with an oral hearing.

Document of arbitration

With this method the claimant has to serve his statement, in writing, within 14 days of a preliminary meeting. The respondent has to serve a written statement giving his defence within a further 14 days. The claimant then has the right to serve a reply to the respondent's defence within a further 14 days.

The arbitrator may decide to interview the parties to receive further clarification of the documents. The arbitrator has to publish his decision within 28 days of receiving the last statement. There is a provision in this method for the respondent to serve a counter claim with his defence, and the other party will also be given a 14 day period to reply to the counter claim.

Full procedure with an oral hearing

The first part of the arbitration is concerned with the exchange of written statements, and follows a similar pattern to the method referred to above under the heading 'Document of arbitration'. The arbitrator then arranges the place, date, and time of the oral hearing, at which both parties will present their case. The arbitrator has to publish his decision within 28 days of the oral hearing.

Short procedure with an oral hearing

This method can only be adopted with the agreement of both parties to the dispute. The oral hearing takes place within 21 days of a preliminary meeting. The parties must send to the arbitrator, and to each other, copies of the documents which will be used at the oral hearing, at least seven days before that hearing. The arbitrator must give his decision within seven days of the hearing.

The Arbitration Act 1996

Aim

The aim of this Act is to improve and clarify existing arbitration law so as to achieve a quicker, cheaper, and fairer way of settling disputes and to promote a philosophy of prevention rather than cure.

Changes

According to a leading lawyer, David Arnold Cooper, key changes brought about by the 1996 Arbitration Act include:

- powers for the arbitrator to cap costs;
- new statutory powers for the arbitrator to act as an inquisitor;
- the arbitrators being given an overriding duty to be fair and impartial;

- the arbitrators also being under duty for parties to present their case without unnecessary cost or delay;
- unwillingness by defendants to cooperate to be taken into account if the plaintiff requires a stay on court action pending arbitration;
- greater power to award compound interest on damages and costs – these powers are now greater than those possessed by the courts;
- very severe limits on the right to apply to appeal from an arbitration award.

In the view of Lord Justice Savile, a particularly important aspect of the Act is the power it gives the arbitrator to decide his own procedures with due regard for time and cost.

> In order to perform the duties laid upon them by the Bill, arbitrators will have to take a proactive role in determining how best to proceed. If they fail to do so, they may find themselves at the wrong end of an application for their removal.

10.16 Adjudication

Method
Adjudication is a dispute-resolution process which is intended to be simple, informal, user friendly, and accessible to all who want to use this method.

Latham Report of 1994
One of the matters dealt with in the Latham Report (see section 3.7) was dispute resolution. The report included the following comment:

> a contract form with a built in adjudication process provides a clear route. If a dispute cannot be resolved by the parties themselves in good faith, it is referred to the adjudicator for decision. Such a system must become the key to settling disputes in the construction industry.

The Housing Grants Construction and Regeneration Act 1996
This Act advances adjudication as a quick and economic method of resolving disputes in the construction industry. It provides a party to a construction contract the right to refer for adjudication a dispute which has arisen under the contract. An adjudicator must be appointed within seven days of a notice being given by one of the parties. The adjudicator is required to reach a decision within 28 days of the dispute being referred to him. A duty is imposed on the adjudicator to act impartially and to take the initiative in ascertaining the facts and the law.

Use
Adjudication is likely to be used for resolving the simpler disputes, with arbitration being used in more difficult disputes and in cases where large amounts of money are involved. Litigation should continue to be viewed as a last resort.

10.17 Site diary

The site diary will be kept by the clerk of works on a daily basis to record anything of importance which happens on the site, including the following:

- time lost by bad weather;
- visitors to the site;
- deliveries of materials;
- start of key areas of work;
- arrival of subcontractors;
- information requested by contractor;
- comments made to contractor, particularly about faulty work;
- discrepancies between work carried out and drawings, for whatever reasons;
- results of site tests.

10.18 Weekly reports

These are often prepared on a standard form (see Figure 11.33) by the clerk of works and sent to the architect. Information given will commonly consist of the following:

- workers on-site, by trade;
- stoppages in hours;
- delays, with reasons;
- plant and materials on-site;
- plant and materials shortages;
- drawings and information received;
- drawings and information given;
- visitors to site.

10.19 Recording progress

One of the requirements of the JCT standard forms of building contracts is that the contractor provides the architect with two copies of his master programme for undertaking the work. If the architect has agreed to a revised completion date for the contract the contractor is also obliged to supply the architect with updated copies of the programme.

The programme is not a contractual document, and the manner in which the contractor undertakes the work is generally at his discretion. However, the contractor's programme will generally provide a useful guide against which the architect can measure the progress of the construction work.

Once work commences on-site, regular meetings will be held (see Figure 11.34 for typical agenda), and one of the most important functions of these meetings is to monitor progress. If any change to the original completion date is envisaged this will generally be recorded in the minutes of the meeting. Progress will also be recorded in the clerk of works' weekly report (see Figure 11.33).

The clerk of works' site diary, which is kept by the clerk of works on a daily basis, is useful in immediately drawing attention to occurrences which can have an effect on the construction programme. Progress photographs also have a useful part to play, and these must obviously be dated so as to provide a pictorial record of progress at particular dates.

10.20 Recording site happenings

The minutes of site meetings, the clerk of works' site diary and weekly reports, and the progress photographs will also be a means of recording all other items which can influence the progress, cost, and standard of the construction work.

The information is invaluable if disputes arise, particularly if they result in claims by the contractor for extra money or an extension of time. People's memories are sometimes inaccurate, and written evidence is generally necessary to settle disputes.

All the architect's instructions must be in writing, and a careful record must be kept as to the dates specific drawings were supplied to the contractor and subcontractors, including the revision letters.

10.21 Information to be provided by the contractor

The JCT standard forms of building contracts place the contractor under an obligation to provide the architect with certain information during the course of the contract. In summary, the contractor must:

- provide and update the master programme;
- return drawings to the architect if requested;
- offer proof, if requested, that materials used comply with the architect's specification;
- give notice of any delays;
- provide information on claims by nominated subcontractors;
- use the necessary documents to adjust the contract sum;
- give notice of fluctuations in the cost of labour and materials from the figures originally entered in the bills of quantities.

10.22 Insurances

The architect has the responsibility of ensuring that work on the site does not begin until the contractor has taken out the insurances necessary to cover any eventuality likely to occur.

The JCT standard forms of contract require the contractor to arrange for the following insurances:

- Insurances will be needed against injury to persons and property due to the negligence of the contractor or by those he is responsible for. This will generally be covered by the contractor's own comprehensive policy, and the architect will need to check that the cover in this policy is adequate and that the premiums have been paid. The appendix in the conditions of contract state the amount of cover required.
- Joint insurance in the names of the employer and the contractor will be required against claims for loss or damage to any property which does not result from the contractor's negligence. This insurance is covered by a provisional sum in the bills of quantities. Before the work commences on-site, the architect gives an instruction to the contractor on how this provisional sum is to be spent. Although this insurance is taken out in the joint names of the employer and the contractor it is the responsibility of the contractor to arrange the insurance and to pay the premiums. The architect will, however, check that the cover is adequate and that the premiums have been paid.
- Insurance of the work against fire and other risks will be needed. Responsibility for the risk may vary from contract to contract, between the employer and contractor. It is important for the architect to check the responsibilities of these two parties so that sufficient cover has been arranged and that the premiums have been paid. The situation tends to be particularly complicated when the building work consists of extensions and alterations to existing buildings.

Ensuring that the right kind of insurance cover has been arranged for all likely eventualities can be a difficult business, and the architect needs to discuss the matter with his client and, if necessary, with the contractor and an insurance broker or other expert before the building work commences.

This is borne out by a case (*Gold* vs *Patman Fotherington*) which came before the courts in 1958. In this case the employer sued the contractor for failing to insure him against the risk of damage to properties adjoining the building site being likely to collapse or subside. During the erection of an office block on the employer's site, piling operations took place and resulted in damage to adjoining properties and the employer was sued by the adjoining owner. In turn, the employer sued the contractor. The employer lost his case against the contractor on the grounds that the obligation imposed by the bills of quantities was for the contractor to insure himself but not the employer.

10.23 Stage L: completion

The main event at this stage is to accept the building on behalf of the client. There is also work to be done in preparing for the handover and matters to be settled after the handover has taken place.

The first activity is a pre-completion check, which consists of the following items:

- Instruct the contractor to give adequate notice of practical completion and check with the aid of the clerk of works that the date given by the contractor is a realistic one. Note that practical completion is the stage when

- all work has been completed in accordance with the contract documents and the architect's instructions,
  - the building is ready for the client, that is, he can take it over for its proper use.
- Inform the client of the proposed handover date and explain the procedure for this stage, including the need to insure the building and contents prior to handover.
- Inspect the building, listing the outstanding work – this list is commonly known as the snagging list – and circulate the list.
- Ensure that services installations are tested and commissioned as agreed at the end of stage K (operations on-site).
- Make sure that 'as-built' record drawings are up to date and ready for issue. Two copies will be supplied – generally one to the client and one to a third party, for example the client's bank. These record drawings will generally include the architect's, consultant's, and subcontractor's drawings.
- Make sure that the building owner's manual, particularly the section dealing with services items, is ready.

When the pre-completion checks have taken place, the handover meeting can be held. The programme for this meeting will generally include the following:

- an explanation by the architect as to the purpose of the meeting;
- a tour of the building during which
  - defects are noted and listed,
  - a check is made that the contractor's property has been, or will be, removed from the site,
  - a check is made that the services are working, meters are read, and fuel stocks are checked;
- the handover, including the following:
  - a set of record drawings,
  - the building owner's manuals, which include information on operating the services and on maintenance,
  - the health and safety file, as required under the Construction (Design and Management) Regulations 1994 (see section 4.16),
  - keys;
- agreement on procedure for the defects liability period.

Following the handover, the Certificate of Practical Completion can be issued. An example is shown in Figure 11.37. The architect issues this to the contractor, with copies to the client and the quantity surveyor. At this stage:

- the contractor is entitled to receive part of the retention fund;
- the defects liability period begins;
- the contractor is no longer responsible for insuring the work;
- the period of final measurement begins;
- any outstanding matters in dispute can be referred to arbitration as they occur (e.g. a dispute on an architect's instruction, or improper withholding of money); however, most items will await completion of the contract.

The employer (client) now takes full responsibility for the building, and the contractor, consultants, and subcontractors explain the workings of the equipment to the employer's staff.

Once the employer takes over the building, the defects liability period commences. This is the period of time, generally six months, when any defects resulting from faulty workmanship have to be put right by the contractor.

The role of the architect in respect of the defects liability period can be summarised as follows:

- The architect, after practical completion, makes sure the contractor has a full list of defects apparent at that stage.
- The architect checks that the contractor is carrying out the work in accordance with an agreed programme.
- If necessary, the architect visits the site to inspect the work.
- The architect asks the client to tell him of any defects which occur during the defects liability period. These defects may be dealt with immediately, or later.
- About three or four weeks before the end of the defects liability period, the architect visits the site, to meet the client and to prepare a list of defects. This is generally done with the clerk of works, and sometimes the clerk of works will undertake this task on his own.
- The architect sends a list of the outstanding defects to the contractor.
- The architect agrees a programme of work.

At the end of the defects liability period the architect has to:

- check with the contractor that all outstanding work has been completed;
- make arrangements for the final inspection;
- make the final inspection, with the client and the contractor, and probably with the clerk of works, quantity surveyor, and consultants also in attendance.

Following the final inspection, the Certificate of Making Good Defects is issued to the contractor. An example is given in Figure 11.38. This signifies the completion of the job and means that the second half of the retention fund is released to the contractor.

10.24 Certificates

On most projects the contractor cannot be expected to wait until the end of the job before he is paid. It is usual therefore for him to be paid by instalments, generally every month, so that he is able to finance the work adequately. This is achieved by the architect issuing certificates, indicating to the employer how much money the contractor is entitled to receive.

In deciding the amount of the certificate, the architect is expected to act as an independent professional and not as the client's agent. In a court case in 1987 (*Michael Sallis and Co. Ltd.* vs *Calil and Calil and William Newman and Associates*) the judge ruled as follows:

It is self evident that a contractor who is a party to a JCT contract looks to the architect to act fairly between him and the building employer in matters such as certificates. . . . If the architect unfairly promotes the building employer's interest by low certification, or merely fails to exercise reasonable care and skill in his certification, it is reasonable that the contractor should not only have the right as against the owner to have the certificates reviewed in arbitration, but should also have the right to recover damages as against the unfair architect.

The certificates issued during the course of the contract are known as 'interim certificates'. When the building is completed, apart from any defects which may come to light during the defects liability period, a 'certificate of practical completion' is issued. When the defects have been made good at the end of the defects liability period a Certificate of Completion of Making Good Defects is issued. The final account is then prepared by the quantity surveyor, to calculate what outstanding money is due to the contractor, and the 'final certificate' is issued. Examples of these certificates are shown in Figures 11.36–11.39.

Interim certificates are issued at periods stated in the appendix to the contract, which is usually at monthly intervals. The normal procedure is for the quantity surveyor to make a valuation to decide how much is due to be paid. The amount will consist of the value of the completed work, and materials delivered to the site for use on the contract, less previous instalments and the amount deducted for retention.

The retention is the sum of money, expressed as a percentage, which is withheld so as to safeguard the employer in case something goes wrong. All the work has to be completed in a satisfactory manner before the retention money is paid to the contractor. The amount of the retention is written in the appendix to the contract, but generally 5% is retained for contracts worth up to £500,000 and 3% for contracts above this figure.

The employer is retaining the money as a trustee for the contractor. In other words, although the employer retains the money it does not belong to him but is held in trust for the contractor until such times as the contractor has fulfilled all obligations. This is important if a situation arises where the employer becomes bankrupt, for it means that creditors would not be able to make claims upon the retention money.

When the architect receives the valuation from the quantity surveyor he issues a certificate to the contractor, except in the case of the local authority edition of the JCT contract, when the certificate is issued direct to the employer.

Under the terms of the contract, the employer is liable to pay the contractor the amount stated in the architect's certificate within 14 days. The architect must, at the time of issuing the certificate, tell the contractor how much of the certificate money is intended for each nominated subcontractor. There is a special form known as a 'direction' which can be used for this purpose. Each nominated subcontractor should also be informed.

10.25 Final account

As has been mentioned in the above section, before the architect can issue his final certificate the quantity surveyor must prepare a final account.

The final account will be a statement of costs, in which the original contract sum is adjusted by items such as variations, fluctuations in the cost of labour and materials from those prevailing at the time the contract was signed, and accounts from nominated subcontractors and suppliers. The contract will stipulate when the final measurement and preparation of the final account must take place.

Any measurement of work necessary for the preparation of the final account will normally be undertaken by the quantity surveyor in conjunction with the contractor. The quantity surveyor has to present his final account to the contractor, and obtain his agreement. When this has been done the final account, sometimes in a simplified form, should be sent to the employer.

Generally both employer and contractor will view the arrival of the final account with considerable interest. The employer will desire to be told of his total commitment, and the contractor will be anxious to receive the remainder of the money due to him.

10.26 Stage M: feedback

'Feedback' is the final stage of the RIBA Plan of Work. Its main purpose is to keep a record of what has happened in the past in order to achieve an improved performance in the future.

The architect has the following two responsibilities after the building is completed.

- The architect has a continuing liability in the case of a building failure. The architect and the contractor have a legal responsibility if there is a failure in the building. This was discussed in chapter 4.
- The architect has a voluntary responsibility to benefit from lessons learnt. In order to benefit from the results of a project, the architect can ask himself a series of pertinent questions. Some examples are given below.
  - Was the job profitable as far as the design team were concerned? If not, why?
  - Did the design process work smoothly?
  - Did the contractor work well?
  - Was there a good working relationship between the design staff and the contractor's staff?
  - Could the design staff, by different detailing, etc., have helped the contractor erect a better building, more quickly?
  - Does the completed building look nice and fit in with its surroundings?
  - Are there any details which were particularly successful, or unsuccessful?
  - Does the building function properly?
  - What does the client think of the building?

Standard documentation

11.1 Introduction

If a building project is to progress smoothly, and to programme, it is vital that everyone involved knows exactly what they have to do and when it has to be done. The architect and architectural technologist have a special responsibility for much of the documentation for this decision-making process. In practice it involves use of written material such as letters, briefing checklists, general checklists, forms, and agendas of meetings.

This chapter includes examples of these types of documentation. With the exception of the British Institute of Architectural Technology's (BIAT's) standard forms (see Figures 11.40–11.49) they relate to the factory and office mentioned in previous chapters of this book. The BIAT forms refer to a development of one-bedroomed and two-bedroomed luxury flats.

Note that the order in which the letters, checklists, forms, and agendas are illustrated reflect the order in which they would be needed in the course of a job, rather than by category.

11.2 Letters

Traditionally, letters are either individually composed or are produced in standard format with blank spaces for filling in for specific situations. In more recent years the advent of word processing has meant that a standard letter format can be adapted to give the impression that the letter was individually produced for a particular project. The letters included in this chapter can be assumed to be mainly of this type.

Letters are illustrated in Figures 11.2, 11.11, 11.14, 11.15, 11.20, 11.22, 11.25, 11.26, and 11.28–11.30.

11.3 Briefing checklists

Many architectural practices have standard briefing checklists to help them obtain all the information they need to know about the requirements of the clients and other interested parties (e.g. the statutory authorities) and information obtained from other sources (e.g. site inspections).

Briefing checklists are shown in Figures 11.1, 11.3, 11.4, and 11.6.

11.4 General checklists

Some architectural practices also make use of standard general checklists to remind their staff of the many tasks which have to be done during the course of a building project. These checklists are of particular value to less experienced architects and architectural technologists, but they can help even the most experienced staff to adopt a systematic approach to their work.

General checklists are given in Figures 11.5, 11.12, 11.13, 11.18, 11.27, 11.31, and 11.32.

11.5 Forms

Standard forms giving information and instructions are widely used for building projects. Some are produced by individual practices, some by professional bodies, such as the Royal Institute of British Architects (RIBA) and BIAT, and others by the statutory authorities.

The following forms are included in this chapter:

● architectural practices, Figures 11.16, 11.21, 11.23, 11.24, and 11.33;
● RIBA, Figures 11.35–11.39;
● BIAT, Figures 11.40–11.49;
● Statutory bodies (i.e. town planning and building control), Figures 11.8–11.10.

11.6 Agendas

An agenda can be considered as a form of checklist. It consists of a list of items which need to be considered at a meeting and help to ensure that nothing is forgotten. After the meeting, a summary of what took place is produced as the minutes of the meeting.

Agendas are illustrated in Figures 11.7, 11.17, 11.19, and 11.34.

Lane & Ralph △ *Architects*

BRIEFING CHECKLIST

PART 1 INFORMATION FROM CLIENT

Generally

1.01 Client's Name. *Mr A Henry – Managing Director*

   Address. *Henry Electronics Ltd.*
   100 Hart Road, London, SW1

   Telephone No.

1.02 Date and Place of Briefing Meeting. *1st March 1996 Client's Office*

1.03 People present. *Mr A Henry, Mr A Lane*

1.04 Client's representative for future queries. *Mr A Henry or, in his absence Mr F McCarthy, Works Manager*

1.05 Type of project. *Factory with office block*

1.06 List any drawings available from client. *Unnumbered plan of site copied from conveyance*

1.07 Names and addresses of any other architects/ professionals involved. *None*

1.08 Client's initial programme requirements. *Buildings completed and occupied by client, September 1997*

1.09 Client's Target Cost. *£1 000 000*

1.10 Any other relevant information available from client.

Approvals at Present Stage

1.11 Has Outline Planning Permission been granted? *No*

   If so, obtain copy or details.

1.12 Has any Local Authority, Government Department, or other authority made any comments on the proposed development? *No*

   If so obtain details.

1.13 Are any activities required in the building for which licences might be required (e.g. Assembly, Music and Dancing, Liquor)? *No*

Site

1.14 If site has not been purchased, what location and plan area is client considering?

1.15 If site has been obtained, state:

Location of site. *Stephen's Industrial Estate, Epsom*

Position of site related to O.S. plan or deed plan etc. *No*

Is client freeholder or leaseholder of site? *Freeholder, but check with Solicitor*

Is any part of the site agriculturally let? *No*

If so, give names and addresses of agricultural tenants.

1.16 Any known easements or rights affecting development of site.
Check with Solicitor

1.17 Existing buildings to be retained or demolished.
Small building to northwest of site can be demolished

1.18 Existing external works to be retained or demolished.

1.19 Existing natural features to be retained or demolished.
Keep mature trees if possible

1.20 Can client give any information on:

Levels? *Mainly flat with knolls around perimeter*

Nature of soil? *probably clay*

Bearing pressure? *not known*

Water table? *no water problems known*

Underground workings, faults, restrictions? *none known*

1.21 Does client know of any private sewers, septic tanks, watercourses, water supply etc., available for this development?

No

1.22 Does client have knowledge of public services available?

Soil sewer.

Surface water sewer. } *Mr Henry believes they are all available around site perimeter*

Water supply.

Gas supply.

Electricity supply. } *Mr Henry believes these are available*

Telephone.

1.23 Names and addresses of adjoining owners, if known to client.

Not known

Preferences

1.24 For any materials, externally and internally. *Likes brick*

1.25 For any structural system or construction. *Wide spans in factory area*

1.26 For any roof type (e.g. flat or pitched.) *Dislikes flat roof*

1.27 For any particular standards and methods or air-conditioning, ventilation, heating, lighting.

air-conditioning for clean-room area

1.28 How important is freedom from maintenance?

very important

Internal Planning and Construction

1.29 Determine and schedule accommodation required, with reference to the following where applicable:

(a) Activity; floor area required; acceptable location (basement, ground, or upper floor) number of occupants and sex.

general production area approx 300 sq m ground floor
clean-room area   "   300 " "   "   "
warehouse   "   700 " "   "   "
office   "   600 " " ground floor or first floor

(b) Circulation spaces.   *Leave to architect*

(c) Any limits to clear heights, spans and openings.

In factory area 4·5m clear height throughout and maximum spans

(d) Any special construction of finishes required.

'clean finish' very important

(e) Floor loading.

(f) Special fixtures e.g. lifts, cranes, conveyors, machine bases, ducts, pits and tanks.

Conversions required

(g) Structural provision for future installations or openings.

Facilities for extension

(h) Special conditions e.g. fumes, dust, noise, vibration, waste disposal, trade effluents, fire protection, mechanical handling, security.

Discuss with Mr McCarthy

1.30   Determine amenities e.g. toilets, washrooms, showers, lockers, changing rooms, rest rooms, first aid, canteen, recreation rooms, kitchen, tea points, cleaner's store, refuse disposal.

All above areas, except for recreation room required

1.31   Any anticipated provision for:
Water storage
Gas meter
Transformers, main switches, distribution switches
Boilers, fuel storage
Ventilation plant, including cooling towers
Lightning protection
Aerials

architects/ consultants to decide

External Planning and Construction

1.32 Site coverage.   *?*

1.33 New accesses from adjoining highways.   *Yes*

1.34 Planting.   *Landscaped site preferred*

1.35 Car Parking – staff and visitors.   *Mr McCarthy to provide information*

1.36 External materials, including signs. *Architects to decide*

1.37 New service roads – type, widths, loads. *Required*

1.38 Gross circulation area. *Mr McCarthy will provide details*

1.39 Service vehicles:

Uncovered parking *Required. Area to be supplied later*

Garaging *not required*

Maintenance provision *"   "*

Loading dock *"   •*

Turn-around space *required*

Petrol storage and pumps *not required*

1.40 Cycle storage *to consider and give architects decision*

1.41 Security:

Fencing *yes*

Gates *yes*

Gate control *yes*

Weighbridge *yes*

1.42 Any special external services requirements e.g. flooding.
No

1.43 Any future extensions to be provided for.
Yes, to both factory, warehouse, and office block

Fig. 11.1 Briefing checklist (obtained from client)

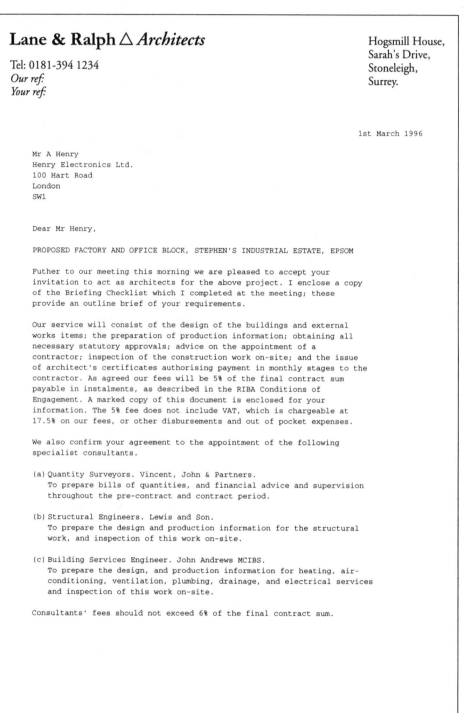

Lane & Ralph △ *Architects*

Tel: 0181-394 1234
Our ref:
Your ref:

Hogsmill House,
Sarah's Drive,
Stoneleigh,
Surrey.

1st March 1996

Mr A Henry
Henry Electronics Ltd.
100 Hart Road
London
SW1

Dear Mr Henry,

PROPOSED FACTORY AND OFFICE BLOCK, STEPHEN'S INDUSTRIAL ESTATE, EPSOM

Futher to our meeting this morning we are pleased to accept your
invitation to act as architects for the above project. I enclose a copy
of the Briefing Checklist which I completed at the meeting; these
provide an outline brief of your requirements.

Our service will consist of the design of the buildings and external
works items; the preparation of production information; obtaining all
necessary statutory approvals; advice on the appointment of a
contractor; inspection of the construction work on-site; and the issue
of architect's certificates authorising payment in monthly stages to the
contractor. As agreed our fees will be 5% of the final contract sum
payable in instalments, as described in the RIBA Conditions of
Engagement. A marked copy of this document is enclosed for your
information. The 5% fee does not include VAT, which is chargeable at
17.5% on our fees, or other disbursements and out of pocket expenses.

We also confirm your agreement to the appointment of the following
specialist consultants.

(a) Quantity Surveyors. Vincent, John & Partners.
    To prepare bills of quantities, and financial advice and supervision
    throughout the pre-contract and contract period.

(b) Structural Engineers. Lewis and Son.
    To prepare the design and production information for the structural
    work, and inspection of this work on-site.

(c) Building Services Engineer. John Andrews MCIBS.
    To prepare the design, and production information for heating, air-
    conditioning, ventilation, plumbing, drainage, and electrical services
    and inspection of this work on-site.

Consultants' fees should not exceed 6% of the final contract sum.

As mentioned at our meeting we would appreciate it if you would check the following matters with your legal advisors.

(a) Confirmation that you have freehold ownership of the site.
(b) Detail any restrictions on the land e.g. rights of way, restrictive covenants, easements.
(c) Supply a plan defining the precise boundaries of the site.
(d) Details of any previous planning permission given for the site.

We will shortly send you a Memorandum of Agreement to formalize the contract between us. Meanwhile we are commencing work on our Feasibility Report.

We would like to thank you for choosing our practice to undertake this project for you. Every effort will be made to provide you with a building which meets all your requirements, within your required time-scale.

If you have any queries please do not hesitate to contact me.

Yours sincerely

Adane

Arnold Lane

Fig. 11.2 Typical letter sent to client after initial meeting

---

Lane & Ralph △ *Architects*

DETAILED BRIEFING AT STAGE B – FEASIBILITY

ROOM/AREA NAME Clean-room

FUNCTION OF ROOM/AREA Assembly of electronic components

SHAPE/PLAN SIZE/HEIGHT 300 square metres floor area 4.5 metres clear height

ROLE OF PEOPLE USING ROOM/AREA AND NO. OF OCCUPANTS
Assembly workers, 35 persons

SPATIAL RELATIONSHIPS Between general production area and warehouse entered via special air-conditioned lobby, as Hart Road factory - take details from factory

SPECIAL FEATURES, INCLUDING LAYOUT, CLEAR SPAN
Squarish shape required, maximum clear span, Generally copy arrangement at Hart Road factory

WALL FINISHES   FLOOR FINISHES   CEILING FINISHES
smooth,   Perforated   Perforated
clean   computer-   illuminated
surfaces   type floor   ceiling

DOOR REQUIREMENTS
Smooth finish, heavy duty, self-closing

FIXTURES
As list supplied by Mr McCarthy

NATURAL LIGHTING REQUIREMENTS
750 Lux

HEATING
Kept to constant 20°C

AIR-CONDITIONING
Yes, downward flow of conditioned air from
VENTILATION perforated ceiling to perforated floor

Fig. 11.3 Part of detailed briefing (obtained from client)

Lane & Ralph △ *Architects*

BRIEFING CHECKLIST

PART 2 INFORMATION FROM INITIAL SITE INSPECTION   24th March 1996

2.01   Notes on Buildings and External works to be demolished or retained
         e.g. size, construction, and condition.

Brick building 4 x 4 m to northwest site about
24 metres from southwest boundary

2.02   Impression of contours.

Fairly flat and level but with knolls very close to
the perimeter of site at the northeast,
northwest and southwest boundary

2.03   Notes on existing natural features, including views, existing trees.

Mature oak tree near the centre of site must
be retained; if possible also retain group of
trees in west corner of site

2.04   Notes on adjoining buildings:

Owners/occupiers   Pound Products Ltd. to southeast
                             boundary

Height   about 7 metres

Construction, materials, condition

Plastic coated sheeting, flat roof - see sketch
attached. Buildings are about 10 years old
Obvious rights enjoyed

Right of support

-Proximity to site

Close to southeast boundary

2.05   Other information. Take photographs, preliminary sketches,
         measurements if necessary and feasible.

Photographs and sketches attached
Public right of way exists along
northwest boundary

Fig. 11.4 Information from site inspection

Lane & Ralph △ *Architects*

SITE AND BUILDING SURVEY CHECKLIST

SITE SURVEY

Overall measurements of site.
Measurements relating buildings to site.
Triangulation of site.
Levels of site and ground levels of buildings, and relate to suitable datum.
Heights, thickness, and materials of boundaries.
Heights, rights of light, and general description of adjacent buildings.
General description of existing buildings on-site.
Fences, railings.
Gates.
Steps, ramps.
Paths.
Paved areas.
Roads, drives.
Landscaping and natural features.
Good and bad views.
Type of soil.
Availability of gas services, with any evidence of location.
Availability of electricity services with details of any overhead lines.
Availability of telephone services with details of any overhead lines.
Availability of water services, with any evidence of location.
Drainage including surface water, soil and waste, gulleys, ventilation
pipes, fresh air inlets, manholes (size and depth), direction and flow.

BUILDING SURVEY

Floor Plans
Overall measurements of the building.
Running measurements in each room picking up door and window openings etc.,
measured to brick jambs.
Floor to ceiling heights.
Through measurements wherever possible.
Diagonal measurements.
Construction joints.
Thickness and construction of all walls.
Particulars and position of columns.
Direction of floor joints and positions of beams and roof beams.
Particulars and positions of roof lights.
Materials and finishes to walls, floors, and ceilings.
Sanitary fittings.
Particulars and sizes of doors and fanlights.
Heights from floor to sill and to head of all windows.
Roof space access.
Stairs and changes of levels.
Ventilators and louvres.
Trim (architraves, skirtings, window boards).
Drainage to show all internal soil and rainwater disposal pipes,
ventilation pipes, internal gulleys, manholes (size and depth), and
direction of flow.

Water supply and other plumbing, including stopcocks, piping runs, insulation, cisterns (sizes and means of support).
Hot water systems, including heater, piping runs, hot water cylinder, expansion-tank.
Heating system, including boiler, plant items, fittings.
Fuel storage.
Electrical installation including external wiring, point of entry, meter, lighting and socket outlets, switches, fittings, and equipment.
Gas installation including meter, piping, points, fittings, and equipment.

Sections (where practicable)
Heights from floor to floor, ceiling heights, and thickness of floors.
Depth of beams.
Height of ridge.
Construction of roof, eaves, and verge.
Construction of staircase, number of treads and direction, dimensions of rise and going.
Damp-proof courses.
Details of window and door sills and heads.

All Elevations
Running measurements to 'pick-up' all door and window openings.
Vertical measurements to 'pick-up' windows, doors, cornices, gutters, ridge, etc.
Position of down pipes, gutters hopper heads, etc.
Materials of walls and roof.
Position and sizes of chimney stacks, vent pipes, etc.
Construction joints.

Generally
Note any defects such as dampness and cause, dry rot and cause, cracks, bulges, recent repairs.

Where other buildings adjoin the site or building under survey, special note should be made of their dimensions, materials, defects, etc.

Take photographs.

Sketch perspectives of special and unusual details.

Fig. 11.5 Site and building survey checklist

Lane & Ralph △ *Architects*

BRIEFING CHECKLIST

PART 3 INFORMATION FROM LOCAL AUTHORITY

Building Regulations
3.01 Name and address of officer concerned.
Cheif Building Control Officer, Town Hall

3.02 Obtain copies of application forms and dates including waiting periods.
Forms obtained, Submit informally to Building Control Officer before making formal submission, then

3.03 Check what structural information is required. *approval likely in 4 weeks*
Full calculation required

3.04 Ask for local knowledge of soil conditions.
Firm Clay

3.05 Building line.

3.06 Hoarding control.
10 metres from southwest boundary

3.07 Any special requirements.
No

Town Planning
3.08 Name and address of officer concerned.
Cheif Development Officer

3.09 Obtain copies of application forms and dates including waiting periods.
Forms obtained. Approval can take 8 weeks after

3.10 Check: *receipt of application*

Zoning *Industrial*

Floor space index, plot ration, or density. *No special requirements*

Car parking requirements *Cater for all employees on-site,*
No parking space available outside
Height restrictions *2 storeys max* *site.*

Access restrictions *Off Pound Road only*

Materials preferences *Use of bricks encouraged*

Tree preservation orders *None*

Planting requirements *None*

3.11 Any special requirements. *None*

Fig. 11.6 Local authority briefing checklist

Lane & Ralph △ *Architects*

FACTORY AND OFFICE BLOCK FOR HENRY ELECTRONICS LTD
STEPHEN'S INDUSTRIAL ESTATE, EPSOM

AGENDA FOR DESIGN TEAM MEETING NO. 1

29th March 1996

1.00 PERSONNEL/ORGANISATIONS

1.01 Introduction of people present at meeting.

1.02 Apologies for absence.

1.03 Design team involved in project.

      Architects: Lane & Ralph

      Quantity Surveyors: Vincent, John & Partners.

      Consulting Structural Engineers: Lewis and Son.

      Consulting Building Services Engineer: John Andrews MCIBS.

      Clerk of Works: C. Robinson.

1.04 Define roles and responsibilities of personnel/organisations.

1.05 Answer questions on fees and conditions of appointment.

1.06 Establish relationships between design team members and client.

2.00 BRIEF

2.01 Background information.

2.02 Briefing and information received to date.

2.03 Further information required from client.

3.00 FEASIBILITY STUDY

3.01 Land survey.

      (a) Scope.

      (b) Responsibility.

3.02 Soil investigation.

(a) Scope.

(b) Responsibility

3.03 Statutory and other authorities

Town planning.

Highways.

Sewers.

Water.

Gas.

Electricity

Define scope of enquiries and
responsibilities of team members
for enquiries.

3.04 Cost implications.

Cost-control methods.

Cost standards and limitations.

Cost plan.

4.00 TENDER AND CONTRACT PROCEEDURE

4.01 Tenders.

4.02 Contract.

5.00 FEASIBILITY REPORT

5.01 Architect's contribution.

5.02 Quantity surveyor's contribution.

5.03 Consulting structural engineer's contribution.

5.04 Consulting building services engineer's contribution.

5.05 Presentation.

Written material.

Drawings.

Style

```
6.00  PROGRAMME

6.01  Land survey.

6.02  Soil investigation.

6.03  Meetings with statutory and other authorities.

6.04  Cost implications.

6.05  Submission of draft contributions by design team members.

6.06  Draft report assembled.

6.07  Final report completed.

7.00  FUTURE MEETINGS

7.01  Main meetings.

         (a) Date.  Time.  Place.

         (b) Persons attending.

7.02  Subsidiary meetings.

         (a) Date.  Time.  Place.

         (b) Persons attending.

8.00  DISTRIBUTION OF MINUTES

         Agree list.

9.00  ANY OTHER BUSINESS
```

Fig. 11.7 Agenda for design team meeting number 1

FOUR Completed Copies of this Form and Plans must be submitted together with ONE Copy of the appropriate Certificate TO:-

EP

BOROUGH PLANNING AND ENGINEERING OFFICER
EPSOM & EWELL BOROUGH COUNCIL
Town Hall, The Parade
EPSOM, Surrey KT18 5BY

Tel No. (0372) 732000

Date received   Date registered

DRAWINGS/PLANS	APPLICATION FOR PLANNING PERMISSION TO DEVELOP LAND OR EXTEND/CHANGE THE USE OF BUILDINGS OR LAND	
Location :		FEE DUE £ 4.560
Block :	Town and Country Planning Act 1990	
Detail :		FEE CHECKED ....
Other :		
CERTIFICATE :		
A B C D		

PLEASE READ THE ACCOMPANYING NOTES FOR APPLICANTS BEFORE COMPLETING ANY PART OF THIS FORM
If extra space is required to answer any question please attach a separate sheet indicating the relevant question(s)

1   Applicant
(In block capitals)

Name   *HENRY ELECTRONICS LTD*

Address   *100 HART ROAD*
LONDON
Post Code *SW1*

Tel No.

Agent (If any) to whom all correspondence will be sent
(In block capitals)

Name   *LANE & RALPH ARCHITECTS*

Address   *HOGSMILL HOUSE SARAH'S*
DRIVE STONELEIGH EPSOM
SURREY   Post Code

Tel No. *0181 394 1234*

2   Address or location of land *Stephen's Industrial Estate*
to which application relates   *Epsom Surrey*

Site must be shown edged RED on the submitted site plan. See Note 7. State site area in Hectares **3·1** or Acres

NOTE: Drawings in support of the application should include plan and elevations to show the relationship of the proposed development to adjacent properties, existing and proposed details and location plan.

3   Brief particulars of proposed development, including the purpose(s) for which the land and/or buildings are to be used.

Single-storey factory of 600 square metres for the assembly of electronic components together with a single-storey warehouse of 700 square metres and a two-storey office block of 600 square metres. Parking spaces to be provided for all people employed at the site, together with lorry parking

4   Particulars of application See notes 3 and 4

Is this application for:-   State Yes or No

(a)	Outline planning permission	*NO*	
or (b)	Full planning permission	*YES*	
or (c)	Approval of reserved matters following the grant of outline permission	*NO*	
or (d)	Continuance of use without complying with a condition subject to which planning permission has been granted	*NO*	
or (e)	Permission for the retention of buildings or works constructed, or for the continuance of a use of land instituted before the date of this application	*NO*	
or (f)	Renewal of unimplemented permission		

If (a) tick any of the following which are to be considered as part of this application

1 Siting   2 Design   3 External appearance
4 Means of access   5 Landscaping

If (c) or (f) state the Date and Number of outline or unimplemented permission

Date .... Number ....

If (d) state the Date and Number of previous permission and Identify the particular condition

Date .... Number ....

The Condition No ....

If (e) state the Date when the buildings or works were constructed or carried out, or the use of the land commenced

Date *2nd June 1996*

FORM TP1 (Part 1) 1991   PLG\TP1-P1

5. Is the permission sought temporary or permanent? *Permanent*. If temporary state for what period ....

If a previous temporary planning permission exists, state the date and number   Date ....   Number ....

6. (a) What is the applicants legal interest in the land? eg Owner, Prospective purchaser, Lessee, etc   *Owner* ....

(b) Does the applicant own or control any adjoining land?   State Yes or No | NO | If Yes it must be shown edged BLUE on the submitted site plan   *See note 7*

7. If the application is for new residential development, state the following:-

Density in dwellings per acre [ ]   Type (House, Flat, etc) ....   Number of Garages or garage spaces [ ]

Total number of dwellings [ ]   Number of storeys [ ]   Number of parking spaces [ ]

Total number of habitable rooms [ ]   Total gross floor area of all buildings (Sq metres/Sq feet) [ ]   *See Note 5*

8. Does the proposed development involve:- (a) Construction of a new access to a highway?   (b) Alteration of an existing access to a highway?   (c) The felling of any trees?

State Yes or No   *See Note 8*   Vehicular   Pedestrian   Vehicular   Pedestrian

If yes indicate positions on plan | YES | | YES | | NO | | NO | [ ]

(d) How will surface water be disposed of? *Connected to local authority sewers*

(e) How will foul sewage be dealt with? " " " " "

9. (a) List details of all external building materials to be used if you are submitting them at this stage   *See note 8*

Roof: *Factory - trough section aluminium sheeting*

Walls: *Golden brown sand faced facing bricks*

Other: *Windows and doors - anodised aluminium*

(b) List any samples that are being submitted   *Brick, aluminium factory roof 'slates' for office roof*

10. List all drawings, plans, certificates, documents etc; forming part of this application   *See notes 7, 8, 11 and 12*

128/1a Site plan - scale 1:200

2b floor and roof plans - scale 1:100

3d Elevations and sections - scale 1:100

11. (a) What is the present use of the land/building? If vacant, what was the land use and when did this cease?

Vacant

Last use was grazing land

(b) What buildings are to be demolished   *Brick store building*

If any state gross floor area (Sq metres/Sq feet) and the current use | 1652 m | ....

12. (a) Are any 'Listed' buildings to be demolished? *See note 10*   (b) Are any 'Listed' buildings to be altered or any non listed buildings in a Conservation Area to be demolished?   State Yes or No | NO |

State Yes or No | NO | If Yes please note that a separate application for Listed Building Consent or Conservation Area Consent will be necessary

Note   1   Form TP1 (Part 2) should now be completed for all applications involving Industrial, Office, Warehousing, Storage, or Shopping development

2   An appropriate Certificate must accompany this application unless you are seeking approval to reserved matters (See notes 11 and 12)

3   A separate Form is required for Building Regulation approval (See note 14) and/or Listed Building or Conservation Area Consent (See Note 10)

PLEASE ENSURE THIS FORM IS SIGNED AND DATED BEFORE SUBMITTING

I/We hereby apply for planning permission for the development described herein and shown on the accompanying plans

Signed   *Adam*   On behalf of   *Henry Electronics Ltd*

Date   *2nd June 1996*   (Insert Applicants name if signed by an Agent)

Fig. 11.8 Town planning application form

TOWN AND COUNTRY PLANNING
(GENERAL DEVELOPMENT PROCEDURE) ORDER 1995
CERTIFICATE UNDER ARTICLE 7

Please complete one of the following Certificates:-

(A)　Complete Certificate A if the applicant is the sole owner of the whole application and there are no leasehold owners with a minimum of seven unexpired years remaining on their lease(s).

OR

(B)　Complete Certificate B if the applicant is not the sole freehold owner or if you or the applicant is a leaseholder, tenant, or prospective purchaser. Having completed Certificate B, please fill in the Notice No. 1 below and send it to the owner(s) or part owner(s) of the application site.

*　If the application site forms part of an agricultural holding and/or there is an agricultural tenant involved, please ask the Council for a revised form of Certificate to complete.

CERTIFICATE A

I hereby certify that:-

No person other than the applicant was an owner of any part of the land to which the application relates at the beginning of the period 21 days before the date of the accompanying application.

None of the land to which the application relates constitutes, or forms part, an agricultural holding.*

Signed *A Henry*　　　　　　　Date *2nd June 1996*

On behalf of *HENRY ELECTRONICS LTD*

CERTIFICATE B

I hereby certify that:-

The requisite notice no. 1 has been given to the owner(s) of the land to which the application relates at the beginning of the period of 21 days before the date of the accompanying application.

None of the land to which the application relates constitutes, or forms part of, an agricultural holding.*

Name and address of owner _____

_____

_____

Signed _____

Date _____

Date of service of notice _____

On behalf of _____

DETACH HERE -

NOTICE No.1

An application for planning permission is being made to Epsom and Ewell Borough Council and you are the owner/part owner of the application site.

Application address _____

_____

Proposed development _____

_____

Name and address of applicant _____

_____

_____

If you wish to make representations on this proposal, please do so within three weeks of receiving this notice to the Borough Planning and Engineering Officer, Epsom and Ewell Borough Council, Town Hall, The Parade, Epsom, Surrey, KT18 5BY.

Signed _____

Date _____

On behalf of _____

Fig. 11.9 Certificate of ownership of land

FULL PLANS SUBMISSION

BUILDING ACT 1984
THE BUILDING REGULATIONS 1991

EPSOM *&* **EWELL**
BOROUGH COUNCIL

TOWN HALL
THE PARADE
EPSOM
SURREY
KT18 5BY

Epsom (01372) 732000
FAX Epsom (01372) 732365

BUILDING REGULATION PLAN NUMBER	BR /	/

PLEASE READ NOTES ON REVERSE SIDE

1.	NAME AND ADDRESS OF OWNER ...HENRY ELECTRONICS LTD 100 HART ROAD LONDON SW1... .... POSTCODE: .... TELEPHONE: ....
2.	NAME AND ADDRESS OF AGENT/BUILDER (Delete as appropriate) LANE & RALPH ARCHITECTS HOGSMILL HOUSE SARAH'S DRIVE EPSOM SURREY .... POSTCODE: .... TELEPHONE: 0181 394 1234
3.	ADDRESS OF PROPOSED WORK Stephen's Industrial Estate Epsom Surrey .... POSTCODE: ....
4.	DESCRIPTION OF PROPOSED WORK Erection of single-storey factory and warehouse and two-storey NOTE: Permission may be required under the Town and Country Planning Acts. office block
5.	USE OF BUILDING assembly of Existing use: .... Proposed use: electronic components Is the building or will the building be put to a designated use under the Fire Precautions Act 1971? Yes/No
6.	OTHER INFORMATION REQUIRED a) Number of storeys: .... b) Surface water drainage: .... c) Foul water drainage: .... d) Does the proposal involve building over a public sewer or drain: Yes/No (see note 2 overleaf)
7.	EXTENSION OF TIME Do you agree to an extension of time if items cannot be resolved within the relevant 5 week period? Yes/No Do you consent to the plans being passed subject to conditions where appropriate? Yes/No
8.	FEE (see separate fee sheets) Schedule 1, number of dwellings: .... Schedule 2, floor area: ....m2 Schedule 3, estimated cost: .... TOTAL FEE ENCLOSED £..............
9.	COMPLETION NOTICE Does the owner require a completion certificate following satisfactory notification and completion of the building work. Yes/No
10.	STATEMENT These plans are deposited in accordance with Building Regulation 11 (1) (b) and are accompanied by the appropriate fee. I understand that the inspection fee will be payable for the work following the first inspection. (Excluding extension under six square metres and works costing under £5,001). Name: ...A LANE............ Date: ...2nd June 1996............ Signature: ...A Lane............

BRFORM/SEPTEMBER 1996

INVESTOR IN PEOPLE

Fig. 11.10 Building regulations application form

Lane & Ralph △ *Architects*

Tel: 0181-394 1234
Our ref:
Your ref:

Hogsmill House,
Sarah's Drive,
Stoneleigh,
Surrey.

Mr O Henry
Henry Electronics Ltd.
100 Hart Road
London SW1

6th June 1996

Dear Mr Henry

Now that you have given us approval of our Scheme Design, I am pleased to tell you
that we are proceeding with our Detail Design Work.

This means that we have reached the stage in the pre-contract part of the project
when any alterations to the brief cannot be made without the possibility of
incurring extra costs and endangering the starting and completion dates on-site.
There is the further complication that any changes could mean that applications for
statutory approvals would have to be resubmitted, which could also lead to delay
and additional costs. We mention this because, as you are aware, we are working to
a very tight programme, and are anxious to meet your required completion date for
the project, and keep the cost within your cost limits.

Yours sincerely,

A. Lane

Fig. 11.11 Typical letter sent to a client at the start of the detail design stage

Lane & Ralph △ *Architects*

1.00 LIST OF DRAWINGS AND SCHEDULES TO BE PREPARED
      N. B. Content of each drawing to be listed, with scales.

1.01 Location drawings.

   (a) Block plans.

   (b) Site plans.

   (c) Floor plans.

   (d) Foundation plans.

   (e) Roof plans.

   (f) Sections.

   (g) Elevations.

1.02 Assembly drawings.

   (a) Use of standard drawings. N.B. Quote detail numbers.

      External walls.

      Wall openings.

      Eaves details.

      Parapet details.

      Roof lights.

      Internal walls.

      Internal wall openings.

      Suspended ceilings.

   (b) Non-standard drawings. N.B. List each drawing.

1.03 Component drawings.

   (a) Use of standard drawings. N.B. Quote detail numbers.

      Windows.

      Doors.

   (b) Non-standard drawings. N.B. List each drawing.

1.04 Schedules

    (a) Windows.

    (b) Doors.

    (c) Ironmongery.

    (d) Manholes.

1.05 Structural drawings.

    (a) Structural steel, general arrangements.

    (b) Structural steel, details.

    (c) Reinforced concrete, general arrangements.

    (d) Reinforced concrete, details.

    (e) Other drawings.

    (f) Schedules.

1.06 Building engineering services drawings.

    (a) Drainage.

    (b) Discharge pipework.

    (c) Electrical.

    (d) Water.

    (e) Heating and a.c.

    (f) Other.

2.00 DRAWING PROCEDURES

2.01 Standard sheet sizes.

2.02 Scales.

2.03 Title panel/job title/job number/numbering system.

2.04 Annotation style — stencil or freehand.

2.05 Use of computers.

2.06 Production of copy negatives.

    List who is to prepare and receive netgatives.

```
3.00  REFERENCING

3.01  Grid.

3.02  Floor levels.

3.03  Floor numbers.

3.04  Room numbers.

3.05  North point.

4.00  AGREE TOLERANCES

4.01  Structure.

4.02  Services.

5.00  SPECIFICATIONS

5.01  Method.

5.02  Contributions from consultants.

5.03  Contributions from subcontractors and suppliers.

6.00  OUTSTANDING INFORMATION REQUIRED

6.01  Client.

6.02  Consultants (structural engineering).

6.03  Consultants (building engineering services).

6.04  Subcontractors and suppliers.

6.05  Agree timetable.
```

Fig. 11.12 Checklist for organisation of production information

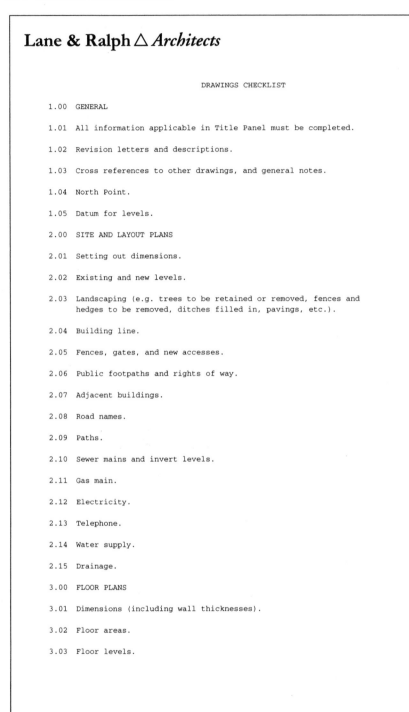

Lane & Ralph △ *Architects*

DRAWINGS CHECKLIST

1.00 GENERAL

1.01 All information applicable in Title Panel must be completed.

1.02 Revision letters and descriptions.

1.03 Cross references to other drawings, and general notes.

1.04 North Point.

1.05 Datum for levels.

2.00 SITE AND LAYOUT PLANS

2.01 Setting out dimensions.

2.02 Existing and new levels.

2.03 Landscaping (e.g. trees to be retained or removed, fences and hedges to be removed, ditches filled in, pavings, etc.).

2.04 Building line.

2.05 Fences, gates, and new accesses.

2.06 Public footpaths and rights of way.

2.07 Adjacent buildings.

2.08 Road names.

2.09 Paths.

2.10 Sewer mains and invert levels.

2.11 Gas main.

2.12 Electricity.

2.13 Telephone.

2.14 Water supply.

2.15 Drainage.

3.00 FLOOR PLANS

3.01 Dimensions (including wall thicknesses).

3.02 Floor areas.

3.03 Floor levels.

3.04 Section lines.

3.05 Room names and/or numbers.

3.06 Floor finishes.

3.07 Beams over (dotted).

      Rooflights over (dotted).

3.08 Services ducts.

3.09 Flues.

3.10 Vertical damp-proof courses.

3.11 Built-in furniture.

3.12 Door numbers, swings.

3.13 Window numbers.

3.14 Stairs (number treads, show directions up and/or down).

3.15 Roof space access.

3.16 Expansion joints.

4.00 ROOF PLANS

4.01 Dimensions

4.02 Falls.

4.03 Gutters and falls.

4.04 Rainwater outlets.

4.05 Roof finishes.

4.06 Parapet copings.

4.07 Maximum and minimum screed thicknesses.

4.08 Flues.

4.09 Vents.

4.10 Rooflights.

4.11 Lightning conductors.

4.12 Expansion joints.

```
5.00  SECTIONS

5.01  Structural and finished floor levels.

5.02  Floor to ceiling (or floor to floor) heights.

5.03  Vertical dimensions.

5.04  Foundation dimensions.

5.05  Ground level (existing and finished).

5.06  Damp-proof courses and membranes.

5.07  Roof pitches.

5.08  Tanking.

6.00  ELEVATIONS

6.01  Floor lines (related to datum).

6.02  Windows, including opening types.

6.03  Sill heights.

6.04  Soil and vent pipes.

6.05  Rainwater pipes and gutters.

6.06  Rainwater heads.

6.07  Expansion joints to brickwork, etc.

7.00  FOUNDATION PLANS

7.01  Dimensions, levels.

7.02  Reinforcement to concrete.

7.03  Position of walls.

7.04  Damp-proof courses.

7.05  Expansion joints.

8.00  DRAINAGE PLANS

8.01  Sewer main (type, i.e. foul, combined, etc.).

8.02  Position of sanitary fittings.
```

8.03 Soil and waste pipe layout.

8.04 Inspection chamber and manhole positions, sizes, inverts.

8.05 Vent pipes.

8.06 Gulleys.

8.07 Grease traps.

8.08 Rodding eyes.

8.09 Cesspool.

8.10 Soakaways.

8.11 Septic tank.

8.12 Rainwater pipes.

8.13 Interceptors.

9.00 ELECTRICAL SERVICES

9.01 Lighting points.

9.02 Power points.

9.03 Switches.

9.04 Rising main.

9.05 Meter cupboard.

9.06 Bell installation.

9.07 Alarm system.

10.00 WATER SERVICES

10.01 Rising main.

10.02 Point of entry first stopcock.

10.03 Cold water storage tank.

10.04 Hot water cylinder.

10.05 Hot water expansion tank.

10.06 Stopcocks.

10.07 Taps.

10.08 Sanitary fittings.

10.09 Fire-fighting equipment.

10.10 Overflow pipes.

10.11 Drain cocks.

11.00 HEATING AND A.C. SERVICES

11.01 Pipework.

11.02 Ductwork.

11.03 Boilers.

11.04 Tanks.

11.05 Pumps.

11.06 Terminal units.

11.07 A.C. plant.

11.08 Louvres.

Fig. 11.13 Drawing checklist

Lane & Ralph △ *Architects*

Tel: 0181-394 1234
Our ref:
Your ref:

Hogsmill House,
Sarah's Drive,
Stoneleigh,
Surrey.

4th July 1996

Porter Construction Ltd.
77 Pembroke Road
Kingston
Surrey

Dear Sirs,

FACTORY AND OFFICE BLOCK, STEPHEN'S INDUSTRIAL ESTATE, EPSOM

We will shortly be inviting tenders for the above project and are writing to ask
if you are interested in being considered for inclusion in the tender list.

If you wish to be considered will you please supply us with the following
information by the 13th July.

1. Minimum and maximum value of individual contracts your company
    is prepared to undertake.

2. Type of contract your company is prepared to undertake.

3. What work is normally undertaken by your own company, and what
    work is subcontracted.

4. The name and address of your company bankers.

5. Details of three contracts undertaken by you during the past
    three years as follows.

    (a) Address of contract.
    (b) Client's name and address.
    (c) Type of project.
    (d) Approximate contract value.
    (e) Start and completion dates.
    (f) Architect's name and address.
    (g) Quantity surveyor's name and address.
    (i) Consulting building services engineer's name and address.

Serious consideration will be given to including your name in the tender list, but
failure to do so will in no way mean your company was considered unsuitable.

Your faithfully,

Alane

Arnold Lane.

Fig. 11.14 Letter asking for information from potential tenderers

Lane & Ralph △ *Architects*

Tel: 0181-394 1234
Our ref:
Your ref:

Hogsmill House,
Sarah's Drive,
Stoneleigh,
Surrey.

11th July 1996

Brown and Taylor
Chartered Architects
44 Ascham Road
Epsom Surrey

Dear Sirs,

FACTORY AND OFFICE BLOCK, STEPHEN'S INDUSTRIAL ESTATE, EPSOM

We have been informed by Porter Construction Ltd that they recently completed a
contract under your supervision. As we are considering inviting them to tender for
an office block and factory development valued at about £1 000 000 we are writing to
ask for your opinion as to their suitability for this contract.

We would therefore be most grateful if you would kindly complete the enclosed
assessment sheet. All the information supplied by you will be treated in the
strictest confidence.

Yours faithfully,

Arnold Lane

Fig. 11.15 Letter to referee about potential tenderer

Lane & Ralph △ *Architects*

ASSESSMENT SHEET ON THE SUITABILITY FOR INCLUDING IN A TENDER LIST

Porter Construction Ltd

FOR A *factory and office block, Epsom*

COSTING IN THE REGION OF £ *1 000 000*

ITEM	PERFORMANCE Please tick		
	Below Average	Average	Above Average
Performance at pre-contract stage			
Performance of administrative staff during contract period			
Performance of site staff			
Ability to keep to programme			
Ability to meet specified quality standards			
Ability to handle subcontractors and suppliers			
Cooperation when problems arose			
Performance in meeting completion date			
Cooperation with regard to settlement of claims			

ANY OTHER INFORMATION

FROM: Name

Address

Signature
Date

Fig. 11.16 Assessment sheet on suitability of tenderer

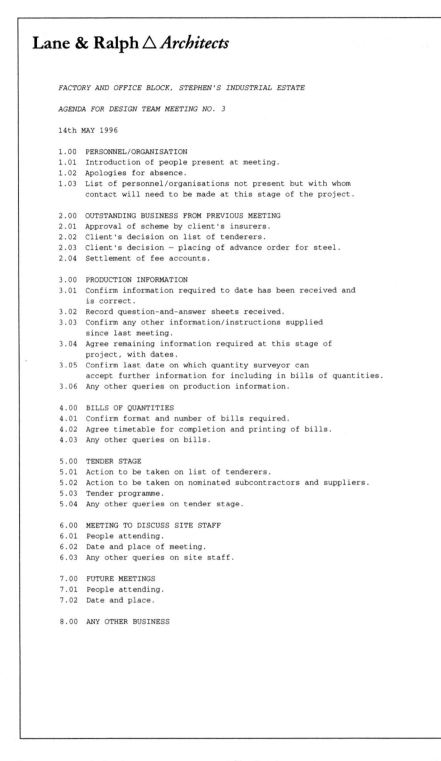

Lane & Ralph △ *Architects*

FACTORY AND OFFICE BLOCK, STEPHEN'S INDUSTRIAL ESTATE

AGENDA FOR DESIGN TEAM MEETING NO. 3

14th MAY 1996

1.00 PERSONNEL/ORGANISATION
1.01 Introduction of people present at meeting.
1.02 Apologies for absence.
1.03 List of personnel/organisations not present but with whom
      contact will need to be made at this stage of the project.

2.00 OUTSTANDING BUSINESS FROM PREVIOUS MEETING
2.01 Approval of scheme by client's insurers.
2.02 Client's decision on list of tenderers.
2.03 Client's decision — placing of advance order for steel.
2.04 Settlement of fee accounts.

3.00 PRODUCTION INFORMATION
3.01 Confirm information required to date has been received and
      is correct.
3.02 Record question-and-answer sheets received.
3.03 Confirm any other information/instructions supplied
      since last meeting.
3.04 Agree remaining information required at this stage of
      project, with dates.
3.05 Confirm last date on which quantity surveyor can
      accept further information for including in bills of quantities.
3.06 Any other queries on production information.

4.00 BILLS OF QUANTITIES
4.01 Confirm format and number of bills required.
4.02 Agree timetable for completion and printing of bills.
4.03 Any other queries on bills.

5.00 TENDER STAGE
5.01 Action to be taken on list of tenderers.
5.02 Action to be taken on nominated subcontractors and suppliers.
5.03 Tender programme.
5.04 Any other queries on tender stage.

6.00 MEETING TO DISCUSS SITE STAFF
6.01 People attending.
6.02 Date and place of meeting.
6.03 Any other queries on site staff.

7.00 FUTURE MEETINGS
7.01 People attending.
7.02 Date and place.

8.00 ANY OTHER BUSINESS

Fig. 11.17 Agenda for design team meeting at bills of quantities stage

Lane & Ralph △ *Architects*

CHECKLIST FOR USE AT STAGE - G - BILLS OF QUANTITIES

1.00 CLIENT: Check the following from client have been incorporated.
1.01 Written instructions.
1.02 Telephone and verbal instruction - confirm to client.

2.00 STATUTORY APPROVALS: Check the following have been incorporated.
2.01 Town planning requirements.
2.02 Building regulations requirements.
2.03 Fire officer's requirements.
2.04 Health and Safety at Work Act inspector's requirements.
2.05 Other statutory requirements.
2.06 Check all consents have been received.

3.00 CONSULTANTS: Check work shown on architect's drawings have been
     incorporated.
3.01 Structural engineers.
3.02 Building services engineers.
3.03 Others.

4.00 ARCHITECTS: Cross-check information on the following.
4.01 Component drawings against relevant assembly drawings.
4.02 Assembly drawings against relevant location drawings.

5.00 SCHEDULES: Check against the following drawings.
5.01 Architect's drawings.
5.02 Structural engineer's drawings.
5.03 Building services engineer's drawings.
5.04 Others.

6.00 SPECIFICATIONS: Check against the following drawings.
6.01 Architect's drawings.
6.02 Structural engineer's drawings.
6.03 Building services engineer's drawings.
6.04 Others.

7.00 QUESTIONS AND ANSWERS SHEETS: Check they are:
7.01 Included in bills.
7.02 Incorporated in drawings.

8.00 TOTAL INFORMATION USE FOR BILLS OF QUANTITIES: Record all
     information supplied and cross-check there is no conflict of information.
8.01 Architect's drawings, schedules, and specifications.
8.02 Structural engineer's drawings, schedules, and specifications.
8.03 Building services engineer's drawings, schedules, and
     specifications.

9.00 PRIME COST AND PROVISIONAL SUMS
9.01 Prime cost sums.
9.02 Provisional sums.

10.00 LATE INFORMATION
10.01 List all items.
10.02 Cover with draft architect's instructions.

Fig. 11.18 Checklist for use at bills of quantities stage

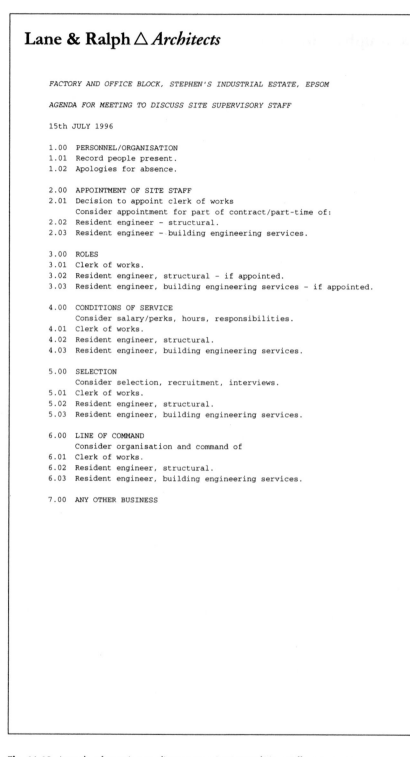

Lane & Ralph △ *Architects*

FACTORY AND OFFICE BLOCK, STEPHEN'S INDUSTRIAL ESTATE, EPSOM

AGENDA FOR MEETING TO DISCUSS SITE SUPERVISORY STAFF

15th JULY 1996

1.00 PERSONNEL/ORGANISATION
1.01 Record people present.
1.02 Apologies for absence.

2.00 APPOINTMENT OF SITE STAFF
2.01 Decision to appoint clerk of works
      Consider appointment for part of contract/part-time of:
2.02 Resident engineer - structural.
2.03 Resident engineer - building engineering services.

3.00 ROLES
3.01 Clerk of works.
3.02 Resident engineer, structural - if appointed.
3.03 Resident engineer, building engineering services - if appointed.

4.00 CONDITIONS OF SERVICE
      Consider salary/perks, hours, responsibilities.
4.01 Clerk of works.
4.02 Resident engineer, structural.
4.03 Resident engineer, building engineering services.

5.00 SELECTION
      Consider selection, recruitment, interviews.
5.01 Clerk of works.
5.02 Resident engineer, structural.
5.03 Resident engineer, building engineering services.

6.00 LINE OF COMMAND
      Consider organisation and command of
6.01 Clerk of works.
6.02 Resident engineer, structural.
6.03 Resident engineer, building engineering services.

7.00 ANY OTHER BUSINESS

Fig. 11.19 Agenda of meeting to discuss appointment of site staff

Lane & Ralph △ *Architects*

Tel: 0181-394 1234
Our ref:
Your ref:

Hogsmill House,
Sarah's Drive,
Stoneleigh,
Surrey.

Porter Construction Ltd
77 Pembroke Road
Kingson
Surrey

15th July 1996

Dear Sirs,

FACTORY AND OFFICE BLOCK, STEPHEN'S INDUSTRIAL ESTATE, EPSOM

We are preparing a list of tenderers for the construction of the above
job and need to know whether you wish to submit a tender.

We give below information relevant to the tender.

GENERAL JOB DESCRIPTION: Single-storey factory with two-storey office block.

JOB LOCATION: Stephen's Industrial Estate, Epsom.

EMPLOYER: Henry Electronics Ltd

QUANTITY SURVEYOR: Vincent, John & Partners.

CONSULTING STRUCTURAL ENGINEERS: Lewis and Son.

CONSULTING BUILDING SERVICES ENGINEERS: John Andrews MCIBS.

APPROXIMATE COST RANGE: £800000 to £1000000.

FORM OF CONTRACT: J.C.T. private edition with quantities.

ANTICIPATED DATE FOR COMMENCING WORK: 17th October 1996.

ANTICIPATED DATE FOR COMPLETION: 18th September 1997.

ANTICIPATED DATE FOR SENDING TENDER DOCUMENTS: 15th August 1996.

ANTICIPATED DATE FOR RETURNING TENDER DOCUMENTS: 19th September 1996.

Please let us know by the 25th July whether you wish to be included in the list of
tenderers. Your acceptance will indicate your agreement to submit a tender in
accordance with the RIBA Code of Practice for Single-Stage Selective Tendering.

Yours faithfully,

A Lane

A. Lane

Fig. 11.20 Letter to potential tenderer

```
TO:

Lane & Ralph
Architects
Hogsmill House
Sarah's Drive
Stoneleigh
Surrey


Dear Sirs,

FACTORY AND OFFICE BLOCK, STEPHEN'S INDUSTRIAL ESTATE, EPSOM

We hereby agree to execute and complete the whole of the works for the above job,
strictly in accordance with the drawings, schedules, specifications, bills of
quantities and conditions of contract supplied
to us for the sum of ...........................................................

...................................................................£............

within a period of .... weeks of being given possession of the site.

We enclose the schedule of rates upon which our tender is based. Our tender will
remain open for acceptance for a period of .... weeks.

Yours faithfully,



Signature...................................

NAME.......................................

ADDRESS....................................

       ....................................

       ....................................

DATE........................
```

Fig. 11.21 Form of tender

Lane & Ralph △ *Architects*

Tel: 0181-394 1234
Our ref:
Your ref:

Hogsmill House,
Sarah's Drive,
Stoneleigh,
Surrey.

15th August 1996

Porter Construction Ltd
77 Pembroke Road
Kingston
Surrey

Dear Sirs,

FACTORY AND OFFICE BLOCK, STEPHEN'S INDUSTRIAL ESTATE, EPSOM

Further to our enquiry dated the 15th July regarding your willingness to tender
for the above job, and your acceptance dated the 18th July, we enclose the
following documents which you will need to prepare your
tender.

1. Two copies of the bills of quantities.
2. One copy of the following drawings and schedules.
   Drawings no. 128/1a, 2b, 3d, 4a, 5, 6a, 7b, 9a.
   Schedules 128/5, 6, 7.
3. Two copies of the form of tender.
4. An addressed envelope for the return of your tender.
   An addressed envelope for the return of your priced bills of quantities.

Your tender is required to reach our office at the above address by 9.00 a.m. 19th
September 1996.

Please confirm the safe arrival of this letter and documents, and your intention
to submit a bona fide tender in accordance with the RIBA Code of Practice for
Single-Stage Selective Tendering by returning and signing the enclosed
acknowledgement form.

You are advised to inspect the site. Please contact the job architect, Maureen
White, tel: 0181-394-1234, to make the necessary arrangements.

Additional production drawings are available for inspection, by arrangement.
Please contact the job architect to agree an appointment to study this additional
information.

Yours faithfully,

Arnold Lane

Arnold Lane

Fig. 11.22 Letter of invitation to tender

```
TO:

Lane & Ralph
Architects
Hogsmill House
Sarah's Drive
Stoneleigh
Surrey



Dear Sirs,

FACTORY AND OFFICE BLOCK, STEPHEN'S INDUSTRIAL ESTATE, EPSOM

CONTRACTOR: PORTER CONSTRUCTION LTD

I acknowledge on behalf of the above contractor the safe receipt of all the tender
documents listed in the accompanying letter which you sent us in connection with
the above contract.

I confirm it is our intention to submit a tender by the date requested in your
letter.

SIGNED..............................

DESIGNATION.........................

DATE.................
```

Fig. 11.23 Acknowledgement of safe receipt of tender documents

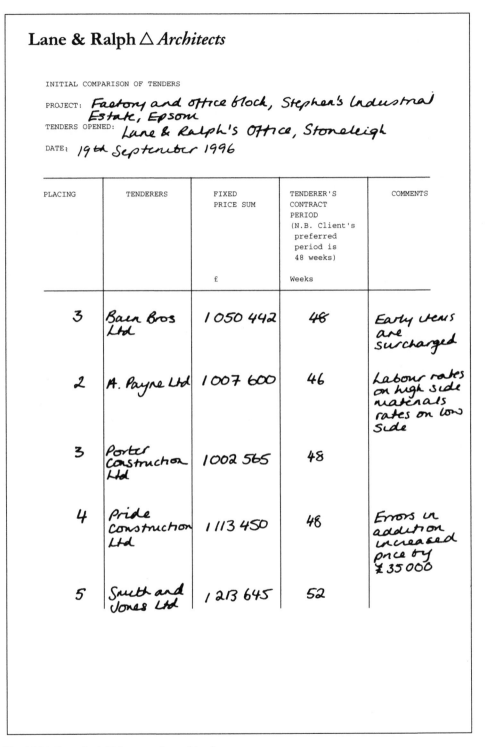

Lane & Ralph △ *Architects*

INITIAL COMPARISON OF TENDERS

PROJECT: *Factory and office block, Stephen's Industrial Estate, Epsom*

TENDERS OPENED: *Lane & Ralph's Office, Stoneleigh*

DATE: *19th September 1996*

PLACING	TENDERERS	FIXED PRICE SUM	TENDERER'S CONTRACT PERIOD (N.B. Client's preferred period is 48 weeks)	COMMENTS
		£	Weeks	
3	*Baen Bros Ltd*	*1 050 442*	*48*	*Early items are surcharged*
2	*A. Payne Ltd*	*1 007 600*	*46*	*Labour rates on high side materials rates on low side*
3	*Porter Construction Ltd*	*1 002 565*	*48*	
4	*Pride Construction Ltd*	*1 113 450*	*48*	*Errors in addition increased price by £ 35 000*
5	*Smith and Jones Ltd*	*1 213 645*	*52*	

Fig. 11.24 Form for initial comparison of tenders

Lane & Ralph △ *Architects*

Tel: 0181-394 1234
Our ref:
Your ref:

Hogsmill House,
Sarah's Drive,
Stoneleigh,
Surrey.

21st September 1996

Porter Construction Ltd
77 Pembroke Road
Kingston
Surrey

Dear Sirs,

FACTORY AND OFFICE BLOCK, STEPHEN'S INDUSTRIAL ESTATE, EPSOM

We are pleased to inform you that the tenders for the above job were opened on the 19th September and your tender was placed lowest.

Subject to a final check being made, and a proper form of contract being entered into, we are recommending to our client that your tender be accepted.

A full list of all tenders received will be sent to you at a later date.

Your faithfully,

Arnold Lane

Fig. 11.25 Letter to successful tenderer

Lane & Ralph △ *Architects*

Tel: 0181-394 1234
Our ref:
Your ref:

Hogsmill House,
Sarah's Drive,
Stoneleigh,
Surrey.

21st September 1996

A. Payne Ltd
Rush Way
Dorking
Surrey

Dear Sirs,

FACTORY AND OFFICE BLOCK, STEPHEN'S INDUSTRIAL ESTATE, EPSOM

We regret to inform you that the tenders for the above job were opened on the 19th
September and that your price was not the lowest submitted.

Although you were unsuccessful on this occasion we wish to thank you for submitting
a tender and assure you that you will not be precluded from being considered for
future tenders.

A full list of all tenders received will be sent to you at a later date.

Yours faithfully,

Arnold Lane (signature)

Arnold Lane

Fig. 11.26 Letter to unsuccessful tenderer

Lane & Ralph △ *Architects*

CHECKLIST OF INFORMATION TO BE GIVEN TO THE CLIENT AT THE
PROJECT PLANNING STAGE

1.00 COST CONTROL
1.01 Only the architect can instruct the contractor — the client must act through
      him.
1.02 Procedure for varying works.
1.03 Procedure for granting an extension of time.
1.04 Procedure for payment of works.
1.05 Arrangements for site meetings.
1.06 Arrangements for site visits.
1.07 Arrangements for reporting on state of job, in respect of progress, costs,
      and other factors.

2.00 CLIENT'S ROLE AS EMPLOYER CONFIRMED
2.01 Dury to give contractor possession of site.
2.02 Rights as to assignment of contract.
2.03 Powers to employ others if contractor does not comply with instructions.
2.04 Obligations regarding insurance.
2.05 Rights and duties in respect of contractor's bankruptcy.
2.06 No liability to nominated subcontractors.
2.07 Powers and duties concerning certificates.
2.08 Rights regarding 'finds'.
2.09 Situation regarding arbitration.

3.00 ARCHITECT'S ROLE EXPLAINED
3.01 Role as agent.
3.02 Quasi-judicial role.
3.03 Custody of contract documents.
3.04 Powers and duties regarding prime cost sums and provisional sums.
3.05 Duty to issue certificates — to be honoured within 14 days.
3.06 Duty to issue certificate of practical completion.
3.07 Powers regarding non-completion.
3.08 Duties relating to nominated subcontractors and suppliers.

4.00 CLERK OF WORKS ROLE EXPLAINED
4.01 Definition of duties, particularly to act under architect as
      inspector of works, but is servant of client.
4.02 Limitations.
4.03 Duties regarding 'finds'.
4.04 Arrangements for payment of salary.

5.00 QUANTITY SURVEYOR'S ROLE EXPLAINED
5.01 Duties regarding variations, provisional sums, and prime cost sums.
5.02 Duties relating to costs involved in 'finds'.

6.00 CONSULTANT'S ROLES EXPLAINED
6.01 Structural engineering.
6.02 Building services engineer.

Fig. 11.27 Checklist of information to be given to client at project planning stage (stage J)

Lane & Ralph △ *Architects*

Tel: 0181-394 1234
Our ref:
Your ref:

Hogsmill House,
Sarah's Drive,
Stoneleigh,
Surrey.

3rd October 1996

Structural Steel Constructions (Polegate) Ltd
Radcliffe Road
Polegate
Sussex

Dear Sirs,

FACTORY AND OFFICE BLOCK, STEPHEN'S INDUSTRIAL ESTATE, EPSOM

Further to your tender for the supply and fixing of the structural steelwork to the factory building we wish to inform you that we have requested the contractor to accept your tender dated the 6th July for the amount stated, inclusive of 2½% discount for payment within the stipulated time.

We enclose for your infomration a list of the tenderers with their tender amounts.

Yours faithfully,

ALane

Arnold Lane

Fig. 11.28 Letter to successful subcontractor

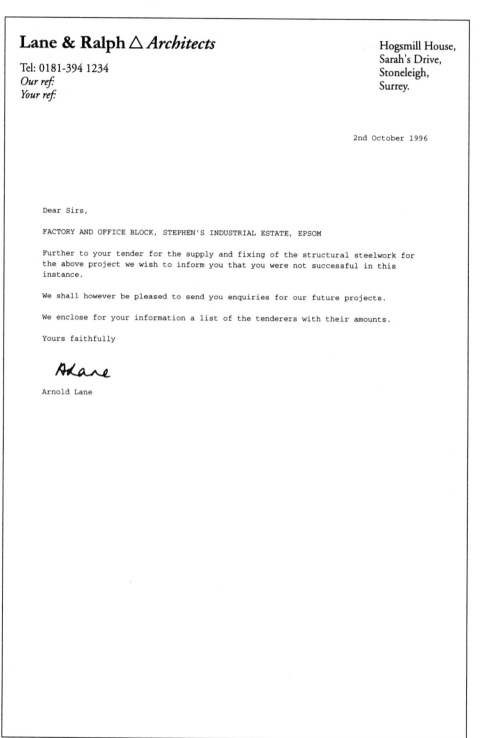

Lane & Ralph △ *Architects*

Tel: 0181-394 1234
Our ref:
Your ref:

Hogsmill House,
Sarah's Drive,
Stoneleigh,
Surrey.

2nd October 1996

Dear Sirs,

FACTORY AND OFFICE BLOCK, STEPHEN'S INDUSTRIAL ESTATE, EPSOM

Further to your tender for the supply and fixing of the structural steelwork for
the above project we wish to inform you that you were not successful in this
instance.

We shall however be pleased to send you enquiries for our future projects.

We enclose for your information a list of the tenderers with their amounts.

Yours faithfully

Arnold Lane

Fig. 11.29 Letter to unsuccessful subcontractor

Lane & Ralph △ *Architects*

Tel: 0181-394 1234
Our ref:
Your ref:

Hogsmill House,
Sarah's Drive,
Stoneleigh,
Surrey.

10th October 1996

Porter Construction Ltd
77 Pembroke Road
Kingston
Surrey

Dear Sirs,

FACTORY AND OFFICE BLOCK, STEPHENS'S INDUSTRIAL ESTATE, EPSOM

This is to confirm that the above site will be handed over to you at 9 a.m. on
Monday 17th October.

From this date until the completion of the contract you will be responsible for the
security of the site, for the safety of anyone entering the site, and for the
security and safety of all partially and completed buildings, and all materials on
the site.

We wish to draw your attention to the following special conditions that apply to
the control of this site.

1. The footpath running alongside the northwest boundary to the site is a public
   right of way and must be maintained at all times.

2. Care must be taken not to damage the buildings immediately adjoining the
   southeast boundary.

3. The mature oak tree near the centre of the site must be protected against
   damage from building operations.

Yours faithfully,

Adane

Arnold Lane

Fig. 11.30 Letter regarding handing over of site to contractor

Lane & Ralph △ *Architects*

ARCHITECT'S GENERAL CHECKLIST DURING OPERATIONS ON-SITE

1.00 GENERAL
1.01 Follow Site Inspection Checklist.
1.02 Check that materials on-site conform to specification and are undamaged.
       N.B. Instructions are to be issued for removal of unsuitable materials.
1.03 Approve sample of materials and workmanship.
1.04 Issue instructions to remove unsatisfactory items of work.
1.05 Keep record of each site visit. Take all necessary action. Maintain records.
1.06 Check site manager is permanently on-site and that contractor's site
       supervision is adequate.

2.00 DRAWINGS
2.01 Check drawings are sent to contractor so as to meet the requirements of his
       agreed programme.
2.02 Check that drawings have been received by the contractor.
2.03 Check that drawings are revised to incorporate all variations and
       instructions.
2.04 Check the clerk of works is maintaining a set of 'as-built' drawings.

3.00 PROGRAMME AND PROGRESS
3.01 Check work is proceeding as agreed programme.
3.02 Check that progress photographs are being taken at regular intervals.

4.00 EXTENSION OF TIME
4.01 Consider claims from contractor for an extension of time.
4.02 Where justified, issue notice of extension of time within the contractual
       time limits.

5.00 NOMINATED SUBCONTRACTORS AND SUPPLIERS
5.01 Check that any outstanding nominations are made in adequate time to suit the
       agreed programme.
5.02 Check that unsuccessful subcontractors and suppliers have been notified of
       results.
5.03 Check instructions regarding subcontractors and suppliers have been issued
       to contractor.
5.04 Check that contractor is not waiting for drawings/information from
       subcontractors or suppliers.
5.05 Check that subcontractors and suppliers are not waiting for
       drawings/information from architects.

6.00 VARIATIONS AND INSTRUCTIONS
6.01 Check that agreed variations and instructions have been formalised by issue
       of appropriate standard forms.

7.00 CERTIFICATES
7.01 Issue all certificates in the strictest accordance with contract.

8.00 PAYMENTS
8.01 Check that payment has been made for work included in certificates, including cost of instructions and variations. N.B. If the client is in default, notify him by recorded delivery, of the consequences.
8.02 Check that payments are being made to subcontractors and suppliers, where such sums have been included in the certificates for that purpose.
8.03 Arrange for client to pay subcontractors and suppliers directly, where contractor is failing to meet his contractual obligations.
8.04 Issue the appropriate certificates in cases where necessary, due to subcontractors or suppliers not meeting their contractual obligations.

9.00 DETERMINATION OF CONTRACT
9.01 Take required action if the client wishes the contract with the contractor to be terminated, and such action is justified.
9.02 Consult the client, and his legal advisors, if the contractor requests that the contract be terminated.

10.00 FEEDBACK
10.01 Record with notes and sketches any aspect of the design and construction of which account should be taken in future projects. File for future use.
10.02 Record any aspect of administrative work of which account should be taken in future projects. File for future use.

Fig. 11.31 General checklist for use during site operations

Lane & Ralph △ *Architects*

1.00 TEMPORARY WORKS
1.01 Suitable siting of temporary buildings, huts, etc.
1.02 Suitable storage of materials – protection, security.
1.03 Suitable protection of finished work.
1.04 Rights of way unobstructed.
1.05 Suitable protection of trees, etc., which are to be preserved.
1.06 Satisfactory boundary hoardings, fencing.
1.07 Setting out correct.
1.08 Bench marks correct.
1.09 Sample panels all right.
1.10 Topsoil spoil heaps all right.

2.00 DEMOLITIONS
2.01 Scope of work all right.
2.02 Temporary supports all right.
2.03 Avoidance of nuisance, danger to adjoining sites, public.
2.04 Items specified to be retained are being retained.

3.00 SUBSTRUCTURE
3.01 Check nature of subsoil compared with trial pits/boreholes.
3.02 Dimensions of excavations correct.
3.03 Safety in excavations being achieved.
3.04 Dewatering procedures all right.
3.05 Adjoining sites and buildings not endangered by excavations.
3.06 Suitable quality of hardcore.
3.07 Suitable quality of blinding.
3.08 Correct placing of reinforcement, including cover.
3.09 Suitable quality of concrete.
3.10 Correct concrete dimensions.
3.11 Damp-proof membranes and tanking all right.
3.12 Ducts through structure correctly sized and positioned.
3.13 Piling work all right – as drawings/specifications.
3.14 Backfilling all right – material and compaction.

4.00 DRAINAGE
4.01 General layout/setting out correct.
4.02 Inverts and gradients correct.
4.03 Drain bedding all right.
4.04 Drain jointing all right.
4.05 Manholes materials and workmanship all right – base, walls, cover.

5.00 STRUCTURAL STEELWORK
5.01 Setting out correct.
5.02 Size of members correct.
5.03 Connections all right.
5.04 Frame square, plumb, and level.
5.05 Corrosion protection – priming.

6.00 *IN SITU* REINFORCED CONCRETE
6.01 Setting out correct.
6.02 Size of members correct.

6.03 Formwork correct and will give required surface finish to concrete.
6.04 Location of reinforcement correct, including cover.
6.05 Size of reinforcement correct.
6.06 Formwork clean.
6.07 Reinforcement clean.
6.08 Openings, holes, fixings, water bars, correctly positioned.
6.09 Striking programme correct.

7.00 PRE-CAST REINFORCED CONCRETE
7.01 Setting out, size, and shape of members correct.
7.02 Finish correct.
7.03 Members have not been damaged during transit of erection.
7.04 Openings, holes fixings, in correct positions.

8.00 BRICK AND BLOCK WALLING
8.01 General setting out correct.
8.02 Walls of correct thickness.
8.03 Openings in correct positions.
8.04 Expansion joints in correct positions.
8.05 Work as sample panels – bricks, blocks, mortar colour, joints.
8.06 Damp-proof courses correct – materials, positions.
8.07 Wall and other ties – correct type and spacings, clean.
8.08 Cavities kept clean.
8.09 Lintels – correct type and bedding.
8.10 Correct reinforcement in calculated brick/blockwork.
8.11 Sliding joint provided.

9.00 CARPENTRY AND JOINERY
9.01 Timber free from defects.
9.02 Timber members of correct size.
9.03 Timber members in correct positions and spacings.
9.04 Timber members correctly fixed and jointed.
9.05 Members primed, protected with preservative.
9.06 Joinery members correctly fixed.
9.07 Weather mouldings, throatings provided.
9.08 Wrot faces provided where required.

10.00 WALL AND ROOF CLADDING
10.01 Correct general extent of work, position of openings.
10.02 Correct materials – outer sheeting, insulation, vapour barrier, lining.
10.03 Correct arrangement of materials.
10.04 Laps, joints, correctly positioned.
10.05 Fixings – correct types and spacings.
10.06 Flashings, trim, weathermoulds, cappings – correct types, positions.
10.07 Mastic provided where specified.
10.08 Prevention of electrolytic action.
10.09 Curtain wall members – correct type, colour, dimensions.
10.10 Curtain wall panels – correct type, colour, dimensions.
10.11 Finished construction weatherproof.

11.00 METALWORK
11.01 Correct type, colour, size of items.
11.02 Correct fixing of items.
11.03 Protection against rust provided.
11.04 Isolation from corrosive materials provided.
11.05 External items weatherproof.

12.00 ROOFING
12.01 Correct falls/pitches provided.
12.02 Outlets provided at lowest points.
12.03 Materials as specified - colour, size, appearance.
12.04 Insulation, vapour barrier provided in correct position, order.
12.05 Skirtings as specified to flat roofs.
12.06 Flashings as specified to flat roofs, including wall chases.
12.07 Correct treatment to ridges and verges of pitched roofs.
12.08 Correct drips, gutters provided.
12.09 All roofs weathertight.

13.00 DISCHARGE PIPEWORK AND SANITARY FITTINGS
13.01 Sanitary fittings as specified provided in correct locations.
13.02 Vertical pipes - located, fixed jointed correctly.
13.03 Horizontal pipes - located, fixed, jointed correctly.
13.04 Horizontal pipes laid to correct falls.
13.05 Traps correctly located.
13.06 Accesses, rodding eyes provided.
13.07 Pipe testing.

14.00 HEATING AND HOT WATER INSTALLATION
14.01 Plant items as specified, correctly located.
14.02 Flues as specified, correctly located.
14.03 Pipe sizes and runs as drawings.
14.04 Valves - types and positions as specified.
14.05 Pipework insulation provided.
14.06 Pipes correctly labelled and identified.

15.00 COLD WATER AND SPRINKLER INSTALLATION
15.01 Plant items as specified, correctly located.
15.02 Pipe sizes and runs as drawings.
15.03 Frost protection provided.
15.04 Valves - types and positions as specified.
15.05 Draining facility provided.
15.06 Pipes correctly labelled and identified.
15.07 Sprinkler heads given protection against paint, dust.

16.00 AIR-CONDITIONING AND VENTILATION
16.01 Plant items as specified, correctly located.
16.02 Duct sizes and runs as drawings.
16.03 Access provided to ducts.
16.04 Louvres provided as specification.

17.00 ELECTRICAL INSTALLATIONS
17.01 Plant items as specified, correctly located.
17.02 Points, outlets, switches, as specified, correctly located.
17.03 Specified cables, correctly run.

17.04 Installation earthed.
17.05 Switchgear identified and labelled.
17.06 Lightning conductor installation correct.
17.07 Communication installation correct.

18.00 FLOOR FINISHES
18.01 Materials as specified provided in correct location.
18.02 Screeds of correct type and quality of finish.
18.03 Other bases all right.
18.04 Accurate falls to channels, gullies.
18.05 Setting out correct.
18.06 Standard of finishes all right. Check under final lighting.
18.07 Skirtings, covers all right.
18.08 Junctions between different finishes all right.

19.00 PLASTERING AND WALL TILING
19.01 Background true and dry enough.
19.02 Metal beads properly fixed.
19.03 Undercoats ready for bonding – scratching.
19.04 Plaster finish all right. Arrises, openings, corners.
19.05 Filling and scrimming of plasterboard joints.
19.06 Regular joints – horizontally and vertically to glazed tiling.
19.07 Treatment at external angles. Top of tiling all right.

20.00 SUSPENDED CEILINGS
20.01 Suspension system at correct height.
20.02 Suspension system correct type, framing arrangement.
20.03 Type of tiles, panels as specified.
20.04 Correct setting out of tiles, panels.
20.05 Lights, grilles, access panels, correctly located.
20.06 Provision for services items – electrical, fire protection.
20.07 Correct finish at walls, head of windows, curtain walling.

21.00 PROPRIETARY PARTITIONS
21.01 Partitions correctly located.
21.02 Type of partition as specified.
21.03 Doors, openings, correctly located.
21.04 Suitable fixings at base, head, ends.
21.05 Provision for services items – electrical, fire protection.
21.06 Correct junctions with other elements.

22.00 GLAZING
22.01 Glass as specified.
22.02 Glass free from defects.
22.03 Facility for slight movement.
22.04 Putty, glazing beads all right.

23.00 PAINTING AND DECORATING
23.01 Correct preparation of surface, freedom from damp.
23.02 Paint of type specified, correct 'thickness'.
23.03 Number of coats as specified.
23.04 Finished work free from 'runs', brush marks.
23.05 Paper wall covering of type specified.
23.06 Wall covering joints all right, openings, skirtings, head.

23.07 General standard of finish acceptable. Check under final lighting.

24.00 IRONMONGERY
24.01 All ironmongery, furniture, supplied as schedules.
24.02 All items fixed, correct no. of screws.
24.03 Latches, locks, bolts open correctly.
24.04 Door springs, closers operate correctly.
24.05 Correct number of keys.
24.06 Doors, windows, open easily, not in need of adjustment.

25.00 CLEANING DOWN
25.01 Floors scrubbed, free from paint splashes.
25.02 Painted surfaces clean, free from faults.
25.03 Glass cleaned, undamaged.
25.04 Sanitary fittings clean, undamaged.
25.05 Lighting fittings clean, undamaged.
25.06 Switch plates, ironmongery, door/window furniture clean.
25.07 Rooms areas, generally immaculate.

Fig. 11.32 Site inspection checklist

Lane & Ralph △ Architects

JOB: *FACTORY AND OFFICE BLOCK, EPSOM*

DATE: *25/11/1996*

CONTRACTOR: *PORTER CONSTRUCTION LTD* WEEK NO. *6*

LABOUR ON-SITE	MON	TUE	WED	THU	FRI	TOTAL	COMMENTS
Labourers	5	5	4	5	4	23	
Bricklayers	5	5	5	4	4	23	
Structural Steelworkers	4	4	4	4	4	20	
Carpenters					2	2	
	14	14	13	13	14	68	

DELAY CAUSED BY	MON	TUE	WED	THU	FRI	TOTAL	COMMENTS
Heavy rain	5	3				8	

| DELAY CAUSED BY | 5 | 3 | | | | 8 | |

	DATE	WEEK NO.
START	17/10/96	1
ORIGINALLY AGREED COMPLETION	18/9/97	48
EXTENSION GRANTED OF WEEKS GIVING REVISED COMPLET.	25/9/97	49
SITE MANAGER'S PRESENT ESTIMATE OF COMPLETION	25/9/97	49

PROBLEMS ON-SITE FOR CONTRACTOR'S OWN LABOUR ITEMS
Difficulty likely in maintaining required number of bricklayers

PROBLEMS ON-SITE FOR SUBCONTRACTORED WORK
Roof cladders (factory building) have not yet confirmed they can commence on-site when required

DRAWINGS AND INFORMATION RECEIVED
Drawing No. 124/2c

DRAWINGS AND INFORMATION REQUIRED
Details of door No's 24 and 32 at junction with steel columns

MATERIALS DELIVERED
Facing bricks, concrete blocks, more structural steel items

VISITORS
Mr Henry (wed) Mr Reason H&SWA Inspector (Fri)

OTHER MATTERS

SIGNED *CRoh*
DATE *25/11/96*

Fig. 11.33 Clerk of works weekly site report

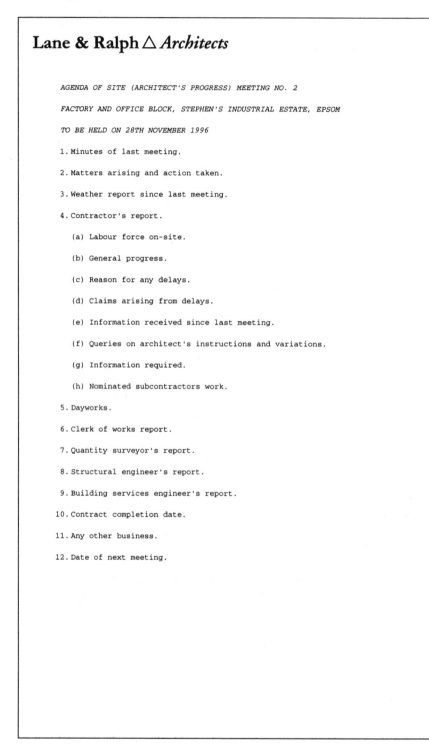

Lane & Ralph △ *Architects*

AGENDA OF SITE (ARCHITECT'S PROGRESS) MEETING NO. 2

FACTORY AND OFFICE BLOCK, STEPHEN'S INDUSTRIAL ESTATE, EPSOM

TO BE HELD ON 28TH NOVEMBER 1996

1. Minutes of last meeting.

2. Matters arising and action taken.

3. Weather report since last meeting.

4. Contractor's report.

   (a) Labour force on-site.

   (b) General progress.

   (c) Reason for any delays.

   (d) Claims arising from delays.

   (e) Information received since last meeting.

   (f) Queries on architect's instructions and variations.

   (g) Information required.

   (h) Nominated subcontractors work.

5. Dayworks.

6. Clerk of works report.

7. Quantity surveyor's report.

8. Structural engineer's report.

9. Building services engineer's report.

10. Contract completion date.

11. Any other business.

12. Date of next meeting.

Fig. 11.34 Agenda of site (architect's progress) meeting

Issued by: LANE & RALPH
address: Hogsmill House, Sarah's Drive
Stoneleigh Surrey

Architect's Instruction

Employer: HENRY ELECTRONICS
address: 100 Hart Road
London SW1

Job reference: AL/124

Instruction no: MW/2

Contractor: PORTER CONSTRUCTION LTD
address: 77 Pembroke Road
Kingston Surrey

Issue date: 2/12/1996

Sheet: 1 of 1

Works
situated at: Factory and office block
Stephen's Industrial Estate
Epsom

Contract dated: 10/10/1996

Under the terms of the above-mentioned Contract, I/we issue the following instructions:

	Office use: Approx costs	
	£ omit	£ add
Revise position of door No's from that shown on drawing No. 124/2e to that shown on drawing No. 124/2f.	—	—

To be signed by or for the issuer named above

Signed _Adare_

Amount of Contract Sum	£	1002 565
± Approximate value of previous Instructions	£	320
± Approximate value of this Instruction	£	1002 885
Approximate adjusted total	£	

Distribution	Original to:	Copies to:		
	☑ Contractor	☑ Employer	☑ Quantity Surveyor	☐ Clerk of Works
		☐ Nominated Sub-Contractors	☐ Consultants	☑ File

F809 for JCT 80/IFC 84/MW 80

© RIBA Publications Ltd 1991

Fig. 11.35 Royal Institute of British Architects (RIBA) form: Architect's instruction

Issued by: *Lane & Ralph*
address: *Hogsmill House Sarah's Drive
Stoneleigh, Surrey*

Employer: *Henry Electronics Ltd*
address: *100 Hart Road
London SW1*

Contractor: *Porter Construction Ltd*
address: *77 Pembroke Road
Kingston Surrey*

Works: *Factory and office block*
situated at: *Stephen's Industrial Estate
Epsom*

Contract dated: *10th October 1996*

**Interim
Certificate**
and Direction

Serial no: **C** *557657*

Job reference: *AL/124*

Certificate no: *1*

Issue date: *14/11/1996*

Valuation date: *11/11/1996*

Contract sum: *£ 1 002 565*

Original to Employer

This Interim Certificate is issued under the terms of the above-mentioned Contract.

Gross valuation inclusive of the value of works by Nominated Sub-Contractors .... £ *85 000*

Less Retention which may be retained by the Employer as detailed on the Statement of Retention .... £ *3 400*

Sub-total £ *81 600*

Less total amount stated as due in Interim Certificates previously issued up to and including Interim Certificate no: .... £

Net amount for payment .... £ *81 600*

I/We hereby certify that the **amount for payment** by the Employer to the Contractor on this Certificate is (in words)

Eighty one thousand six hundred pounds

I/We hereby direct the Contractor that this amount includes interim or final payments to Nominated Sub-Contractors as listed in the attached *Statement of Retention and of Nominated Sub-Contractors' Values*, which are to be discharged to those named in accordance with the Sub-Contract.

All amounts are exclusive of VAT

To be signed by or for the issuer named above

Signed *Adare   for Lane & Ralph*

[1] Relevant only if clause 1A of the VAT Agreement applies. Delete if not applicable.

[1] The Contractor has given notice that the rate of VAT chargeable on the supply of goods and services to which the Contract relates is *17½* %

[1] _____ % of the amount certified above is .... £

[1] Total of net amount and VAT amount (for information) .... £

This is not a Tax Invoice

F801 for JCT 80

© RIBA Publications Ltd 1990

Fig. 11.36 Royal Institute of British Architects (RIBA) form: Interim certificate

Certificate of

Practical Completion

Issued by: *Lane & Ralph*
address: *Hogsmill House, Sarah's Drive*
Stoneleigh Surrey

Employer: *Henry Electronics Ltd*
address: *100 Hart Road*
London SW1

Job reference: *AL/124*

Certificate no: *1*

Contractor: *Porter Construction Ltd*
address: *77 Pembroke Road*
Kingston Surrey

Issue date: *20/9/97*

Works: *Factory and office block*
situated at: *Stephen's Industrial Estate*
Epsom

Contract dated: *10th October 1996*

Under the terms of the above-mentioned Contract,

I/we hereby certify that Practical Completion of

*Delete as appropriate

*1. the Works

*2. Section No. _____ of the Works

was achieved on

_____*18th September*_____ 19 *97*

To be signed by or for the issuer named above

Signed __*A Lane*__ for *Lane & Ralph*

Distribution	Original to:	Duplicate to:	Copies to:	
	☑ Employer	☑ Contractor	☑ Quantity Surveyor	☐ Clerk of Works
			☐ Consultants	☑ File

F853 for JCT 80/IFC 84/MW 80

© RIBA Publications Ltd 1991

Fig. 11.37 Royal Institute of British Architects (RIBA) form: Certificate of practical completion

Certificate of
Completion of

Making Good Defects

Issued by: *Lane & Ralph*
address: *Hogsnull House, Sarah's Drive*
Stoneleigh, Surrey

Employer: *Henry Electronics Ltd*
address: *100 Hart Road*
London SW1

Contractor: *Portee Construction Ltd*
address: *77 Pembroke Road*
Kingston Surrey

Works: *Factory and office block*
situated at: *Stephen's Industrial Estate*
Epsom

Contract dated: *10th October 1996*

Job reference: *AL/124*

Certificate no: *1*

Issue date: *10/11/97*

Under the terms of the above-mentioned Contract,

I/we hereby certify that the defects, shrinkages and other faults specified
in the schedule of defects delivered to the Contractor as an instruction have
in my/our opinion been made good.

This Certificate refers to:

*Delete as
appropriate

*1. the Works referred to in the
Certificate of Practical Completion

No. *MW/13*   dated *20th September 1997*

*2. Section No. _____ of the Works referred to in the

Certificate of Practical Completion

No. _____ dated _____

*3. the part of the Works identified in the
Statement/Certificate of Partial Possession by the Employer

No. _____ dated _____

To be signed by or for
the issuer named
above

Signed *Adare   For Lane & Ralph*

Distribution	Original to:	Duplicate to:	Copies to:	
	☑ Employer	☑ Contractor	☑ Quantity Surveyor	☐ Clerk of Works
			☐ Consultants	☑ File

F807 for JCT 80 / IFC 84 / MW 80   © RIBA Publications Ltd 1990

Fig. 11.38 Royal Institute of British Architects (RIBA) form: Certificate of making good defects

Issued by: *Lane & Ralph*
address: *Hogsmill House Sarah's Drive*
Stoneleigh Surrey

Final Certificate

Employer: *Henry Electronics Ltd*
address: *100 Hart Road*
London SW1

Serial no: *A MW/14*

Job reference: *AL/124*

Contractor: *Porter Construction Ltd*
address: *77 Pembroke Road*
Kingston Surrey

Issue date: *13/11/1997*

Contract sum:

Works: *Factory and office block*
situated at: *Stephen's Industrial Estate*
Epsom

Contract dated: *10th October 1996*

File copy

This Final Certificate is issued under the terms of the above-mentioned Contract.

The Contract Sum adjusted as necessary is .... £ *1 025 605*

The total amount previously certified for payment to the Contractor is .... £ *975 050*

The difference between the above-stated amounts is .... £ *50 555*

I/We hereby certify the sum of (in words)

Fifty thousand five hundred and
fifty five pounds

as a **balance due**:

*Delete as appropriate

*to the Contractor from the Employer.

*to the Employer from the Contractor.

All amounts are exclusive of VAT

To be signed by or for the issuer named above

Signed _____ *A Lane* _____ *for Lane & Ralph* _____

The terms of the Contract provide that, subject to any amounts properly deductible by the Employer, the said balance shall be a debt payable from the one to the other as from the

[1] Delete as appropriate. See cover notes for provision in particular contract.

[1] 14th/21st/28th day after the date of this Certificate.

[2] Relevant only if clause 1A of JCT 80 VAT Agreement, clause A1 of IFC 84 Supplemental Conditions or clause B1 of MW 80 Supplementary Memorandum applies. Delete if not applicable.

[2] The Contractor has given notice that the rate of VAT chargeable on the supply of goods and services to which the Contract relates is _____ %

[2] _____ % of the amount certified above is .... £ _____

[2] Total of balance due and VAT amount (for information) .... £ _____

This is not a Tax Invoice

F852 for JCT 80/IFC 84/MW 80

© RIBA Publications Ltd 1990

Fig. 11.39 Royal Institute of British Architects (RIBA) form: Final certificate

BRITISH INSTITUTE OF ARCHITECTURAL TECHNOLOGISTS

Confirmation
of Instructions

Practice Name: *Margery Jones* COPY
Associates
Address: *145 Washington Avenue, Eastbourne
E. Sussex*
Date: *1st July 1997*

Job No: *MJ/8/54*

To: *Coast Developments Ltd
Coast House, Coast Road, Brighton, Sussex*

For:

I/We thank you for your instructions and confirm that I/we shall be pleased to act
for you in connection with

I/We understand that I/we shall be responsible, under the terms of this agreement, for the following items
which shall be carried out where applicable in accordance with the BIAT current Conditions of Engagement,
as copy enclosed. I/We should be pleased to receive written confirmation from you that these conditions are
acceptable.

Work Stages

Stage O: Survey

Stage A: Inception
Initial meeting with client to discuss brief and determine cost limits, to advise on
the need for independent consultants such as Engineers, Quantity Surveyors,
etc; and to give advice on possible types of contract and tender.

Stage B. Feasibility Studies
Preparation of sketch drawings to illustrate tentative proposals for discussion
and development with client, and for preliminary discussions with authorities,
etc.

Stage C: Final Scheme Drawings
Preparation of final scheme drawings and details; submission to client and
suitable for submission under the Town and Country Planning Acts.

Stage D. Detail Design
Commencing production information drawings for contractors use. Develop
scheme to a stage suitable for submission under Building Acts, Regulations and
other statutory requirements, and completion of applications for statutory
approvals where necessary.

Stage E: Production Information
Proceeding with production information including drawings, schedules and
specifications suitable for the purposes of a tender.

Stage F: Contract Preparation and Administration
Inviting building contractors and specialist sub-contractors and suppliers to
submit formal tenders and quotations for work. Considering offers received and
making recommendations thereon to the client. Preparing contract documents
as necessary and arranging for their execution. Giving instructions to appointed
contractors on behalf of the client, inspecting work in progress to determine
whether the contractor is generally fulfilling his obligations under the contract,
carrying out other administrative duties entailed. Certifying interim applications
for payment on account of work carried out, considering and agreeing final
payment due under the contract. Supplying client with set of "as built" drawings,
service drawings and maintenance manual, if required. (For projects having a
construction value of less that £20,000 this stage will be charged on a quantum
merit basis).

Variations if applicable

The fees for carrying out this work will be £   at an hourly rate of £
at   % of the total contract sum (or estimated sum for abortive work)
at an agreed lump sum of £ *60 000—*
These fees are exclusive of prints, travelling, local authority fees and VAT. Accounts will be rendered in
stages as work proceeds.

Signed: *Margery Jones*

Principal/Partner/Director

Fig. 11.40 British Institute of Architectural Technology (BIAT) form: Confirmation of instructions

BRITISH INSTITUTE OF ARCHITECTURAL TECHNOLOGISTS

Instruction

Practice Name: *Margery Jones Associates*
Address: *145 Washington Avenue Eastbourne*
E Sussex

Employer: *Coast Developments Ltd*
Address: *Coast House Coast Road Brighton*
Sussex

Contractor: *Phillips Construction Ltd*
Address: *77 New Road Polegate Sussex*

Works: *24 Luxury flats in two blocks*

Situate at: *Seafront Parade Eastbourne Sussex*

No: *2*

Sheet one of.....*1*

Job ref: *MJ/8/54*

Date: *12th December 1997*

Under the terms of the Contract dated:

I/We issue the following instructions. Where applicable the Contract sum will be adjusted
in accordance with the terms of the relevant Condition.

Instructions	For office use: £ omit	Approx. costs £ add
Demolish brick built garages in northwest corner of site and remove all materials from site		*400*

To be signed by or for the practice named above.

Signed *A Jones   for Margery Jones Associates*

Notes

Amount of Contract sum £	*1 025 000*
Approximate value of previous instructions £	*200*
£	
Approximate value of this instruction £	*400*
Approximate adjusted total £	*1 025 600*

✓To Contractor   Copies to: ✓Employer   ✓Clerk of Works
                                      Structural Consultant   Electrical Consultant
                                      ✓Quantity Surveyor   ✓file
                                      Heating Consultant   Others

Fig. 11.41 British Institute of Architectural Technology (BIAT) form: Instruction

BRITISH INSTITUTE OF ARCHITECTURAL TECHNOLOGISTS

Certificate

Practice Name: *Margery Jones Associates*
Address: *145 Washington Avenue*
Eastbourne E Sussex

Employer: *Coast Developments Ltd*
Address: *Coast House Coast Road Brighton*
Sussex

Certificate No: *2*

Job ref: *MJ/8/54*

Contractor: *Phillips Construction Ltd*
Address: *77 New Road Polegate Sussex*

Date: *24th Feb 1998*

Works: *24 Luxury flats in two blocks*

Situate at: *Seafront Parade Eastbourne Sussex*

Contract date: *14th November 1997*

For payment of Interim/Final Contractor's Account dated:

Contract sum as tender date	£	*1 025 000*
Adjustments as per instruction nos. *1 and 2*	£	*600*
Revised contract sum	£	*1 025 600*
Gross sum	£	*100 000*
Less retention at *3* %	£	*3 000*
	£	*97 000*
Less Total value previously certified	£	*40 000*
Amount due	£	*57 000*

In accordance with the Contract as above I/We hereby certify that the amount as detailed above is due from the Employer to the Contractor.

Value of this certificate   £ *57000*
Amount in words *Fifty seven thousand pounds*

This certificate is due for settlement within *7* days of the date of issue to the Employer
Contractor: This certificate included the value of works executed by any nominated Subcontractors as detailed on attached Notification.
All the above amounts are exclusive of V.A.T.
The issue of this Certificate is not for and shall not be taken as evidence that any work or materials or goods or workmanship is or are accepted as conforming to description or being in accordance with the contract

To be signed by or for the practice named above.

Signed: *L Jones*   *for Margery Jones Associates*

✓Original to Employer   copies to: ✓Contractor   ✓Quantity Surveyor   ✓File   Others

Fig. 11.42 British Institute of Architectural Technology (BIAT) form: Certificate

BRITISH INSTITUTE OF ARCHITECTURAL TECHNOLOGISTS

Notification

of Amounts included
in Certificate

Practice Name: *Margery Jones Associates*
Address: *145 Washington Avenue*
Eastbourne E Sussex

Employer: *Coast Development Ltd*
Address: *Coast House Coast Road Brighton*
Sussex

Nominated
Sub-Contractor: *Plumb (shortbored piling systems) Ltd*
Address: *44 Station Way Seaford Sussex*

Job ref: *MJ/8/54*

Date: *24th Feb 1998*

Works: *24 Luxury flats in two blocks*

Situate at: *Seafront Parade Eastbourne Sussex*

I/We inform you that under the terms of the Contract dated:
A Certificate has been issued to the Employer
The Contractor has been directed that the Certificate includes the
following amount due to you.

Certificate No: *2*   Date: *24th February 1998*

Instalment No: *1*   Valuation date: *16th February 1998*

Gross Total to date	Total Retention	Previously certified	Balance in Certificate
£ 40 100	£ 1 200	—	£ 38 900

The amount shown takes no account of any discounts to which the
Contractor may be entitled.
All the above amounts are exclusive of V.A.T.

Signed: *M Jones*   *for Margery Jones Associates*

To be signed by
or for the practice
named above.

√ Sub-Contractor   √ File

Fig. 11.43 British Institute of Architectural Technology (BIAT) form: Notification of amounts included in
Certificate

BRITISH INSTITUTE OF ARCHITECTURAL TECHNOLOGISTS

Direction

Amounts included
in interim certificate
for nominated
sub-contractors

Practice Name: Margery Jones Associates
Address: 145 Washington Avenue
Eastbourne E. Sussex

Employer: Coast Developments Ltd
Address: Coast House Coast Road
Brighton Sussex

Contractor: Phillips Construction Ltd
Address: 77 New Road Polegate Sussex

Job ref: MJ/8/54

Date: 24th Feb. 1998

Works: 24 Luxury Flats in two blocks

Situate at: Seafront Parade Eastbourne Sussex

In accordance with the Contract dated:

I/We direct that the following amounts are included on the interim certificate
detailed below and are due to be paid to the subcontractors listed.

Certificate No: 2   Date: 24th Feb. 1998

Valuation date: 16th February 1998

Nominated Sub-Contractor	Total to date	Total Retention	Previously certified	Balance included in Certificate
Plumb (Shortbored piling Systems) Ltd	£ 40000	£ 1200	–	£ 38 900

No account has been taken in the amounts shown for any discounts
to which the Contractor may be credited.

All amounts are exclusive of VAT.

Proof of Discharge should be provided by the Contractor.

Signed: MJones   for Margery Jones Associates   To be signed by or
for the practice
named above.

Original to Contractor ✓   Copies to: ✓ Employer   File
✓ Quantity Surveyor

Fig. 11.44 British Institute of Architectural Technology (BIAT) form: Direction

BRITISH INSTITUTE OF ARCHITECTURAL TECHNOLOGISTS

Notification of
Extension of Time

Practice Name: *Margery Jones Associates*
Address: *145 Washington Avenue*
Eastbourne Sussex

Employer: *Coast Developments Ltd*
Address: *Coast House Coast Road*
Brighton Sussex

Contractor: *Phillips Construction Ltd*
Address: *77 New Road Polegate Sussex*

Works: *24 Luxury Flats in two blocks*

Situate at: *Seafront Parade Eastbourne Sussex*

In accordance with the Contract dated: *14th November 1997*

Notice is given that the date for completion, namely

Date: *27th July 1998*

is extended by reason of: *Altering flats 7 and 8 in Block A*
into one flat, including installation of air
conditioning

arising out of the Contractor's written notice

Dated: *14th May 1998*

The revised Date(s) for completion are confirmed as

Date(s): *10th August 1998*

Signed: *MJones for Margery Jones Associates*

Serial no:

Job ref: *MJ/8/54*

Date: *27th July 1998*

To be signed by
or for the practice
named above.

Original to Contractor   Copies to: ✓Employer   ✓File
                                     ✓Quantity Surveyor   Others
                                     ✓Structural/Civil Engineer
                                     ✓Clerk of Works
                                     ✓Services Consultant

Fig. 11.45 British Institute of Architectural Technology (BIAT) form: Notification of extension of time

BRITISH INSTITUTE OF ARCHITECTURAL TECHNOLOGISTS

Certificate of
Practical
Completion
or Partial Completion

Practice Name: *Margery Jones Associates*
Address: *145 Washington Avenue*
Eastbourne Sussex

Employer: *Coast Developments Ltd*
Address: *Coast House Coast Road*
Brighton Sussex

Contractor: *Phillips Construction Ltd*
Address: *77 New Road Polegate Sussex*

Works: *24 Luxury flats in two blocks*

Situate at: *Seafront Parade Eastbourne Sussex*

Job ref: *MJ/8/54*

Date: *24th August 1998*

In accordance with the contract and amendments, dated:
I/We certify that, subject to the completion of any outstanding items, and/or making good
of any defects, shrinkages, and other faults which appear during the defects liability period.

(delete a or b as necessary)

---

a: The works were in my/our opinion practically complete on: *24th August 1998*

and that the said defects liability period will end on: *24th February 1999*

---

b: A part of the Works, namely:

the approximate value of which I/We estimate to be: £

was taken into possession on:

and that in relation to this part of the works, the defects liability period
will end on:

I/We declare that a certificate for one moiety of the retention monies deducted under
previous certificates in respect of the Works or part of the works is to be issued in
accordance with the Conditions of Contract and amendments.
The issue of this Certificate is not for and shall not be taken as evidence that any work or materials
or goods or workmanship is or are accepted as conforming to description or being in accordance with
the contract

To be signed by
or for the practice
named above.

Signed: *M Jones   for Margery Jones Associates*

✓Original to Contractor   Copies to: ✓Employer   ✓File
                                              Structural Consultant   Others
                                              ✓Quantity Surveyor
                                              Heating Consultant
                                              ✓Clerk of Works
                                              Electrical Consultant

Fig. 11.46 British Institute of Architectural Technology (BIAT) form: Certificate of practical completion or
partial completion

BRITISH INSTITUTE OF ARCHITECTURAL TECHNOLOGISTS

Certificate of
Making Good
Defects

Practice Name: *Margery Jones Associates*
Address: *145 Waddington Avenue*
Eastbourne Sussex

Employer: *Coast Developments Ltd*
Address: *Coast House Coast Road*
Brighton Sussex

Contractor/Sub-contractor: *Phillips Construction Ltd*
Address: *77 New Road Polegate Sussex*

Job ref: *MJ/8/54*

Date: *7th Sept 1998*

Works: *24 Luxury flats in two blocks*

Situate at: *Seafront Parade Eastbourne Sussex*

Contract date: *14th November 1997*

of expiry of defects liability period: *24th February 1999*

Date of making good defects: *3rd September 1998*

I/We certify that under the terms of the Contract all defects
as set out in the snagging schedule have been made good as far as reasonably
can be ascertained by visual inspection

Signed: *MJones   for Margery Jones Associates*

To be signed by
or for the practice
named above.

The issue of this certificate will result in the release of the residue at
retention percentage held after the issue of Certificate of Practical
Completion.

✓Original to Contractor   Copies to: ✓Employer   ✓File
                                              ✓Clerk of Works   Others
                                              ✓Quantity Surveyor

Fig. 11.47 British Institute of Architectural Technology (BIAT) form: Certificate of making good defects

BRITISH INSTITUTE OF ARCHITECTURAL TECHNOLOGISTS

Certificate of
Non-Completion

Practice Name: *Margery Jones Associates*
Address: *145 Washington Avenue*
Eastbourne E. Sussex

Employer: *Coast Developments Ltd*
Address: *Coast House Coast Road*
Brighton Sussex

Contractor: *Phillips Construction Ltd*
Address: *77 New Road Polegate Sussex*

Works: *24 Luxury flats in two blocks*

Situate at: *Seafront Parade Eastbourne Sussex*

Serial no:

Job ref: *MJ/8/54*

Date: *10th August 1998*

Under the terms of the contract dated: *14th November 1997*

I/We certify that in my/our opinion

the whole/part of the works namely   *Electrical Services*

have not been completed and ought reasonably to have been completed by

Date: *10th August 1998*

after due allowance for any extension of time granted under the terms
of the Contract.

Signed: *MJones   for Margery Jones Associates*

To be signed by
or for the practice
named above.

Original to Contractor   Copies to: Employer   ✓File
                          ✓Quantity Surveyor   Others
                          Structural/Civil Engineer
                          ✓Clerk of Works
                          Services Consultant

Fig. 11.48 British Institute of Architectural Technology (BIAT) form: Certificate of non-completion

BRITISH INSTITUTE OF ARCHITECTURAL TECHNOLOGISTS

COPY

Certificate of
Inspection

Practice Name:

Address:

Address of Property:

WHEREAS   A : I/We have been engaged by (1)_____
to design and obtain Local Authority approval for, and carry out, periodic inspections during
construction of (2)_____
by agreement and confirmation of instructions dated_____

or A : I/We have been provided by (1)_____
with copies of drawings and specifications together with (3) _____
_____
and have been engaged to carry out periodic inspections during construction of
(2)_____by agreement and confirmation of
instructions dated _____.

B : (4)_____ (the funder) has agreed to advance money
to (1)_____ in consideration of these certificates.

HEREBY CERTIFIED 1 : I/We have made periodic visits to the property to inspect the progress and quality of the
works and to check that they are being executed generally in accordance with the contract
documents[(5) as provided to me/us.]

2 : The works have now reached _____ stage of construction and insofar as
reasonable visual inspection allows on such periodic visits (subject as excluded below),
the construction satisfies the requirements of paragraph 1 hereof.

Exclusions (6) (i) :
(ii) :
(iii) :

The issue of this Certificate is not for and shall not be taken as evidence that any work or materials
or goods or workmanship is or are accepted as conforming to description or being in accordance
with the contract. For the avoidance of or removal of doubt it is mutually decided acknowledged and
agreed that the Certificate of Inspection or any other Certificate issued by the architectural
technologist is not intended to and shall not operate as conclusive evidence that any of the work
or materials or goods or workmanship conforms to description or is in accordance with the contract.

Signature of
Inspecting Officer:

Date:

(7) : "The certifier has no power of instruction to the contractor in respect of faulty materials
or workmanship"

Guidance notes : (1) Insert client's name
(2) Insert nature of building
(3) Insert list of other documents, i.e. engineers' calculations, builders' quotes, etc.
(4) Insert bank of building society requiring certificate of inspection.
(5) Delete if design carried out by the certifier.
(6) Enter "none" or list items not covered by this certificate.

Note: It may be that the certifier is not the designer - in which case liability for the drawings should be
excluded. This is in addition to any specific exclusions of a technical nature.

: it may be that the client at (1) is the contractor in which case No. (7) will apply - otherwise this
clause should be deleted. [Under these circumstances and insofar as the certifier sees things that
he is unhappy with he should seriously consider his professional duty to warn or notify those who
rely upon this certificate].

Fig. 11.49 British Institute of Architectural Technology (BIAT) form: Certificate of inspection

Appendix 1: Glossary

Abstracting
The third stage in the preparation of bills of quantities in which similar types of dimensions (i.e. cubic, squared, and linear) are brought together on sheets called the abstract.

Agent
Someone who represents a person or firm in business matters. In a building project the architect or architectural technologist acts as the client's agent and has the authority to spend money on his behalf.

Agre'ment certificate
Certificates granted by an independent testing organisation, called the British Board Agre'ment, stating that the manufacturer's products have satisfactorily passed agreed tests. Subsequent to the granting of the certificate strict quality control has to be continued.

Appraisal
The examination and testing of building materials and components and an evaluation as to their appropriateness for a specific purpose.

Arbitration
A technical court to settle disputes which cannot be resolved by the parties involved. The arbitrator is an independent third person (often an architect or surveyor) who hears all the arguments and gives a ruling, which must be accepted by both parties to the dispute.

Architect's certificate
A notice from the architect, generally written on a standard form, informing the employer that he is under a contractual obligation to pay the contractor for work done.

Architect's instruction
Further drawings, details, and instructions issued by the architect to the contractor, after the issue of the contract documents. They are generally given on a standard form.

Architectural practitioner
A professional person with expertise in architectural design and technology, who is in practice as an architect or architectural technologist.

Assembly drawing
A drawing which shows how the parts of a building are constructed and how they meet at junctions. An example of an assembly drawing is a 1: 5 detail at the cill position of a window.

Balancing
Final adjustment of water and air flows in pipes and ducts of heating and air-conditioning systems to ensure that each radiator and terminal unit receives the optimum amount of water or air.

Bankruptcy
The state of affairs when a person is unable to meet his debts as they become due. For a limited company, the process of becoming bankrupt is called liquidation.

Billing
The final stage in the preparation of bills of quantities, which consists of writing the bills from previously prepared information (i.e. at the 'casting' stage) into its final form.

Bills of quantities
A contract document generally prepared by quantity surveyors to enable contractors to estimate the cost of a proposed building. It describes and details the materials and labour needed to construct the building shown on the designer's drawings.

BRE digests
Reports published by the Building Research Establishment (BRE), providing suc-
cinct consideration of building topics, including materials, structures, services,
design, building methods, defects, and repairs.

British Standards (BS) [or British Standards Specification (BSS)]
Document issued by the British Standards Institution to lay down a minimum
standard for materials and components (e.g. walling blocks and doors) used in
the construction and other industries.

British Standards Institution
The organisation responsible for the preparation and publishing of British Standards
and Codes of Practice.

Buildability
Something that is easily built because of the use of uncomplicated design and
construction techniques.

Builder's work
Work undertaken by the main contractor to meet the requirements of a subcontractor.

Building owner
The traditional term to describe the client in a building project. This term is
interchangeable with the general term 'client', and the contractual term 'employer'.

Building regulations
Regulations concerned with safeguarding the safety and health of occupants of
completed buildings. They deal with matters such as safe methods of design,
standards of construction, and selection and use of materials.

Building surveyor
A specialist in building construction who investigates and reports on buildings and
who is often involved in the design, specification, and supervisory work for the
repair, rehabilitation, alteration, and extension of existing buildings.

Building team
Those people who are collectively involved in the design and construction of a
building, generally the client, architect, architectural technologist, quantity sur-

veyor, consulting structural engineer, consulting building services engineer, contractor, site manager, foreman, subcontractors and suppliers, and the clerk of works.

Bye-law
A law made by local authorities and public bodies, under powers given to them by parliament.

Certificate of practical completion
A certificate issued when a building has been completed, apart from making good any minor defects.

Civil engineering
The design and construction of unroofed structures, such as roads, bridges, tunnels, harbours, dams, airstrips, irrigation systems, and similar unroofed structures.

Client
The person for whom a service or product is provided. In the case of a building project, the service is provided by the architect and other members of the design team, and the product is the building, provided by the contractor. The term is interchangeable with 'employer', which is the term used in the building contract, and the term 'building owner', which is the traditional term used to describe the client.

Code of Practice (CP)
A code of good practice, issued by the British Standards Institution to cover workmanship in specific areas (e.g. building drainage, and brick and block masonry).

Collateral warranty
A guarantee which, in the case of a building, commits the designer to guarantee future purchases of the building, as well as the original owner, that the building will be fit for the purpose for which it is built.

Common law
This originally meant the law which is common throughout England, as opposed to local rules. It is now taken to mean the unwritten law (i.e. all law other than the enacted law imposed by legislation).

Completion
The stage in a building contract when all the work has been done.

Component drawing
A drawing which shows the shape, dimensions, assembly, and other details of components, such as windows.

Conservation area
An area with particular attractive or historic features which is protected under the town and country planning acts against unsuitable developments. The local district or county council declares an area to be a conservation area. The aim is to enhance such areas, and planning applications are scrutinised with special care in these areas.

Consultant
A person who provides specialist advice and information. In the case of building projects, the term is most likely to refer to structural engineers and building services engineers, who take responsibility for these areas of a project. The term is also used for experienced architects (often retired partners) who give advice on architectural and construction matters to architectural practices.

Contingency sum
A sum of money included in the contract price of a building project to cover the cost of extra work which it is not possible to anticipate at the design stage of the project.

Contract
A business agreement between two parties. In the subject under consideration it is between the employer (client) and the contractor (builder).

Corporation tax
A tax imposed by the government and paid by companies on their net profits. The actual rate depends on how much profit is made.

Cost control
The process of taking all possible steps to ensure that the final cost of the building is in accordance with the client's requirements and ability to pay. The duty of exercising cost control rests with the design team, particularly the quantity sur-

veyor, and is pursued from the first approximate estimate, throughout the project, until the final account.

Cost limits
The total amount of money the client is prepared to spend on the building he requires.

Cost plan
A plan for allocating the available money among the various elements (e.g. substructure, walls, roof, etc.) of the proposed building.

Cost plus contracts
Forms of contracts used for very urgent jobs when there is not time to wait until the drawings are available. The client pays the contractor the actual cost of the job (i.e. the flat rate) plus an agreed percentage for overheads and profit.

Cubing
A method of obtaining an approximate estimate. The volume of the building is calculated (in cubic metres) and then multiplied by a sum representing the cost per cubic metre of the building's volume.

Daywork
Work which is difficult to measure, price, and be included in the bills of quantities in the normal way. The work is listed on daywork sheets which show the hours worked by the various tradespeople, materials and plant used, and other charges. In practice it means that the contractor recoups all his costs, including a percentage for overheads.

Defects liability period
A period stated in the contract, but usually six months, after the employer takes over the building when all defects due to faulty materials and workmanship must be made good.

Delays
Circumstances which prevent the contractor from completing the work in accordance with the agreed programme. The delay may be caused by the contractor, employer, architect, or for reasons beyond the control of the parties to the contract.

Design-and-build contract
A form of contract in which the contractor is responsible for both the design and the construction of the building.

Design brief
Statement by the client of the requirements for the building he has commissioned. It will generally include information on the accommodation, quality of construction and finishes, total cost of the project, and the time-scale within which he wants the building to be constructed.

Design team
Those members of the building team who are particularly involved in the design, as opposed to the construction aspects, of a building project. They are usually considered to be the client, architect, architectural technologist, quantity surveyor, consulting structural engineer, and consulting building services engineer.

Determination
The determination of a contract prior to all work being completed. The determination can be initiated by either the employer or the contractor.

Development plan
A plan prepared by the local district or county council to protect the environment and to achieve a balanced allocation of the available land to meet the various needs. Among other things it stipulates the type of development (e.g. houses, factories, or offices) in a particular area.

Divided responsibility
An obligation which is shared between two or more people, for example where someone is given a 'fix only' contract, and a second person or firm is responsible for supplying the materials.

Door schedule
A list of doors for a building project, giving details of location, sizes, types, ironmongery, etc. It will generally form a part of the contract documents.

Dry construction
Use of materials and constructional techniques (such as suspended ceilings) which do not involve the use of any wet materials (such as plaster or mortar).

Easement
Rights acquired to benefit from someone else's land, such as the right of way over a piece of land, the right to lay and maintain drains under a person's land, and the right of support to a building.

Elements
The main parts of a building, such as the roof, floors, walls, and staircases.

Employer
A legal term used to describe the client, particularly in relation to the building contract. The terms – 'client' and 'employee' are interchangeable.

Employer's liability insurance
An insurance taken out by the contractor to idemnify the employer for any claims resulting from injury or death of any person on the construction site.

Environment
The strict meaning is 'surrounding objects', but in relation to architectural design procedures it can be taken to mean the things which surround a building or building site, including the climate.

Estimate
A prediction as to the cost of undertaking specified building work. Initially, contractors think of this as a net cost, to which overheads and profits, etc. are added at the tender stage.

Extension of time
The procedure to extend the date for completion of a building project from that stated in the contract. It also sets back the date on which the contractor is liable to pay damages because he has not completed the building work by the contractual date.

External works
Construction works located outside the perimeter of a building, mainly consisting of earthmoving, landscaping, roads and external pavings, drainage, external furniture, and fencing and external walls.

Feedback

The process of learning by experience gained during the course of a building project. Successful and unsuccessful aspects of the project are recorded and lessons are learned for application to future projects.

Fenestration

The architectural arrangement of windows and other openings in a building.

Final account

The account which is prepared and paid after all building work is completed. It takes into consideration all variations, remeasurements, fluctuations in labour rates and materials prices, and all other factors affecting the total cost of the project. It tells the client what the total cost of the building project is and how much money remains to be paid to the contractor.

Final certificate

The certificate issued after the final account has been prepared, which releases all outstanding monies due to the contractor after completion of all work, including making good any defects. Since the introduction of the 1985 Building Regulations the term 'final certificate' is also used to describe the certificate issued by an approved inspector to signify the completion of building work.

Final completion

The time when all work has been done, including items which have 'come to light' during the defects liability period (usually six months after practical completion).

Final inspection

The inspection by the architectural practitioner at the time of final completion.

Financial control

Regular checks, generally by the contractor's surveyor, that a specific project is not losing money. This is achieved by comparing the unit rates entered into the bills of quantities at the time the contractor prepared his estimate with the actual cost of the work as revealed by the cost of the work completed given in each monthly statement.

Finishing schedule

A list of rooms and spaces for a building project with information on the floor, wall, ceiling, and other finishes. It will generally form a part of the contract documents.

Fire certificate
A certificate issued by the fire officer (fire brigade), under the Fire Precautions Act 1971, certifying that a building (such as a hotel, office, shop, or factory) has been inspected and the means of escape, alarms, and fire equipment is satisfactory.

Firm
A term which has no legal significance but is used to denote partners and others carrying on a business together.

Fit-out
A term, sometimes used in building projects when referring to specialist finishing trades, such as the erection of proprietary partitions, suspended ceilings, purpose-built joinery items, cupboards, and shelves.

Fluctuations clause
A clause in a building contract which allows for a price adjustmkent to take account of changes in materials and labour costs since the contract was signed.

Force majeure
In respect of a building contract it means an event beyond the contractor's control (e.g. a strike or a flood).

Form of tender
A single-page document, completed and signed by the main contractor, which states all the key information about the project for which a tender is being submitted, for example project name, tender price, land time required to complete the project.

Freezing of the design
The term used to indicate the stage when the members of the design team jointly agree that there will be no further changes in the design of the proposed building, particularly in respect of its siting, size, shape, and general arrangement.

Frustration of contract
Situation in which a contract has to be terminated due to some unforeseen and unavoidable event.

General attendance
The provision by the main contractor of temporary works items such as scaffolding and services which can be used by the subcontractors.

Grant
Money given by the government, generally to people in financial need, to help pay the cost of repairing and renovating old houses.

Handing over (or handover)
The stage in a building project when the employer takes over the responsibility of the building from the contractor. Although the contractor may still have some items of work to complete at the handing over stage, the employer is legally responsible for the building.

Harmonisation
The use of common standards within all the countries in the European Union.

Health and Safety Executive (HSE)
The government department concerned with standards of health, safety, and welfare in industry.

High-rise building
Commonly considered to be a building with more than eight storeys.

Indemnity insurance
An insurance policy taken out by a professional person, such as an architect or architectural technologist, to protect that person against claims by the client for negligence, errors, omissions, etc.

Industrialised building
A method of building involving a large amount of prefabrication and standardisation.

Infrastructure
The basic system of roads, services, and communications which enables a country to function efficiently.

Interim certificate
Certificates issued at regular intervals, generally every month, to pay the contractor for work carried out to date, including all materials on-site for immediate use.

International standards
Standards issued by the International Standards Organization.

International Standards Organization (ISO)
The organisation, based in Geneva, which coordinates the work of national bodies (such as the British Standards Institution) and produces international standards.

Joint Contracts Tribunal
A body composed of representatives of various bodies concerned with building contracts [e.g. the Royal Institute of British Architects (RIBA), the Royal Institution of Chartered Surveyors (RICS), and the Building Employers Confederation (BEC)] who prepare standard forms of building contracts.

Kitemark
The trademark of the British Standards Institution used by manufacturers whose products conform to British Standards.

Landscaping
The land-shaping, planting, and laying of roads and pavings in the land surrounding a building.

Lead-in time (or lead time)
The period of time between the award of a contract to a contractor and the time he actually starts work on-site. During the lead-in time the contractor organises his labour, materials, and plant, and generally gets ready to begin construction.

Legislation
Laws, for example acts such as the Fire Precautions Act 1971, and regulations such as the Building Regulations 1991.

Local authority
An elected body of members forming the council, together with a separate body of paid staff (e.g. planning officers and building control officers) who administer services in a specific area of the United Kingdom. They have a separate legal entity

from central government, but no powers except those granted to them by the government, such as powers to administer town planning and building regulations.

Location drawing
A drawing which locates and identifies spaces and parts of a building, such as rooms, doors, and drainage. Examples of location drawings are 1:100 plans, elevations, and sections.

Low-rise building
Commonly considered to be a building with from one to eight storeys.

Main contractor
One of the two parties to a building contract. He has overall responsibility to construct the building, including control of subcontractors and suppliers.

Making good defects certificate
Certificate issued by the architect and architectural technologist authorising a payment to the contactractor when all defective work has been made good.

Measured item
An item of work included in the bills of quantities.

Memorandum of Agreement
A document signed between the client and the architect agreeing the conditions of the architect's appointment, including the extent of the services the architect will provide and the fees he will receive.

Multidiscipline practice
A professional firm in which its members are trained and experienced in different disciplines. In the building industry this could mean, for example, a firm containing architects, architectural technologists, quantity surveyors, structural engineers, building services engineers, and town planners.

National building specification (NBS)
A form of building specification published by the Royal Institute of British Architects (RIBA) which uses the CI/SfB (Construction Industry/Samarbetskommitten for Byggnadsfragor) coding system and provides details of materials and workmanship under separate headings.

Negligence

Failure by someone (e.g. in the case of a building contract, the architect or architectural technologist) to take the care which should have been taken and, as a result of this carelessness, causes damage to another party (e.g. the client).

Nominated subcontractor

A subcontractor nominated by the architect or architectural technologist to carry out specialist work on the site.

Non-nominated subcontractor

A subcontractor selected by the contractor (as opposed to the architect) to carry out specialist work on the site. Also given the name of domestic subcontractor.

Organisational framework

In relation to the design team this term means the breaking down of the team into groups giving each group specific tasks to undertake in order to achieve the overall objectives of the design team.

Package deal

Another name for a design-and-build contract.

Practical completion

The stage when the building is completed and is in a fit state to be taken over by the employer for its intended use. The defects liability period commences from this date.

Practical completion certificate

The certificate issued by the architect or architectural technologist authorising a payment to the contractor at the practical completion stage.

Pre-contract

The stage of a building project prior to the contractor taking possession of the site and beginning work.

Prime cost (PC)

A sum added by the contractor to his tender to cover work by a nominated subcontractor or goods supplied by a nominated supplier.

Production information
The total information, including drawings, schedules, and specifications, produced by the design team to facilitate the erection of the building.

Provisional sum
A sum of money included in the bills of quantities to cover an item for which detailed information is not available at the time the bills are prepared.

Public limited company
A company listed on the Stock Exchange and therefore able to raise money as required from the general public by selling shares in the company and able to transfer the shares from one investor to another. To be listed the company must have a stipulated minimum amount of capital.

Quality assurance (QA)
The adoption of methods which assure customer needs are met in respect of products and services.

Quality control
The process of ensuring that the standards set in the drawings, specifications, and other contractual documents for workmanship and materials are complied with.

Quotation
A firm price given for goods to be supplied, or work which has to be done. Unless the quotation clearly states that the price may be varied, it becomes fixed as soon as it is accepted by the customer. This is different from an estimate, which is considered to be a probable cost of supplying goods or of undertaking work.

Remeasurement
The measurement of quantities of work at the site after it has been done, as opposed to measuring work from drawings prior to work commencing.

Restrictive covenant
Undertakings to restrict the use of one piece of land so that the occupiers of other pieces of land may benefit. An example is not to change the appearance of a building.

Retention
A sum of money deducted from each valuation (see 'valuation') so as to protect the employer in case things go wrong. The amount is not generally more than 5 per cent of the valuation.

RIBA plan of work
A scheme prepared by the Royal Institute of British Architects (RIBA), showing the content and order of the architect's work. The work is divided into stages, and all significant events are listed. It is fully described in the *Architect's Job Book*, published by RIBA Publications.

Sample
A specimen of a product or component, such as a brick, tile, or window, which is submitted to, and approved by, the designer as being suitable for use in the proposed building.

Sample panel
A specimen of a piece of work, such as a panel of brickwork, which is prepared so that the architect can examine and approve it as being of a suitable standard for use in the proposed building.

Schedules
The presentation of information in a tabulated form for items such as doors, windows, ironmongery, finishes, and manholes.

Self-finished
Materials in which the finish is applied during manufacture (e.g. anodised aluminium).

Services
Water, gas, air, electricity, and waste products, supplied or collected in pipes, ducts, or cables, to serve the building occupier's needs in respect of heatng, lighting, plumbing, etc.

Specification
A document giving a written description of materials to be used, and construction methods to be employed, in the construction of a building.

Squaring
The second stage in the preparation of bills of quantities, in which sets of dimensions 'taken off' in the previous stage are multiplied together to obtain squared or cubic values, or left in a linear form.

Standard Method of Measurement (SMM)
A document which details the way each item in the bills of quantities should be measured.

Statutory undertaker
An organisation committed by law to provide a public service. Since privatisation, few of these now remain. Gas, water, and electricity undertakings have become service companies.

Statutory work
Something which is required to be done because of a written law such as the Building Regulations.

Structural floor level
The level of the structural concrete, as opposed to the floor finish.

Structure
The load-bearing part of a building (e.g. structural steel or reinforced concrete frame, brick walls, floors and roof).

Subcontract
A contract between a main contractor and a subcontractor.

Subcontractor
A person or firm employed to carry out part of the building work (e.g. on suspended ceilings or the electrical installations).

Subletting
The employment of a subcontractor.

Submission
The complete tender package submitted by the main contractor, including the completed form of tender, priced bill of quantities, tender bond, and supporting documents requested by the employer or his agent.

Substructure
The parts of a building below ground level (e.g. foundations and basement).

Superstructure
The parts of a building above ground level.

Supplier
A person or firm employed to supply goods (e.g. windows or bricks).

Supply only
Arrangement whereby materials or components are brought to a site by one firm, and fixed by another.

Taking off
The first stage in the preparation of bills of quantities, in which dimensions taken from drawings are entered onto sheets of paper.

Temporary works
Work which needs to be done as part of a building project but which will not remain in the finished building (e.g. site huts, temporary roads and services, timbering for earthworks support during excavations, shoring, and scaffolding).

Tender
An offer by a contractor to erect, for a specified sum, in a specified time, and under stated conditions, the building work described in the contract bills of quantities, specification, and drawings.

Tender documents
Documents supplied to the contactor to enable him to prepare a tender.

Tender figure
The sum of money forming part of the tender.

Tendering
The operation of sending out the tender documents to the contractor so that he can prepare a tender price.

Tort
A word of French origin meaning 'a wrong'. A tort is a civil wrong imposed by the law, as opposed to contractual liability which is imposed by consent between the parties to a contract. Torts include trespass, nuisance, and negligence.

User requirements
A summary of precisely what type of building and facilities are needed by the proposed occupier of a building.

U value
A thermal transmittance coefficient which measures the quantity of heat in watts which will flow from the inside to the outside of one square metre of construction when there is a 1°C difference between internal and external temperatures.

Valuation
A calculation by the quantity surveyor of the amount due to be paid to the contractor for work done and materials to be charged to the site. As interim certificates are generally issued at monthly intervals, valuations will also generally be made every month.

Value added tax (VAT)
A tax charged by the government on each business transaction involved in supplying goods and services. Work in the construction of new buildings is zero rated, and no tax is charged on demolition. The full VAT rate of 17.5% is charged on maintenance work and on repair and improvement work.

Variation order
An addition, omission, or alteration to the contract, issued to the contractor by the architect or architectural technologist, generally on a standard form.

Appendix 2: Abbreviations

AA	Architectural Association
ABT	Association of Building Technicians
ACA	Association of Consultant Architects
ACAS	Advisory, Conciliation and Arbitration Service
ACE	Association of Consulting Engineers
AFNOR	Association Française de Normalisation; the French national standard, equivalent of the British Standard (BS)
AI	Architect's instruction
ANB	Adjudicator Nominating Body
ARB	Architect's Registration Board [formerly the Architect's Registration Council of the United Kingdom (ARCUK)]
ARCUK	Architect's Registration Council of the United Kingdom, now the Architects' Registration Board (ARB)
ASHVE	American Society of Heating and Ventilation Engineers
ASI	Architects and Surveyors Institute
ASTM	American Society for Testing and Materials
BBA	British Board of Agre'ment
BCIS	Building Cost Information Service
BEC	Building Employers Confederation
BIAT	British Institute of Architectural Technology
BOQ	Bills of quantities [also abbreviated to BQ]
BPF	British Property Federation
BQ	Bills of quantities (also abbreviated to BOQ)
BRE	Building Research Establishment
BS	British Standards
BSI	British Standards Institution
BSRIA	British Services Research and Information Association
BSS	British Standard Specification
BT	British Telecommunications
BTEC	Business and Technical Education Council
BUILD	Building Users Insurance Against Latent Defects
CAD	Computer-aided design (or draughting)
CAS	Clients Advisory Service [Royal Institute of British Architects (RIBA)]

CAWS	Common Arrangement of Work Section
CDM	Construction (Design and Management) [Regulations 1994]
CE	Comité Européen; European committee for standardization; see also below
CE	European conformity mark; see also above
CEN	Comité Européen de Normalization; Central European committe for standardization
CIArb	Chartered Institute of Arbitrators
CIBSE	Chartered Institute of Building Services Engineers
CIOB	Chartered Institute of Building
CIOC	Chartered Institute of Construction
CI/SfB	Construction Industry/Samarbetskommitten for Byggnadsfragor (the latter of which is the Swedish Coordinating Committee for the Building Industry)
CITB	Construction Industry Training Board
CORGI	Confederation for the Registration of Gas Installers
COW	Clerk of Works
CP	Code of Practice
CPD	Construction Products Directive; see also below
CPD	Continuing professional development; see also above
DIN	Deutsches Institut für Normung; the German national standard, the equivalent of British Standard (BS)
DoE	Department of the Environment [now the Department of the Environment, Transport and the Regions (DoETR)]
DoETR	Department of the Environment, Transport and the Regions [formerly the Department of the Environment (DoE)]
EC	Eurocode, code of practice; see also below
EC	European Community (officially, European Communities); see also above
EEA	European Economic Area
EN	Euronorm; a European Standard
ETA	European Technical Approval
FCEC	Federation of Civil Engineering Contractors
FFL	finished floor level
FOC	Fire Officers Committee
FPA	Fire Protection Association
GW	Government Works
H&SWA	Health and Safety at Work Act
HMSO	Her Majesty's Stationery Office (now The Stationery Office)
HNC	Higher National Certificate
HND	Higher National Diploma
HSE	Health and Safety Executive
IAAS	Incorporated Association of Architects and Surveyors
ICE	Institution of Civil Engineers
IEE	Institution of Electrical Engineers
ILA	Institute of Landscape Architects
IMechE	Institution of Mechanical Engineers

ISE	Institution of Structural Engineers
ISO	International Standards Organization
JCT	Joint Contracts Tribunal
LA	Local authority
NBS	National Building Specification
NCVQ	National Council for Vocational Qualifications
NFBTE	National Federation of Building Trade Employers
NHBC	National House Builder's Council
NJC	National Joint Consultative Committee of Architects, Quantity Surveyors and Builders
NJCBI	National Joint Committee for the Building Industry
NS	Nominated supplier
NSC	Nominated subcontrator
NTS	Not to scale
NVQ	National Vocational Qualification
PAYE	Pay as you earn
PC	Prime cost
PLC	Public limited company
preENVs	pre-standards (EN standards, defined above)
PS	Provisional sum
PSA	Property Service Agency
QA	Quality assurance
QAS	Quality assurance standards
QM	Quality management
QS	Quantity surveyor
RE	Resident engineer
RIAI	Royal Institute of Architects in Ireland
RIAS	Royal Incorporation of Architects in Scotland
RIBA	Royal Institute of British Architects
RICS	Royal Institution of Chartered Surveyors
RSUA	Royal Society of Ulster Architects
RTPI	Royal Town Planning Institute
SAAT	Society of Architectural and Associated Technicians
SFL	structural floor level
SMM	*Standard Method of Measurement* (booklet)
SVQ	Scottish Vocational Qualification
TRADA	Timber Research and Development Association
TQM	Total quality management
UDC	Universal Decimal classification; see also below
UDC	Urban development corporation; see also above
Uniclass	Unified Classification for the Construction Industry
UCATT	Union of Construction, Allied Trades and Technicians
VAT	Value added tax
VDU	Visual Display Unit
VO	Variation order

Questions

A series of questions are given below, which the reader can attempt, so as to check whether the contents of the book have been assimilated. If the reader is unable to answer a specific question, a reread of the sections of the book indicated in brackets would be advisable.

1. Describe the historical development of the architect from his original role, to his present role as a leader of the design team (§§1.2, 2.2, and 3.2).

2. Explain the need for a 'design team framework' today [§§2.3 and 3.10).

3. List the professional skills required by an architectural technologist (§2.7).

4. Describe how the education of architectural technologists has changed since the forerunner of the British Institute of Architectural Technology (BIAT) was formed in 1965 (§2.8).

5. What is the justification for the professional institutions insisting that their members undertake continuing professional development (CPD), and what methods are generally acceptable to the institutions (§2.9)?

6. Describe the architect's responsibilities towards the client during the contract stage (§2.10, 10.2, and 10.23).

7. Describe the concepts of quality assurance (QA) and quality management (QM) (§§2.12 and 2.13).

8. What is the reason for the European Union (EU) directive making architects in one member country eligible for registration in other member countries (§2.14)?

9. Summarise the various modes of practice which may be used by architects and architectural technologists (§3.2).

10. List the advantages and disadvantages of using a design-and-construct organisation for a building project (§3.3).

11. Describe two ways of undertaking a building project, other than the traditional way of using an independent architect and a main contractor who was awarded the contract after competitive tendering (§§3.5 and 3.6).

12. Summarise the content of the Latham Report (§3.7).

13. List typical goals which would be expected on a construction project operating under a partnering system (§3.8).

14. By means of diagrams indicate three different examples of organisational frameworks in architectural practices (§3.10).

15. List six good habits which should be adopted as part of the day-to-day work philosophy of an architectural practice (§3.12).

16. State six requirements necessary to achieve good communications in an architectural practice (§3.15).

17. Describe the benefits that computers can contribute in the field of communications (§3.18).

18. State three different methods which architects and architectural technologists can use to charge for their services (§3.22).

19. Describe how the client's brief is established (§§3.26, 3.27, 8.2, and 8.4)

20. Describe the various methods used by architects and architectural technologists to obtain work (§3.28).

21. List the items which architects and architectural technologists would normally expect their professional indemnity insurance to cover (§4.3).

22. Explain the significance of 'professional negligence' in an architectural practice (§§4.6–4.14).

23. Summarise the role of the client, the designer and the planning supervisor, in respect of the Construction Design and Management (CDM) Regulations 1994 (§4.15 and 4.16).

24. Describe the purpose and content of the CDM safety file (§4.16).

25. Outline the legal position regarding protection against infringement of copyright in the UK (§4.17).

26. Describe the effect on British Standards that have been brought about by British membership of the European Union (§5.5).

27. Describe the use of computers in an architectural practice (§§)5.6, 5.7, 6.10, and 8.11).

28. Describe what the 'Internet' has to offer the architectural practitioner (§5.7).

29. Describe the Royal Institution of Chartered Surveyors' Building Cost Information Service (§5.12).

30. Summarise the main features of the CI/SfB Construction Industry/Samarbets-kommitten for Byggnadsfragor) system (§5.16).

31. Summarise the things the architect and architectural technologist employer has

to provide for his employees to meet the requirements of the current health, welfare, and safety legislation (§6.6).

32. Describe the position with regards to redundancy for employees in an architectural practice (§6.15).

33. Describe the constraints imposed on design by the client (§7.2).

34. Explain the influence on the appearance of a building resulting from the designer's views on architecture (§7.3).

35. Explain the meaning of the following terms: architectural composition, unity, duality, mass, proportions, scale, contrast, regulating lines, and harmony (§7.3).

36. Describe the constraints imposed on a design by the 'user requirements' (§7.4).

37. Explain why it is sensible to consider the sciences of anthropometrics and ergonomics when designing a building (§7.5).

38. Describe the ways in which the designer of a building can respond to the needs of the disabled (§7.6).

39. Describe the constraints imposed on a design by the site (§7.7).

40. Describe the constraints imposed on a design by the environment (§7.8).

41. Describe the constraints imposed on a design by 'cost limits' (§7.9).

42. Explain the difference between the total cost of a project and the cost value to the client (§7.9).

43. Explain how the cost of a job is affected by the building market (§7.9).

44. Describe the constraints imposed on a design by legal requirements (§7.10).

45. Describe the effects of building regulations on a design (§§7.11 and 8.24).

46. Describe the effects of the town planning acts on a design (§§7.12 and 8.25).

47. Define what is meant by the terms 'trespass', 'nuisance', and 'easements' (§§7.13, 7.14, and 7.17).

48. Define what is meant by a 'party wall' and summarise the extent of the Party Wall etc. Act 1996 (§7.16).

49. Describe the effect of building engineering services on a design (§7.l8).

50. Describe how information and instructions are relayed from the design team staff to the site staff during the building process (§§8.6, 8.8, 10.5–10.9, and 10.17–10.20).

51. Describe what is discussed at pre-contract meetings and the purpose of such meetings (§§9.2–9.15).

52. Describe different methods of communicating design outcomes to the client (§§9.2–9.6).

53. Briefly describe the items covered by the pre-contract stages A–J of the Royal Institute of British Architecture's Plan of Work (§§9.2, 9.3, 9.5, 9.7–9.11, and 9.15).

54. Describe the information required to obtain approximate estimates of a project (§§9.3 and 9.4).

55. Explain why it is necessary at a certain stage of the project to 'freeze' the design (§9.8).

56. Describe the procedures to be followed to convert a tender into a contract (§§9.11–9.14).

57. Describe the information required to enable competitive tenders to be obtained (§9.13).

58. Describe the importance of accurate record-keeping during the course of building work (§§10.2, 10.5, 10.8, 10.14, and 10.17–10.20).

59. Describe the importance of quality control during the course of building work (§§10.3 and 10.4).

60. Briefly describe the items covered by the contract stages K–M of the RIBA Plan of Work (§§ 10.2, 10.23, and 10.26).

61. Describe the methods of payment for building work (§§10.7, 10.8, 10.24, and 10.25).

62. Describe how the progress of work on a building site is recorded (§§10.17–10.20).

63. Describe specific information which the contractor has to supply to the architect during the contract period (§10.21).

Sources of information

Introduction

Various acts, regulations, documents, books, and publications were either referred to in this book or influenced the book's contents.

Acts

Complicated contemporary societies such as ours need rules which are capable of handling various economic, social, health, welfare, safety, environmental, and other problems which may arise. One method of making rules is by passing an act of parliament. Many such acts affect the construction industry, both in respect of building design and construction and in respect of the way the completed buildings are used. The list of such acts named under this section have (or have had) an influence on the subject of architectural design procedures and have been referred to during the research and writing of this book.

For an 'in-depth' study of the subject of architectural design procedures it is recommended that students should study such sources of information for themselves.

Acts are available from The Stationery Office. Enquiries should be sent to:

Customer Services
The Stationery Office
51 Nine Elms Lane
Vauxhall
London SW8 5DR
Tel.: 0171 873 0011
Fax: 0171 873 8247

Ancient Monuments and Archaeological Areas Act 1979
Arbitration Acts 1950, 1975, 1979, and 1996
Architects Act 1997
Architect's (Registration) Acts 1931 and 1938
Building Act 1984
Clean Air Act 1969
Companies Acts 1947, 1967, 1985, and 1989

Consumer Arbitration Agreement Act 1988
Control of Pollution Act 1974
Copyright Act 1956
Copyright, Designs and Patents Act 1988
Defective Premises Act 1971
Disabled Discrimination Act 1995
Employment Protection (Consolidation) Act 1978
Explosive Acts 1875 and 1923
Fire Precautions Act 1971
Health and Safety at Work Act 1974
Highways Acts 1959, 1971, and 1980
Housing Grants, Construction and Regeneration Act 1996 (Also referred to as the
    1996 Construction Act)
Insolvency Act 1986
Limitations Act 1939
London Building Act (Amendment) Acts 1939
Nuclear Installations Act 1965
Partnership Act 1890
Party Wall etc. Act 1996
Planning and Compensation Act 1991
Planning (Consequential Provisions) Act 1990
Planning (Hazardous Substances) Act 1990
Planning (Listed Buildings and Conservation Areas) Act 1990
Private Street Works Act 1961
Public Health Acts 1990 and 1991
Registration of Business Names Act 1916
Sex Discrimination Act 1975
Social Security Act 1975
Third Parties (Rights Against Insurers) Act 1930
Town and Country Planning Act 1990
Unfair Contract Terms Act 1977

Regulations

Other methods of making and enforcing behaviour are by regulations, orders in council, statutory instruments, and bye-laws. These rely on delegated powers. There is no time for parliament to be involved with every detail of every piece of legislation which modern society requires. It is therefore common practice for parliament to provide the framework of an act – this is known as an enabling act – and then to grant authority to someone else to devise and control the detailed regulations. The Building Regulations are one of the best known examples of delegated legislation. They are laws made under the Building Act 1984 to control the layout, materials, and construction of buildings, and the health and safety of occupiers, particularly in case of fire.

Building Regulations (Amendment) Regulation 1994
Construction (Design and Management) Regulations 1994
Construction (Health, Safety and Welfare) Regulations 1996
Fees for Applications and Deemed Applications (Amendment) Regulations 1997
Management of Health and Safety at Work Regulations 1992
Town and Country Planning (Fees for Applications Amendment) Regulations 1997
Workplace (Health, Safety and Welfare) Regulations 1992

Town and country planning orders

Town and Country Planning General Development Order 1988
Town and Country Planning (General Development Procedure) Order 1995
Town and Country Planning Use Classes Order 1985
Use Class Order 1987

Health and Safety Executive publications

The Health and Safety Executive (HSE) is a government department with authority under the Health and Safety at Work Act 1974 to advise and enforce standards of health, welfare, and safety in industry. Priced and free publications are available by mail order form:

HSE Books
Customer Services Department
PO Box 1999
Sudbury
Suffolk
CO10 6FS
Tel.: 01787 881165
Fax: 01787 313995

The following HSE publications have been referred to in this book.

Health and Safety Regulation – a Short Guide
Workplace – Health, Safety and Welfare

Joint Contracts Tribunal standard forms of building contract

The following Joint Contracts Tribunal (JCT) standard forms of building contracts are published by the JCT and are obtainable from:

RIBA Publications
Finsbury Mission
39 Moreland Street
London
ECV 8BB

Tel.: 0191 251 0791
Fax: 0171 608 2375

JCT Form of Agreement for Minor Works 1980
JCT Intermediate form of Building Contract 1984
JCT Prime Cost Contract 1992
JCT Standard Form of Management Contract 1987
JCT Standard Form, Local Authorities with Quantities 1980
JCT Standard Form, Local Authorities with Approximate Quantities 1980
JCT Standard Form, Local Authorities without Quantities 1980
JCT Standard Form, Private with Quantities 1980
JCT Standard Form, Private with Approximate Quantities 1980
JCT Standard Form, Private without Quantities 1980

RIBA Publications

The following RIBA publications were referred to in this book and can be obtained from RIBA Publications at the address given in the previous section.

Code of Professional Conduct 1991
Cox, S., Hamilton, A. 1991: *Architect's Handbook of Practice Management*
Cox, S., Hamilton, A. 1994 *Architect's Guide to Job Administration under the CDM Regulations 1994*
Cox, S., Hamilton, A. 1995: *Architect's Job Book 1995*
Guidance for Clients on Fees 1994
Standard Form of Agreement for the Appointment of an Architect 1992
Standard forms for use on building projects:
    Architect's instruction
    Interim certificate
    Certificate of practical completion
    Certificate of making good defects
    Final certificate
Uniclass Manual

British Institute of Architectural Technology publications

The following may be obtained from:

British Institute of Architectural Technology
397 City Road
London
ECV1 1NE
Tel/Fax: 0171 278 2206

Code of Conduct
Conditions of Engagement
Conduct and Disciplinary Procedures

Practice Guidance Notes
Standard forms for use on building projects:
  Confirmation of instructions
  Instruction
  Certificate
  Notification of amounts included in certificate
  Direction
  Notification of extension of time
  Certification of practical completion or partial completion
  Certificate of making good defects
  Certificate of non-completion
  Certificate of inspection

Royal Institution of Chartered Surveyors publication

The following is available from the Royal Institution of Chartered Surveyors, London.

Standard Method of Measurement of Building Works (SMM7) 1987

Journals and technical press publications

Journals of professional institutes
Architectural Technology, published by the British Institute of Architectural Technology, London, covering architectural technology, particularly information on the use of computers in architectural practices.
Construction Manager, published by the Chartered Institute of Building, London, covering particularly matters relating to project management and contracts, including contract law.

Technical press
These include law reports. The following are particularly recommended.

Building Design, published weekly by Morgan Grampian.
Building, published weekly by The Building.

Miscellaneous

Belcher, J. 1907: *The Essentials of Architecture.*
Briggs, M.S. 1962: *Concise Encyclopaedia of Architecture.* London: J.M. Dent.
Clamp, H. 1993: *The Shorter Form of Building Contract.*
Consumer Arbitration Agreement 1988; available from The Stationery Office, London.
Goldsmith, S. 1976: *Designing for the Disabled: The New Paradigm.*

Hammond, J. *Understanding Human Engineering.*

Jones, N.F., Berman, D. 1985: *The JCT Intermediate Form of Building Contract.* Oxford: Basil Blackwell.

Lancaster, O. 1948: *Pillar to Post.* John Murray.

Latham Report 1994: *Constructing the team: joint review of procurement and contractual arrangements in the United Kingdom construction industry: final report.* London: The Stationery Office.

Osborne, D.J. *Ergonomics at Work.* Chichester: John Wiley.

Parris, J. 1990: *The Standard Forms of Building Contract.* Oxford: Basil Blackwell.

Pheasant, S. *Bodyspace.* London: Taylor & Francis.

Ray-Jones, A., Clegg, D. 1976: *CI/SfB Construction Indexing Manual.* London: RIBA Publications.

Robertson, H. 1955: *The Principles of Architectural Composition.* London: Architectural Press.

Speaght & Stone, A.J. 1996: *Architect's Legal Handbook – The Law for Architects.* Guildford: Butterworth.

Recommended reading

The following publications and books provide useful additional reading material.

The British Standard Specifications are published by the British Standards Institution, London, and are available for most materials and components used in the building industry. The full list is too long to include here, but details can be obtained from the British Standards Institution.

The British Standard Codes of Practice are published by the British Standards Institution, London, and are available covering design and workmanship for most building activities. Again, the full list is too long to include here, but details can be obtained from the British Standards Institution.

The British Standards Institution is also responsible for publishing the English language versions of European Standards.

Building Research Establishment Digests are published each month by the Building Research Establishment, Garston, Watford; they review and assess the effectiveness of building techniques and materials.

I also recommend the following books.

Chudley, R. 1995: *Building Construction Handbook*. Harlow: Longman.
Fletcher, B. (Sir). 1975: *A History of Architecture*. London: Architectural Press.
Lawson, B. *How Designers Think*. Guildford: Butterworth.
May, A. (Sir). 1995: *Keating on Building Contracts*.
Spon 1998: *Spon's Architect's and Builder's Price Book 1998*. London: E&FN Spon.
Stephenson, J. 1995: *Building Regulations Explained*. London: E & FN Spon.
Tutt, P. and Adler, D. 1979: *New Metric Handbook*. Guildford: Butterworths.
Willis, A.J., Willis, C.J. 1991: *Specification Writing for Architects and Surveyors*.

Index